New Cooperative Banking in Europe

Marco Migliorelli
Editor

New Cooperative Banking in Europe

Strategies for Adapting the Business Model Post Crisis

palgrave
macmillan

Editor
Marco Migliorelli
IAE Université Paris 1 Panthéon-Sorbonne
(Sorbonne Business School)
Paris, France

ISBN 978-3-030-06687-1 ISBN 978-3-319-93578-2 (eBook)
https://doi.org/10.1007/978-3-319-93578-2

Softcover re-print of the Hardcover 1st edition 2018

Cover illustration: VanReeel, iStock / Getty Images Plus

This Palgrave Macmillan imprint is published by the registered company Springer Nature Switzerland AG
The registered company address is: Gewerbestrasse 11, 6330 Cham, Switzerland

Foreword

The idea of this book came from several meetings I had with professors, practitioners and students that, like me, are passionate by the theme of cooperative banking. Many of them advocate that the cooperative model, axed on membership, democratic governance, proximity and commitment to social values, represented during and in the aftermath of the Great Crisis a valuable anchor for businesses and households and that such a model should be further encouraged. Others claim that cooperative banks were, in the longer term, not shielded from the drawbacks of the economic turmoil and progressively weakened their capacity to generate a distinctive value proposition, in particular due to the reluctance to adapt their business model to the changed competitive scenario.

The possibility to enrich this debate is what inspired this collective work. The convergence towards the joint-stock company model or the necessity of some deep evolution in crucial aspects of the cooperative paradigm was often at the heart of the discussions I had on the possible future of cooperative banking in Europe.

Many changes have already occurred in the cooperative banking sector in Europe since the explosion of the Great Crisis. The book summarises the most important ones. Nevertheless, cooperative banking is far from being in a phase of new maturity. Structural low profitability, stricter regulation and the entrance of fintech companies in the market of banking services are some of the elements that will keep shaping the market. For this reason, the book also deepens the analysis on how the inherent and unique cooperative values could still be effectively leveraged in the banking market in the years to come.

IAE Université Paris 1 Panthéon-Sorbonne (Sorbonne Business School)
Paris, France

Marco Migliorelli

Preface

The cooperative banking segment in Europe counts more than 3000 banks and has more than 200 million customers. This book, which is in the form of an edited collection, aims at providing a clear understanding on how European cooperative banks have been evolving to take into account the new competitive scenario as resulted from the Great Crisis blasted in Europe in 2008.

The cooperative banking business model is unique in the financial sector. Such uniqueness derives from some inherent and indeed interconnected characteristics. Firstly, from the specific ownership structure, backed by the concepts of *membership* and *democratic governance*. Members have in principle equal weight in the key decision-making processes ("one head–one vote") and no new members can normally be excluded. Secondly, from the application of the principle of *proximity* (link with the territory), which mainly steers the cooperative banks' operational activity. Cooperative banks' operations are in fact focused first of all on their members and in the area where they are based. Thirdly, from promoting *mutualism* and the gone-with *limited profit-seeking nature*. Most of the cooperative banks have statutory constraints and specific rules as concerns the distribution of the profits.

Thanks to these characteristics, cooperative banks have traditionally guaranteed an important countercyclical role and have showed above-the-average capitalisation levels, in line with a mitigated risk appetite. Despite that, the cooperative banking system has been put under an unprecedented pressure as a result of the Great Crisis. Factors such as exceptionally low interest rates, low profitability generated by traditional banking services (which are the backbone of the cooperative banking business), the marked growth in the level of non-performing loans in many countries and the increasing regulatory burden have produced a significant shift in the competitive scenario, to which many cooperative banks have not yet completely adapted. For these reasons, it is of extreme interest to observe how cooperative banks have been reacting in the attempt to preserve their unique business model and, at the same time, to keep providing credit to the economy.

To do that, this book is structured in ten chapters. In Chap. 1, Simon Cornée, Lucrezia Fattobene and Marco Migliorelli present an overview of the key characteristics of the cooperative banking segment in Europe. To this extent, the chapter describes the presence of the cooperative banks over Europe, identifies the key organisational models in use and performs a structured review of the existing literature on cooperative banking and relationship lending.

In Chap. 2, Eric Meyer provides an analysis of the performances of cooperative banks in recent years. He first gives an overview on their main economic and financial results and then focuses his dissertation on the key factors that have modified the competitive scenario since the beginning of the Great Crisis, with a specific focus on low interest rates.

Chapter 3, written by Marco Migliorelli, analyses the lending behaviour of cooperative banks vis-à-vis commercial and savings banks during and after the crisis, in order to verify if a specific lending pattern has existed. This allows the author to assess whether the traditional countercyclical attitude of cooperative banks during downturns can be confirmed or put under question.

In Chap. 4, Marco Migliorelli gives an introduction of the banking regulatory framework in the European Union with respect to cooperative banks. To this extent, the chapter discusses the main adaptations needed to the relevant regulation in order to take into account the cooperative banking singularities and includes an overview of the main impacts of regulation on the cooperative banking business model.

Chapter 5 presents the major reforms undertaken country-wise in the cooperative banking sector from the beginning of the Great Crisis to date. In this respect, Hans Groeneveld presents the case of Rabobank in the Netherlands, Roberto Di Salvo and Juan Sergio Lopez analyse the recent reforms occurred in Italy and Francesco Di Leo summarises the other main national-level initiatives and events.

Chapter 6, written by Eric Lamarque, is dedicated to the discussion of the cooperative banks' governance. The author first presents the specific impact of the Basel III provisions on the governance of cooperative banks. Then, he analyses the relevant existing governance structures and related challenges. Finally, he proposes a possible way to introduce innovation in governance models.

In Chap. 7, Tiphaine Gorlier, Géraldine Michel and Valérie Zeitoun analyse to what extent the concept of *proximity* needs to be reinterpreted in the digital era. To this extent, they argue on how digitalisation can be a powerful lever to foster a solid relationship with members and clients and how the cooperative brands, engraved by unique values, can become a symbolic anchor to keep conveying a sentiment of *proximity*.

In Chap. 8, Silvio Goglio and Ivana Catturani discuss the key trends that will keep shaping cooperative banks in the next years and possible strategic reactions. In this respect, they address the importance of reaffirming the role of membership, of leveraging the unique relationship with the clients, of exploring the possibilities given by digitalisation and of evaluating the different concentration options for smaller cooperative banks.

In Chap. 9, Giorgio Caselli examines the benefits that may derive from a plurality of ownership types, business models and corporate objectives in the banking sector. To this extent, the main challenges that the current regulatory framework in the European Union might pose to the cooperative banking model, along with how the proportionality principle could help address some of these challenges, are also discussed.

Finally, in Chap. 10, Marco Migliorelli summarises the main issues and trends discussed in the book and presents some concluding remarks.

Paris, France Marco Migliorelli

Acknowledgements

I would like to thank the contributors. This book would have not come to fruition without their strong expertise and exceptional commitment.

Contents

Notes on Editor and Contributors

Editor

Marco Migliorelli is a researcher in finance at the IAE of the University Paris 1 Panthéon-Sorbonne (Sorbonne Business School) and an economist at the European Commission.[1] He holds a PhD in Banking and Finance from the University of Rome Tor Vergata. His main research interests include cooperative banks, green finance and financing instruments innovation.

Contributors

Giorgio Caselli is a research fellow at the Centre for Business Research of the University of Cambridge. He completed his PhD in Financial Economics at Cranfield University. His research interests lie at the intersection of business economics and finance, with a specific focus on how firm behaviour shapes macroeconomic outcomes.

Ivana Catturani is a research fellow and lecturer at the University of Trento and a researcher at Euricse. She obtained her PhD in Economics and Management at the University of Trento. Her research activity is focused on cooperative financial institution, with a particular focus on their governance issues and their relevance for the local development.

[1] The contents included in this book do not necessarily reflect the official opinion of the European Commission. Responsibility for the information and views expressed in the book lies entirely with the authors.

Simon Cornée is an associate professor at the Faculty of Economics of the University of Rennes 1 and a researcher at the CREM-CNRS and at the CERMi. His research interests lie at the interaction of finance, governance and social economy, with a focus on social finance and cooperative studies.

Francesco Di Leo is a PhD in Banking and Finance from the University of Rome Tor Vergata. He is an accountant, auditor, independent advisor and lecturer of financial intermediaries. His research interests cover sustainable value in banking and banking regulation.

Roberto Di Salvo is the deputy general manager at Federcasse and the general manager at Fondo di Garanzia dei Depositanti del Credito Cooperativo (the deposit insurance scheme for cooperative credit banks in Italy). He previously worked at the Bank of Italy. He earned his MPhil in Banking and Finance at University College of North Wales. His fields of interest include banking and monetary economics.

Lucrezia Fattobene is a research fellow at Polytechnic University of Marche and at the University of Rome Tor Vergata. She earned her PhD in Management from the University of Rome Tor Vergata. Her main research interests are in the fields of corporate governance, behavioural finance and neuroeconomics.

Silvio Goglio is an associate professor of Political Economy at the University of Trento and coordinator of the research area in cooperatives and development at Euricse. His research interests include collective efficiency and local governance, institutional changes and economic performance, local and cooperative credit and regional development.

Tiphaine Gorlier is a professor at IPAG Business School. Her main research interests are rooted in the field of consumer-brand relationships, especially on the concept of proximity. Previously, she held various positions in the industry dealing with operational marketing, customer relationship management and e-commerce.

Hans Groeneveld is a professor of Financial Services Cooperatives at Tilburg University and director of International Cooperative Affairs at Rabobank. He is the author of many publications on the theme of cooperative banks in Europe.

Eric Lamarque is the dean of the IAE of the University Paris 1 Panthéon-Sorbonne (Sorbonne Business School) where he is also a professor and director of the Research Chair Management and Governance of Financial Cooperatives. He is the author of several publications on the theme of cooperative banks in Europe.

Juan Sergio Lopez is the head of the Research and International Relations Department at Federcasse. He previously worked at the World Bank. He holds an MPhil from the Social Policy Research Unit of the University of Sussex. His fields of interest include applied economics, banking and monetary economics.

Eric Meyer is a professor at the University of Münster, where he is also the director of the Institute for Cooperatives. He is the author of several publications on the theme of cooperative banks in Europe, particularly in Germany.

Géraldine Michel is a professor at the IAE of the University Paris 1 Panthéon-Sorbonne (Sorbonne Business School) and director of the Research Chair Brands and Values. She is the author of several books and has published articles in the field of brand in international journals. Her current research interests are brand management, social representation, values and conviviality.

Valérie Zeitoun is an associate professor at the IAE of the University Paris 1 Panthéon-Sorbonne (Sorbonne Business School), where she teaches consumer behaviour and qualitative methodologies. Her research focuses in particular on the mechanisms and issues of the consumer-brand relationship.

List of Figures

List of Tables

CHAPTER 1

An Overview of Cooperative Banking in Europe

Simon Cornée, Lucrezia Fattobene, and Marco Migliorelli

1.1 Cooperative Banks: Origins and Fundamental Principles in Today's World

Cooperation is a crucial behavioural principle of human social life (Rilling et al. 2002; Gintis et al. 2004), and it is key to our survivorship (Harari 2012). Considering that natural selection is based on the success of the

We are immensely grateful to Professor Alessandro Carretta for his precious suggestions. We would also like to thank professors Gianmario Raggetti, Vincenzo Farina and Gianni Nicolini for their useful advices. As concerns the specific contribution of each author, Lucrezia Fattobene authored Sects. 1.1, 1.2, and 1.3, Simon Cornée authored Sects. 1.4, 1.5, 1.6, and 1.7, Marco Migliorelli assured coordination, revision and quality control.

S. Cornée (✉)
University of Rennes 1, Rennes, France
e-mail: simon.cornee@univ-rennes1.fr

L. Fattobene
Polytechnic University of Marche, Ancona, Italy

University of Rome Tor Vergata, Rome, Italy

M. Migliorelli (ed.), *New Cooperative Banking in Europe*,
https://doi.org/10.1007/978-3-319-93578-2_1

single individual, the explanation of the existence of social cooperation among nonrelatives has long been a dare for evolutionary biologists. Despite the progress on this apparent paradox, the question on how the cooperative behaviour evolved can still be considered one of the 25 most challenging interrogatives that researchers will have to deal with (Pennisi 2005). There are several advantages associated with cooperation. Firstly, cooperation positively affects the efficiency of the production process, quantitatively increasing the resource production capabilities. Secondly, it increases the variety and the quality of goods and services individuals can acquire. Thirdly, in a fluctuating environment as the world we live in, cooperation represents an insurance against variability (Barker et al. 2017).

In the first half of the nineteenth century, in Germany, Friedrich Wilhelm Raiffeisen perceived these advantages and understood that a way to fight the poverty spread among rural population was to foster people *to help themselves.* The Stein-Hardenberg Reforms in the agriculture sector, which led to the so-called *bauernbefreiung* (peasant liberation), had the effect to create a new social context characterised by the free circulation of people and the increased availability of the labour force. If, on the one hand, the process of liberalisation of the farmers had the consequences of enriching opportunities in the agriculture sector as a whole thanks to an increase of the productivity rate, on the other hand, it caused higher unemployment, in particular in remote rural areas. This, in addition to the *gewerbefreiheit* (freedom of trade), which eliminated the protection insured by corporations, caused a widespread impoverishment of farmers, whose life conditions worsen remarkably. In this situation of misery and dissatisfaction of a large part of the population, Friedrich Wilhelm Raiffeisen realised that the core of the problem had to be addressed to the lack of adequate capital in the rural environment. He believed that to interrupt the vicious circle by which the inadequacy of available monetary resources generated even more misery, the rural system had to rely on the opportunities *within* the system, applying the *selbsthilfe* (self-help) principle, rather than struggle to collect resources from the outside (Raiffeisen 1866).

M. Migliorelli
IAE Université Paris 1 Panthéon-Sorbonne (Sorbonne Business School), Paris, France

While the dissolution of the ancient feudal system was impoverishing inhabitants of the rural areas, the industrial revolution that mainly concerned urban and suburban locations undermined the stability of small businesses and craftsmen, who needed working capital and fresh resources to renew their activities. Independently from Raiffeisen, Franz Hermann Schulze-Delitzsch proposed the view by which the individual improves his conditions relying on his own initiative and, whenever his effort would not be sufficient to overcome difficulties, joining forces and cooperation would promote the success (Tamagnini 1960).

At that time, credit institutions were lending only large amounts of resources backed by collaterals and the existing credit system was not adequate to provide for the new financial needs of farmers and artisans in rural and urban areas respectively. It was in this climate of difficulties that, in Germany, the two personalities of Raiffeisen and Schulze-Delitzsch, even if with different political and social views,[1] found a humus to conceive the modern cooperative credit system. The common aim was to improve the life conditions of a large part of population that, from the ongoing socio-economic, political and technological changes was obtaining only alienation and misery. Besides sharing the so-called mutualist model, the Raiffeisen and Schulze-Delitzsch cooperative banks exhibited several operative differences. Raiffeisen's cooperatives were located in rural and small urban areas and their activity was confined to narrow districts, the parish, in order to ensure that individual members knew each other well. The structure was a *solidarity-based liability* of all the members for possible debts (*one for all—all for one*) and, except for the treasurer who was paid a salary, the administrative roles were carried on an honorary basis. The loans granted were long term, the involvement with non-credit activities was permitted and no dividends were paid on shares. Schulze-Delitzsch's cooperative banks, instead, were located in urban areas and admitted as members people living in the city or in part of it. Opposite to the Raiffeisen's model, in the Schulze-Delitzsch's model liability was limited, managers (and not exclusively treasurers) were paid, short-term loans were granted with the possibility of renewals, non-credit activities were permitted and dividends were paid on shares. In a few decades, starting from Germany, Raiffeisen and Schulze-Delitzsch's models spread

[1] Raiffeisen's cooperative movement has religious and Christian roots, while Schulze-Delitzsch is a liberal figure who sees in credit cooperation a means to provide workers *equality of opportunities* rather than equality itself.

rapidly across neighbouring countries. Nevertheless, historical aspects and country-specific characteristics fostered a no uniform development of the cooperative movement, which translated in sharp differences among European cooperative systems.[2]

Today's cooperative banks have mainly maintained the mutualist model of the past,[3] not as a reminiscence but rather as the basis of their resilience. Even in a growing heterogeneity of organisational models and operational practices, all cooperative banks are today backed by the fundamental principles of:

- *Membership and democratic governance*: ownership is equally shared between all the cooperative members and the "one head—one vote" rule is adopted in the key decision-making processes.
- *Proximity*: cooperative banks collect savings and grant credit prevalently at a local level and mainly to small and medium enterprises (SMEs),[4] households and associations.[5]
- *Prudent management*: cooperative banks are committed to promote the development of communities they serve by adopting a low risk-taking approach.

Other important widespread cooperative banking principles in today's world, but which are indeed applied with different intensity and operational characteristics in different countries, are that *member shares are not marketable but redeemable at face value* (which implies that members do not participate to the net assets) and that a *large part of the profits has to be retained* (in order to represent the main source of capital generation, which is hence considered an intergenerational resource).

[2] For a comparative presentation of European cooperative systems, which includes also credit cooperatives and credit unions, see Karafolas (2016).

[3] According to the International Co-operative Alliance (ICA), a cooperative bank is "an autonomous association of persons united voluntarily to meet their common economic, social, and cultural needs and aspirations through a jointly-owned and democratically-controlled enterprise. Cooperatives are based on the values of self-help, self-responsibility, democracy, equality, equity and solidarity. In the tradition of their founders, co-operative members believe in the ethical values of honesty, openness, social responsibility and caring for others".

[4] For an overview of the role of cooperative banks and other smaller institution in financing SMEs and small midcaps in Europe, see Lang et al. (2016).

[5] While in the past membership was necessary to be able to request a loan, nowadays cooperative banks serve also non-members. This, in addition to the heterogeneity of clients, challenges the functioning of the cooperative banks' governance.

As *stakeholder value banks*, opposite to *shareholder value banks*, the primary business objective of cooperative banks is then to maximise stakeholders' interests in the long-term rather than a short-term maximisation of profits (Ferri et al. 2014). This attitude, the governance structure and the local orientation jointly encourage the incentive not to assume excessive risks. *Proximity*, by promoting relationship contract structures, allows softening the agency problem that is inherent in any bank-firm relationship and provides a competitive advantage in enhancing trust (Kay 2006). Moreover, *proximity* and *democratic governance* ensure that the economic and social fabric of the local community finds appropriate representation (Carretta 2011). Notwithstanding these premises, cooperative banks should not be considered philanthropic association but rather as *dual bottom line institutions* whose profitability, efficiency and stability objectives are intertwined with deeply rooted local and social goals (Ayadi et al. 2010).

1.2 Types of Cooperative Banking Groups and Networks

Throughout the years, the need to increase efficiency and reach economy of scale or scope has led in many cases cooperative banks to evolve from small local entities to increasing integrated national groups or networks. As a matter of fact, the group or network structure is today adopted in almost all the European countries. By reflecting the cooperative principles, the general architecture of a cooperative group or network is typically an inverted pyramid whose basis is represented by members that belong to local banks, which, in turn, own a central bank. This two-tier structure may evolve in a three-tier structure when the figure of regional bank is collocated between local entities and central bodies. The central body is usually in charge of the governance and may have the power to control affiliates, even though it is owned, wholly or partially, by those affiliates. The main operational functions of the central body of the group or network are to provide liquidity, cash clearing and access to national central banks and financial markets. In this respect, banking cooperatives groups or networks usually work according to the *principle of subsidiary*. Local entities are responsible for the core activity of managing both personal and business relationships with clients and members and supporting local communities, while the other tiers of the inverted pyramid carry on specialised activities that can hence be considered outsourced (e.g. in the areas of asset management or, in the most sophisticated groups or networks, even investment banking). If on the one hand the group or network structure offers the advantages of centralised business functions (which became necessary in particular to ensure sufficient level of efficiency with the increasing pressure of competition), on the other hand, it may imply lower autonomy and independence of local entities in managing their business. Nevertheless, an important characteristic of cooperative groups or networks that compensate reduced autonomy of local entities is the internal mutual support which binds members to different degrees of *solidarity*.[6]

In this general framework, it is possible to detect two main types of models of cooperative banks conglomerates in Europe, on the basis of their specific organisational structure: *basic* and *integrated models*.[7] In *basic models*, cooperation and centralisation are limited. However, local banks are associated in accordance with statutory or legal provisions and own the central institution, which is able to facilitate access to financial markets and guarantees centralised liquidity management. These banks do not have an Institutional Protection Scheme (IPS) as identified by the Art. 113(7) of the Capital Requirements Regulation (CRR)[8,9] or a cross-guarantee scheme. *Integrated models* of cooperative banks are the most

[6] Moreover, in case of groups, the level of integration influences whether the entities which compose the group report either consolidated or individual report or figures (e.g. local and central German institutions report separately while in Finland and in Netherland consolidated figures are reported for the whole group) (Ayadi 2017).

[7] This classification is the one usually proposed by the European Association of Co-operative Banks (EACB). From a theoretical perspective, other main classifications of cooperative networks are described in the literature. Di Salvo (2002) distinguishes among networks centralised at national level, centralised at regional level, decentralised but legally integrated and decentralised but integrated on a voluntary base. According to the level of integration and decentralisation, Desrochers and Fischer (2005) identify the three categories of atomised systems, consensual networks and strategic networks.

[8] IPS is defined in the Capital Requirements Regulation (CRR) as "a contractual or statutory liability arrangement which protects those institutions and in particular ensures their liquidity and solvency to avoid bankruptcy where necessary". Even if from an accounting point of view IPSs cannot be considered banking groups, they have been defined "flexible groups" given that they are allowed by regulators to apply prudential requirements similar to those applied by members belonging to consolidate groups. The main difference between IPSs and consolidated groups is that in the former banks have a higher level of independence and are not under the control of a single entity. For an overview of IPS in the euro area, please see Choulet (2016).

[9] Regulation (EU) No 575/2013 of the European Parliament and of the Council of 26 June 2013 on prudential requirements for credit institutions and investment firms and amending Regulation (EU) No 648/2012.

common in European countries. Banks of this type share ownership structure and common features of advertising, brand name and products with all the banks that belong to the group, creating a strong identity in customers' perception. The variation in the degrees of integration of the management, centralisation of the control and independence of local entities also permits to detect three different kinds of ***integrated models: networks with an IPS, integrated cooperative networks*** and ***consolidate cooperative groups.*** In ***networks with an IPS***, banks remain largely independent in their daily activity but are tied by arrangements that ensure liquidity and solvency in case of bankruptcy. Local institutions within the network are individually supervised at national level. In ***integrated cooperative networks*** (as recognised by Art. 113(6) CRR), a parent-subsidiary relationship exists between the central bank and local entities, with the former having a number of control powers on local entities and the latter keeping political control on the central institution. Banks of this type may be supervised by the European Central Bank (ECB) (because of the size of the agglomerate), based on consolidated accounts. ***Consolidate cooperative groups*** (in line with Art. 10 CRR) are characterised by the highest degree of integration, which permits to consider the central body and local or regional banks as a single entity, even for what it concerns specific prudential requirements. In this sense, consolidated accounts are considered for monitoring the solvency and the liquidity of all the group entities. In this type of groups, the central bank has the mandate to supervise and instruct the management of local or regional banks. Moreover, the banks typically benefit from a cross-guarantee scheme. Figure 1.1 synthetises the main differences between the models discussed.

The differences in size, associated with other features of diversity, such as member and clients base, may also suggest a different classification of cooperative banks in two subgroups. On the one side, it is possible to observe small cooperative banks or banking conglomerates whose activities are predominantly directed to the home market and which have both low domestic market share and have a scarce or no international focus. On the other side, it is there are large cooperative banking groups that beside a relevant presence in the national market have also significant foreign activities (Groeneveld 2017).

From the discussion above, it is evident that the current landscape of the cooperative banking system in Europe comprises a vast diversity of cooperative banks and models, reflecting the variety in political, social, and economic environment and national legal frameworks (e.g. Karafolas 2016;

	BASIC MODELS	INTEGRATED MODELS		
		Networks with an IPS	*Integrated cooperative networks*	*Consolidated cooperative groups*
Main legal references	Art. 400(2)(d), 422(8) CRR	Art. 113(7) CRR	Art. 113(6) CRR	Art. 10 CRR
Institutional Protection Scheme	No	Yes	No	No
Cross-guarantee scheme	No	No	Yes	Yes
Degree of centralisation	Very Low	Low or Medium	High	Very High
Examples of groups or networks	Polish and Hungarian cooperative banks	BVR (DE), Fachverband der Raiffeisenbanken (AT)	Crédit Agricole, Crédit Mutuel, BPCE (FR)	OP-Pohjola (FI), Credito Agricola (PT), Raiffeisen Luxembourg (LU)

Fig. 1.1 Main organisation models in cooperative banking. Notes: Authors' elaboration

Ayadi et al. 2010; Alexopoulos and Goglio 2009). Nevertheless, the necessity to evolve into larger cooperative banking groups or networks represents a significant commonality in the heterogeneity of the cooperative banking system. As a by-product of this tendency, a growing degree of hybridisation of the offer can be today observed, taking shape through the proposal of a vast set of banking and financial services for all the types of customers.

1.3 Size and Geographical Presence of Cooperative Banks in Europe

Starting from the nineteenth century, cooperative banks have represented central players in European economic and financial systems (Fonteyne 2007). More than one century after, several waves of external competitive environmental changes, which included liberalisation, globalisation and innovation, led to the progressive modernisation and sophistication of the cooperative banks' structures while preserving the inherent principles of *membership and democratic governance*, *proximity* and *prudent management* (Boscia et al. 2009, 2010). In particular since 2008, the banking industry as a whole had also to face critical events such as the last financial crisis and the crisis of the sovereign debt, with all the consequences these events implied. The overall contraction of the economy, the reduction in the interest rates and the increase in regulatory burden affected in turn banks' profitability. In some European countries, cooperative banks have not ridden out the storms, thus disappearing or ending to occupy only a marginal role. Nevertheless, the majority of the cooperative banks managed to overcome difficulties. Some early studies conducted immediately after the crisis revealed that cooperative banks reported in general better performances than other organisational forms (e.g. Birchall and Ketilson 2009).[10] Yet, the last crisis eventually highlighted the resilience of the model of *stakeholder value banks* which, compared to their peers, have been less impacted. The amount of total assets of the entire banking sector showed more variability than that of the cooperative banks over the years of the crisis (Groeneveld 2017).[11] Higher capitalisation, lower dependence on financial markets and lower risk taking probably had a stabilising effect in particular on relatively small cooperative entities. Consistently, larger cooperative banking groups with a high level of hybridisation displayed a resistance similar to other joint-stock banking groups.

Data based on latest available statistics issued by the European Association of Co-operative Banks (EACB) for 24 cooperative banking groups or networks in 20 European countries[12,13] reveals that the number of cooperative banks' members reached 82 million in 2016.[14] In this respect, Fig. 1.2 shows the members' distribution for the major European cooperative banking groups and networks.[15] The observed disparity in

[10] Becchetti et al. (2016) document that over the period 1998–2010, cooperative banks display a lower proportion of derivatives over total assets, lower earnings volatility and higher loans/total assets ratios than commercial banks.

[11] The overview is released by TIAS School for Business and Society with the support of the EACB.

[12] Key statistics and financial indicators are made available by the EACB on a yearly basis and are openly accessible via the association's website. Last data consulted refers to the "Key statistics – Financial indicators 2016" factsheet.

[13] Dezelna Banka Slovenije d.d. (SI), Volksbanken (AT), Central Cooperative Bank (BG), Banque Raiffeisen (LU), SZHISZ (HU), LCCU Group (LT), Association of Cooperative Banks of Greece (GR), Cooperative Central Bank (CY), Nykredit (DK), Credito Agricola (PT), Creditcoop (RO), KZBS (PL), BCC (IT), BCC (ES), UNACC (ES), Raiffeisenbanken (AT), OP Financial Group (FI), Raiffeisen Schweiz (CH), Rabobank (NL), Crédit Mutuel (FR), BPCE (FR), Crédit Agricole (FR), Volks-Raiffeisenbanken (DE), Building Societies (UK).

[14] In this respect, member base appears even more relevant if expressed as member-to-population ratio, which equalled 19.2 per cent in 2015 with member growth that exceeds population growth (Groeneveld 2017). In addition, the number of members has even grown from the beginning of the crisis.

[15] Only cooperative banking groups whose number of members is more than one million are considered. The following groups are not represented: Dezelna Banka Slovenije d.d. (SI), Volksbanken (AT), Central Cooperative Bank (BG), Banque Raiffeisen (LU), SZHISZ (HU), LCCU Group (LT), Association of Cooperative Banks of Greece (GR), Cooperative Central Bank (CY), Nykredit (DK), Credito Agricola (PT), Creditcoop (RO), KZBS (PL).

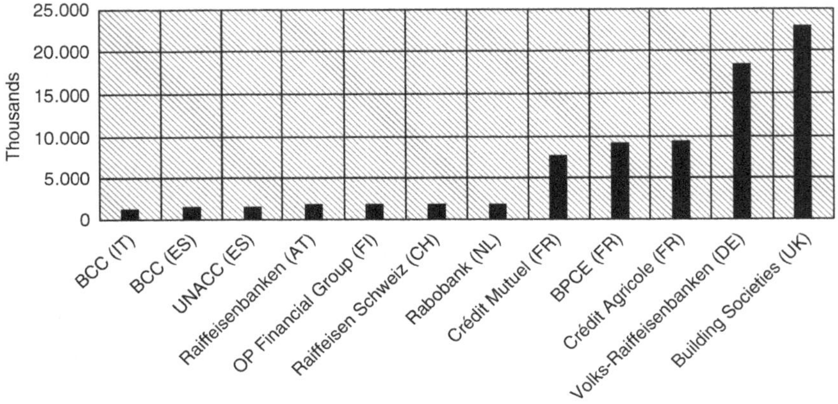

Fig. 1.2 Number of members for major European cooperative banking groups and networks. Notes: Authors' elaboration on data EACB. Data as of 31/12/2016

the number of members reflects cooperative banks' different attitude towards *membership*, by which some countries do actively recruit members while others do not, but also different individual market positioning. As far as it concerns the number of clients, in 2016 it reached more than 210 million all over Europe.[16] As for the number of members, also the number of clients is very different among countries, ranging from a few thousands for the LCCU Group (Lithuania) to a maximum of 52 million for Crédit Agricole (France). Correspondingly, the number of branches varies from a minimum of 42 (Banque Raiffeisen, Luxembourg) to a maximum of 11,787 (Volks and Raiffeisenbanken, Germany). To this extent, the cooperative banks' branch market share in 2015 peaked to 31.5 per cent, and from the beginning of the crisis, other banks closed more branches than cooperative banks (11.0 per cent versus only 3.5 per cent). This data on branches in particular suggests that in a world that is always more virtual, cooperative banks have managed so far to ensure their physical presence fairly well (Groeneveld 2017). The significant disparateness in political, social, and economical characteristics of European countries is also conveyed through the differences in asset size of cooperative banks, presented in Fig. 1.3. The ratio of the largest (Crédit Agricole, France)

[16] These figures include both retail and business clients.

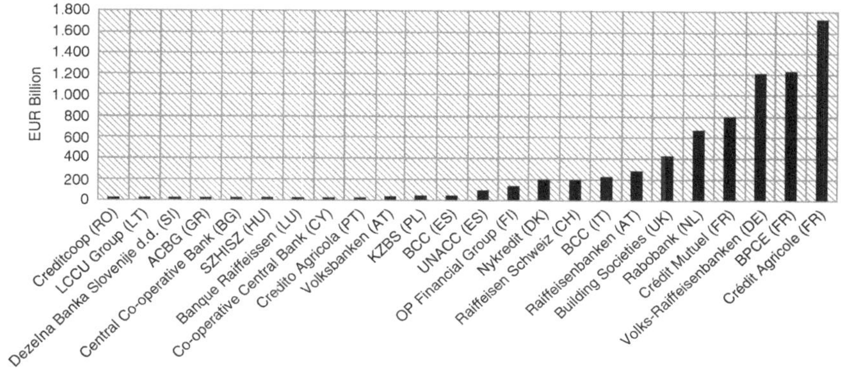

Fig. 1.3 Total assets for major European cooperative banking groups and networks. Notes: Authors' elaboration on data EACB. Data as of 31/12/2016

to the smallest (Creditcoop, Romania) institution is more than 7000.[17] Some cooperative groups have reached remarkable dimensions and sophistication.[18] Four cooperative conglomerates such as Crédit Agricole, BPCE and Crédit Mutuel in France and Rabobank in the Netherlands are today among the 20 largest European banks by assets and 11th, 19th, 37th and 43rd in the ranking of the largest banks in the world, respectively (Standard and Poor 2017).[19]

Finally, some descriptive statistics on the domestic market share of major cooperative banks over Europe as concerns domestic deposits, loans and mortgages are presented in Table 1.1. Overall, these figures confirm

[17] This huge difference is driven by the fact that Credicoop role in Romanian banking system is minor, for several reasons such as the high competition with commercial banks, the reputational problem of credit cooperative organisations and the perceptions of the communist system influence (Pirvu and Banica 2016).

[18] In terms of corporate governance, belonging to large financial integrated conglomerates has positive and negative effects. On one side, governance complexity increases and the efficacy of managers and board members' control on the central institutions become controversial, with a risk of misalignments of interests. On the other side, some corporate governance mechanisms work better when institutions belong to networks since the monitoring role was played by the apex organisation and the pressure exerted by the peers within the network.

[19] In this respect, Fig. 1.3 shows the total assets for all the Volks-Raiffeisenbanken in Germany, which are organised in the form of a *network with an IPS* and do not consolidate. For this reason, they cannot be mentioned among the largest banks in Europe.

Table 1.1 Domestic market shares for cooperative groups and networks

		Domestic market share (%)		
		Deposits	*Loans*	*Mortgages*
Austria	Österreichische Raiffeisenbanken	30.2	28.6	26.0
	Österreichischer Volksbanken	3.5	4.3	7.9
Bulgaria	Central Cooperative Bank	5.7	4.3	1.8
Cyprus	Cooperative Central Bank	26.0	22.0	36.0
Denmark	Nykredit	5.4	30.8	41.2
Finland	OP Financial Group	38.5	35.4	39.4
France	Crédit Agricole	24.4	21.4	30.2
	Crédit Mutuel	15.5	17.1	20.1
	BPCE	21.5	20.7	26.2
Germany	Cooperative Financial Network	21.4	21.1	28.5
Greece	Association of Cooperative Banks of Greece	1.0	0.8	n.a.
Hungary	SZHISZ	10.0	8.0	8.4
Italy	Federcasse (BCC)	7.7	7.2	9.8
Lithuania	LCCU Group	2.0	1.0	1.0
Luxembourg	Banque Raiffeisen	22.0	14.0	14.0
The Netherlands	Rabobank	34.0	n.a.	21.0
Poland	National Union of Cooperative Banks (KZBS)	9.8	7.2	2.2
Portugal	Credito Agricola	6.8	4.5	3.0
Slovenia	Dezelna Banka Slovenije d.d.	3.1	2.2	n.a.
Spain	Unión Nacional de Cooperativas de Crédito (UNACC)	6.0	4.5	n.a.
	Banco de Crédito Cooperativo (BCC)	2.2	2.6	n.a.
United Kingdom	Building Societies Association	18.4	n.a.	21.5

Notes: Authors' elaboration on data EACB. Data as of 31/12/2016. n.a. stands for not available

the relevance of cooperative banks over Europe.[20] If the weight of cooperative banks in terms of bank deposits and loans can be estimated to about one-fifth in the European Union as a whole (Fiordelisi and Mare 2014), the presence of the cooperative banks turns to be of systematic importance in key European countries, such as Austria, France, Germany and the Netherlands.

[20] When considering major cooperative banking groups only, data reveals that over the years 2011–2015, deposit and loan market shares improved by 0.5 and 1.1 per cent to 21.9 and 22.3 per cent, respectively (Groeneveld 2017).

1.4 Cooperative Banks and Relationship Banking[21]

Relationship banking can be defined as the provision of financial services by a financial intermediary to the market on the basis of both hard and soft information, this latter obtained through a long-term engagement and continuous interaction with the client. Cooperative banks are by far the most important relationship banking institutions.[22] In this respect, relationship lending is the main lending technology they use, opposite to the traditional transaction lending technologies[23] massively adopted in particular by commercial banks (Leyshon and Thrift 1999).

Relationship banking is particularly effective in SMEs financing. In fact, by adopting relationship lending, cooperative banks hold a noticeable expertise in serving informationally opaque borrowers. This expertise stems mainly from the intensive use of qualitative information derived from the establishment of long-term credit relationships. Engaging in repeated interactions entails beneficial effects for both parties, allowing them to reach pareto-superior outcomes compared to what they could get in spot-market transactions. Repeated lender-borrower interactions enhance cooperative behaviour and mutual trust, which in turn facilitate the flow of soft information between parties (Uzzi and Lancaster 2003). A sort of implicit arrangement is then formed: borrowers are ready to deliver more private information on their financial situation to the lenders, provided that they have a reasonable guarantee to benefit from credit availability at a reasonable price. At the same time, lenders make the implicit promise of ensuring further credit availability to borrowers as they have a clear view of the latter, thanks to the high-quality soft knowledge they have gathered (Sharpe 1990; Guille 1994; Rivaud-Danset 1996).

[21] This section largely draws on Cornée (2014). We gratefully thank *Journal of Entrepreneurial and Organizational Diversity* for authorising the use of excerpts from the original article.

[22] In many instances, banking institutions that follow the same organisational pattern (i.e. a decentralised decision-making) may exhibit quite a similar behaviour in their lending practices (e.g. DeYoung et al. 2004; Scott 2004). This is especially the case for other stakeholder-oriented banks, such as community banks and savings banks. This justifies why the studies reviewed in this section are not specifically conducted on cooperative banks. There exists very little research comparing cooperative banks with their commercial counterparts, the studies being generally carried out on the banking industry as a whole.

[23] Examples of transaction lending technologies are financial statement lending, asset-based lending and small business credit scoring.

Regardless of the indicator used to this scope,[24] empirical evidence reports quite univocally that for the borrowing firm, stronger lending relationships result in a lower probability of being rationed (Uzzi 1999; Lehmann and Neuberger 2001; Cole et al. 2004) or in a reduced recourse to more expensive sources of financing, such as trade credit (Petersen and Rajan 1994). This evidence shows that banks amplify credit availability directly through facilitated debt provision, but they can also do it indirectly by reducing collateral requirements. The repeated interactions in long-term credit relationships allow lenders to condition their credit terms on the past repayment behaviour of borrowers. By repeatedly repaying their debt rather than defaulting, borrowers can positively alter lenders' beliefs about their creditworthiness (Fehr and Zehnder 2006). By strengthening their creditworthiness over time, borrowers build a reputation with lenders. Reputation can act as an intangible asset which may be pledged by small entrepreneurs to compensate their lack of real assets, thereby circumventing the problems associated with collateral requirements. Empirical evidence unambiguously supports this argumentation by documenting that stronger relationships are associated with reduced collateral requirements (e.g. Berger and Udell 1995; Degryse and Van Cayseele 2000).[25]

Another reason explaining the cooperative banks' reliance on relationship lending lies in the specificities of their decision-making processes. Both theory and evidence suggest that relationship lending will be more likely to deliver efficient outcomes in small or decentralised banks, which are characterised by few managerial layers. Loan officers are more predisposed to collecting and adequately exploiting high-quality soft information, which is typically embedded in social relationships, under the condition that they have a sufficient authority on the bank's fund allocation (Stein 2002; Berger et al. 2005). By contrast, large, centralised banks with multiple layers of management and more hierarchical decision-

[24] There exist many empirical works highlighting the benefits associated with relationship lending in terms of credit availability. Methodologically speaking, the strength of lending relationships is generally measured via three indicators: its duration (defined as the number of years the bank has offered loans, deposits or other financial services to the firm), its scope (proxied by the quantity of financial services contracted by the firm) and its exclusivity (evaluated in terms of the bank being the firm's sole debt provider).

[25] A possible distinctive role of cooperative banks in helping SMEs to access finance and even to indirectly reach the financial markets is discussed by Migliorelli and Dessertine (2017) in the framework of the introduction of new market-oriented financing instruments in the EU agriculture to finance environmentally friendly practices.

making processes will be more inclined to rely on arm's length transactions with their borrowers, low transferability of soft facts within the organisation resulting in prohibitive internal contractual costs (Liberti and Mian 2009). The analysis of cooperative banks' organisational architecture supports this view. In spite of the significant consolidation and integration they have undergone, cooperative banks still exhibit a more decentralised decision-making process than do their commercial counterparts (Ory and Lemzeri 2012). Loan approval decisions in cooperative banks are also more likely to be based on proximity and mutual trust, as more discretion is granted to loan officers in the lending process (Abdesselam et al. 2002). On a similar note, the management of credit lines, which crystallises the quality of the interactions, may be more flexible. In contrast, loan officers in commercial banks have less managerial latitude and adopt a more technical approach to lending and credit-granting decisions, which depend on the firm's financial statements and on credit analysts' sector expertise. Credit lines granted to borrowers are also proportionally less important in terms of volume, and more stringently managed (Abdesselam et al. 2002).

Finally, cooperative banks rely more on relationship lending as a result of their ownership structure. The way equity is held and traded is still a major distinctive feature between cooperatives, which usually are not listed in stock markets, and commercial banks, which are often listed corporations (Ory et al. 2006). Subsequently, commercial banks are considerably more exposed to the pressure and discipline exerted by stock markets. The pursuit of shareholder value maximisation may also impact the lending strategy of commercial banks. Typically, they are incited to invest in assets that are currently profitable to meet the short-term profitability constraints dictated by shareholders.[26] In contrast, cooperative banks are notably less subject to market pressure and their goal is not profit maximisation, at least in the short run, but rather their members' consumer surplus, through the provision of financial services at moderate prices to retail clients (Hesse and Cihac 2007).[27]

[26] Orléan (1999) provides an in-depth theoretical analysis explaining how the microstructural features of financial markets lead to short-term profit maximisation.

[27] Even though cooperatives may not face short-term market constraints, they need to attain a certain level of profitability in the medium or long term to be competitive in the industry. On the whole, cooperatives' profitability constraint is not dictated by short-term pressure exerted by stock markets but rather by medium or long-term product market (Gianfaldoni and Richez-Battesti 2005). The medium or long-term profitability constraint is

However, relationship lending may also bring about undesirable side effects for SMEs. The principal effect is an informational *hold-up* for borrowers. By trading with only one bank, a borrower may, over the course of the relationship, become captive to their incumbent bank since (s)he is unable to signal their quality to other banks as their debt provision relies mainly on soft, non-transmittable knowledge (Sharpe 1990).[28] Lenders may in turn take advantage of their bargaining power and extract rents from lending relationships by raising their interest rates (Boot 2000; Von Thadden 1995). The findings of Angelini et al. (1998) are of great interest as regards in particular cooperative banks. The authors report a *hold-up* effect for borrowers trading only for commercial banks and not for borrowers that are members of a credit cooperative. This echoes the conclusions reached by Cornée et al. (2012), which experimentally show that lenders exhibiting stronger social preferences do not take advantage of their bargaining power to charge a higher interest rate to their borrowers. Subsequently, borrowers who benefit from fairer credit offers have a lower propensity to taking excessive risks in their investment choices. Reciprocity may thus act as a powerful mechanism against moral hazard (Fehr et al. 2009). Altogether, these studies reveal that cooperative banks guarantee credit availability and are less stringent for collateral requirements when long-term credit relationships are established. In this respect, they may act similarly to their commercial counterparts. Nevertheless,

more in line with the temporality of relationship lending. Financing young or de *novo* small borrowing firms is seldom fully profitable in the short-term. When a bank finances small businesses via relationship lending, it makes a substantial investment in the first interactions, which is then amortised over several periods, through repeated interactions with the businesses. In other words, lenders subsidise borrowers in early periods and get reimbursed for this subsidy thereafter (Petersen and Rajan 1995). Such a long-term strategy may be feasible for cooperative banks, but rather incompatible with their commercial counterparts that may be subject to short-term shareholder maximisation. Similarly, a fiercely competitive credit market may be destructive to the formation of mutually beneficial relationships between lenders and borrowers. Lenders are reluctant to assist informationally opaque borrowers and consequently accept lower returns upfront if they fear that the future benefits associated with this early assistance may be reaped by competitors (Petersen and Rajan 1995).

[28] To mitigate this "hold-up" problem, SMEs increasingly favour multiple sources of capital. By trading with several banks and by pitting one against the other, borrowers can reduce the cost of their debt. Nonetheless, multi-banking strategies affect the cost of capital in various ways. As explained in the rest of this section, the quality of debt supply (i.e. capital availability and reduced collateral requirement) deteriorates along with the number of financiers, thereby incurring indirect financing costs that will eventually be embedded in the interest rate.

even though limited, evidence shows that cooperatives appear to grant a better treatment to borrowers as regards sharing the rent generated by credit relationships.[29]

1.5 Characteristics of the Support of Cooperative Banks to the Economy

Cooperative banking has been given considerably more attention by the economic researchers since the outbreak of the Great Crisis. A growing body of empirical work seeks to analyse how the governance and ownership characteristics of cooperative banks affect not only their own behaviour but also the entire banking system. These specificities are generally examined in a comparative perspective: the merits of cooperative banks are relatively assessed against the practices of other banks, chiefly commercial, capitalistic banks, which are deemed to represent the standard banking institutions.

The archetypical model of credit cooperatives, as outlined above, has undergone significant changes over the last century to form large banking groups (Ayadi et al. 2010). Even though cooperative banks have pursued hybridisation strategies by evolving in some cased into full-service universal banks or by entering into activities that were not inherently entrenched, such as corporate and investment banking (Ory and Lemzeri 2012), they still appear to be anchored to their business basics and firmly adhere to traditional intermediation.[30] In the context of France, Gianfaldoni and Richez-Battesti (2005) show that cooperative banks are by far the main external funders of SMEs and households. Labye et al. (2002) and Ayadi et al. (2010) generalise these findings to Europe by showing that cooperative banks are major retail banking players in most EU countries. More formal proof of cooperative banks' support to the real economy is brought by Becchetti et al. (2016). The authors first report that cooperative banks display a higher loan-to-asset ratio, a higher proportion of their total

[29] In any case, empirical evidence regarding the *hold-up* hypothesis is still somehow contradictory. For instance, D'Auria et al. (1999), Degryse and Van Cayseele (2000), and Degryse and Ongena (2005) report that longer relationships result in a higher interest rate charged to borrowers. Berger and Udell (1995), Uzzi (1999), as well as Berger et al. (2007) reach an opposite conclusion. Moreover, many studies (e.g. Elsas and Krahnen 1998; Machauer and Weber 1998; Lehmann and Neuberger 2001) show no significant effect.

[30] Nonetheless, the current developments of microfinance practices in Europe imply that cooperative banks have somehow drifted away from their original goal of facilitating access to credit to non-bankable.

income stemming from the interest margin and a lower reliance on complex financial operations, such as derivatives trading. They then show these accounting measures, specifically an increase in the loan-to-asset ratio, are positively correlated with the value-added growth of the manufacturing sector. In line with these findings, Coccorese and Shaffer (2018) document that cooperative banks enhance local economic development.

A few studies have analysed whether cooperative banks play a distinctive role in the transmission of the monetary transmission (within the stream of literature that tries to analyse the so-called *bank lending channel*). In this respect, while some works focus on the quantities (e.g. specific loan supply policies provided by cooperative banks), there is only indirect evidence on the prices (e.g. specific interest rate pass-through mechanisms provided by cooperative banks). Regarding the quantities, Ferri et al. (2014) show that, following a monetary contraction (i.e. an increase in the short-interest rate), cooperative banks restrain their loan supply to a lesser extent than do commercial banks. These less procyclical lending policies conducted by cooperative banks help maintain longer-term bank-customer relationships and smooth access to credit for borrowers. Meriläinen (2016) goes further in this direction, since he documents that lending growth in cooperative banks, as compared to that in commercial banks, is more regular and markedly less sensitive to negative shocks, such as the last financial crisis and the sovereign debt crisis. Becchetti et al. (2016) further qualify this view by indicating that cooperative banks' difference in terms of their proportion of loans to total assets did not increase during the financial crisis but actually tightened a bit, hence suggesting that the growth pace of cooperative banks' loan assets, albeit quite unresponsive to macroeconomic shocks, is slower than that of their total assets. Nevertheless, Migliorelli and Brunelli (2016) observe a limitation to the countercyclical role of cooperative banks in terms of lending provision with respect to the south-west part of the euro area, which includes the economies hit more severely by the crisis. Regarding the interest-rate-setting behaviour, the evidence relates to research endeavours aimed at examining the general impact of relationship banking, and not the precise influence of cooperative banking. For example, Bolton et al. (2013) report that Italian relational banks, compared to transactional ones, charged a higher spread before the crisis but offered more favourable continuation-lending terms in response to the crisis.[31] This fits the idea that relational banks tend to smooth the price effects of monetary tightening events (Gambacorta 2008).

[31] Yet, some evidence suggests that cooperative banks also charge lower interest rate in non-crisis times (e.g. Cornée et al. 2017).

1.6 Stability of Cooperative Banks

The impact of cooperative banks on stability can be assessed at both individual and sector level. To get a sense of the key contributions on this issue, it is useful to understand how the main empirical proxy of stability, the *z-score*, is constructed. The *z-score* is defined as follows: $z - score = \frac{k + \mu}{\sigma_\mu}$, where k is the level of capitalisation (equity-to-asset ratio), μ is the return on assets and σ_μ is the standard deviation of the return on assets, as a proxy for return volatility (e.g. Mercieca et al. 2007). Assuming the normality of bank returns, the *z-score* measures the number of standard deviations a return realisation has to fall in order to deplete equity (Hesse and Cihac 2007). The higher the *z-score*, the less probable for a bank to become insolvent, and the higher is the bank's stability. At the individual level, the evidence indicates that the cooperative banks display higher average *z-scores* than do their commercial counterparts, suggesting that their business model is more stable (Hesse and Cihac 2007; Chiaramonte et al. 2015; Köhler 2015). In reality, this result conceals two distinct effects: the denominator of cooperative banks' *z-score* is much lower than for other banks, highlighting a much lower volatility of cooperative banks' returns, which more than offsets their lower level of profitability and capitalisation, detected by lower values at the numerator at their *z-scores*.

At the sector level, Hesse and Cihac (2007) show that a higher share of cooperative banks increases stability (again measured by *z-score*) of an average bank in the same banking system. However, this is only an average effect based on all types of banks, insofar as weak commercial banks' soundness is negatively affected by a larger presence of cooperative banks. Chiaramonte et al. (2015) generally confirm these findings, but indicate that the stabilising power of cooperative banks is specifically detectable during the crisis years and above a certain market share threshold. Lastly, the stabilising effect attributable to cooperative banks is more likely to be observable in competitive environment (Fiordelisi and Mare 2014; Chiaramonte et al. 2015). In general, the higher stability of cooperative banks stems from the very nature of their business, namely their adherence to traditional intermediation activities, which are markedly less volatile than market activities. Retail activities remain cooperative banks' crucial activity and usually provide them with a stable source of revenue. In diversified cooperative banking groups, basic intermediation activities operated by local banks may act as a buffer, which in bad times dampens losses from market operations and corporate investment activities undertaken by central bodies (Ory and Lemzeri 2012).

In literature, stability is also assessed with respect to the assets and liabilities sides of banks' balance sheets separately. On the assets side, cooperative banks not only have more loans as a proportion of their assets, but they also exhibit a more prudent lending behaviour. In this respect, Iannotta et al.'s study (2007) shows that cooperative banks hold a loan portfolio of better quality and display lower asset risk than do both private and public banks. This finding can be rationalised by the fact that relationship lending, which is more intensively used by cooperative banks, ensures more informed credit-granting decisions and, subsequently, fewer defaults (Grunert et al. 2005; Cornée 2017). On a related note, Meriläinen (2017) documents that loan loss provisioning is proportionally less important and less cyclical in cooperative banks, hence suggesting that they are more risk-adverse than their commercial equivalents. On the liabilities side, cooperative banks appear to benefit from more stable sources of funding. In a context where depositors are increasingly taking control of their banking relationships, Brunetti et al. (2016) investigate households' decision to switch bank and report that cooperative banks are nine per cent less likely to be discarded by these households. This is not due to commercial-based behaviour such as high remuneration of deposits (Cornée et al. 2017) or the practice to lock in customers by imposing high switching costs (Egarius and Weill 2016). On the contrary, it is mainly the consequence of non-commercial factors embedded in *membership*. Members derive a special value from the relationship with their cooperative bank, which cannot be reducible to purely material benefits. This sort of cement, based inter alia on local community involvement, allows a lasting relationship even in context in which trade becomes more fluid and barriers are broken down (Fulton 1999). Thanks to this social attachment, cooperative banks have stickier deposits, which should impact positively their financial stability and ability to meet prudential liquidity requirements.

1.7 Cooperative Banks and Savings Banks

Saving banks are considered, at the same level of cooperative banks, *stakeholder value banks*.[32] Savings banks can be found in almost every country in Western Europe, but they are especially prominent in large central

[32] The earliest savings banks were established in late eighteenth century, but they became more common at the turn of the nineteenth century as welfare institutions. Savings banks were typically set up by groups of socially minded, wealthy individuals or public authorities.

European countries and in Scandinavia, with more than 30 per cent of the market share in Germany, Austria and Norway (Meriläinen 2016).[33] In most European countries, savings banks share four common institutional features (Ayadi et al. 2009). First, they focus on savings mobilisation and retail banking activities. Second, they have a non-profit status and are committed to a dual objective, as they are expected to fulfil a social mission while being financially viable. Third, their operations are generally restricted to a geographical region, which is defined by the legal status of the public or private entity sponsoring them. Last, they are usually decentralised, autonomous elements of larger networks, which allow them to achieve economies of scale for, inter alia, information systems, marketing or representation functions.

In all these respects, savings banks do not significantly differ from cooperative banks. The main criterion of demarcation between the two types of institutions lies on the contrary in their ownership structure. Unlike cooperative banks, savings banks are not owned by (a part) of their customers. Instead, the capital is typically held by local public authorities (e.g. municipalities or regions) or by private foundations whose starting capital originates from donative financing. In publicly owned savings banks, public authorities retain the control rights, while in privately owned banks, the board of directors is self-perpetuating (appoints itself and its successors). With regard to the receipt of residual earnings in savings banks, the profit beyond the upkeep is not distributed to owners since there exist no owners or members in any proper sense, but rather shared by customers (Hansmann 1997).

They were accordingly organised either as a public law regime or as foundations or associations with a non-profit mission. They were mandated to foster the *spirit of thriftiness* among underprivileged people, by providing them safe savings facilities. The resources were invested in safe, liquid assets, such as government securities. Precautionary savings for life events and retirement render were intended as a means of addressing vulnerability and reducing dependence on charitable aid. Later, their mission was extended to delivering, at reasonable terms, credit and ancillary services for those who were rationed out, such as low-income households, SMEs, and local public investment projects (Ayadi et al. 2009).

[33] Private ownership is predominant in Scandinavian and Italian savings banks. In contrast, in Germany and Austria, savings banks are publicly owned and represent alongside cooperative and commercial banks an essential component of the so-called *three-pillar system* (Bülbül et al. 2013). In Germany, they total up to 50 million customers (ESBG 2013). In Spain, privately owned savings banks historically constituted a major component in the banking sector, but their market share drastically shrank after the last financial crisis

There exists very little theoretical work on the effect of being a savings bank versus being a cooperative bank on the adherence to the foundational values and on the consideration of customers' interests. In a collective action perspective, one may assume that when control rights are clearly identifiable, as is often the case in public savings banks, the exercise of control over managers is possibly easier and more effective than in cooperative banks, wherein capital ownership is widely diffuse (Bülbül et al. 2013). At the same time, member exit and withdrawal of the member share, which is a powerful mechanism to discipline managers in cooperative banks, does not exist by definition in savings banks (Ayadi et al. 2009, 2010). In addition, it is possible that in cooperative banks, customers' desiderata are embodied more satisfactorily by directors (and thus managers), as the latter democratically represent, perhaps imperfectibly, the former. No such representative system exits in savings banks. Altogether, the difference between the two constitutive categories of stakeholder banks largely remains within the empirical realm. The studies mentioned in the previous section generally include dummy variables that permit to capture the differential effects between cooperative banks and savings banks. Interestingly, the two groups exhibit similarities in their activities and contribution to financial stability. However, most studies report that the results are generally less robust for savings banks than for cooperative banks. First, the statistical and economic significance is usually lower for savings banks. Second, country-specific analyses show that the sensitivity to the national context is more pronounced in the case of savings banks. Third, smoothing effects and relational dynamics, which are consistently detectable for cooperative banks, especially in times of crisis, are not always observable in savings banks.

References

Abdesselam, R., Cieply, S., & Le Pape, N. (2002). Les facteurs de différentiation des banques mutualistes et AFB en matière de financement des PME-PMI. *Revue d'Economie Financière, 67*, 121–131.

Alexopoulos, Y., & Goglio, S. (2009). *Financial Deregulation and Economic Distress: Is There a Future for Financial Co-Operatives?* Euricse Working Papers, No. 001/09.

Angelini, P., Di Salvo, R., & Ferri, G. (1998). Availability and Cost of Credit for Small Businesses: Customer Relationships and Credit Cooperatives. *Journal of Banking & Finance, 22*(6–8), 925–954.

Ayadi, R. (2017). Banks' Business Models in Europe: Are Cooperative Banks Different? In E. Miklaszewska (Ed.), *Institutional Diversity in Banking: Small Country, Small Bank Perspectives*. London: Palgrave Macmillan.

Ayadi, R., Llewellyn, D., Schmidt, R. H., Arbak, E., & De Groen, P. W. (2009). *Investigating Diversity in the Banking Sector in Europe: Performance and Role of Savings Banks*. Brussels: CEPS Paperbacks.

Ayadi, R., Llewellyn, D., Schmidt, R. H., Arbak, E., & De Groen, P. W. (2010). *Investigating Diversity in the Banking Sector in Europe: Key Developments, Performance and Role of Cooperative Banks*. Brussels: CEPS Paperbacks.

Barker, J. L., Bronstein, J. L., Friesen, M. L., Jones, E. I., Reeve, H. K., Zink, A. G., & Frederickson, M. E. (2017). Synthesizing Perspectives on the Evolution of Cooperation Within and Between Species. *Evolution, 71*, 814–825.

Becchetti, L., Ciciretti, R., & Paolantonio, A. (2016). The Cooperative Bank Difference Before and After the Global Financial Crisis. *Journal of International Money and Finance, 69*, 224–246.

Berger, A. N., Miller, N. H., Petersen, M. A., Rajan, R. G., & Stein, J. C. (2005). Does Function Allow Organizational Form? Evidence from the Lending Practices of Large and Small Banks. *Journal of Financial Economics, 76*(2), 237–269.

Berger, A. N., Rosen, R. J., & Udell, G. F. (2007). Does Market Size Structure Affect Competition: The Case of Small Business Lending. *Journal of Banking & Finance, 31*(1), 11–33.

Berger, A. N., & Udell, G. F. (1995). Relationship Lending and Lines of Credit in Small Firm Finance. *Journal of Business, 68*(3), 351–381.

Birchall, J., & Ketilson, L. H. (2009). *Resilience of the Cooperative Business Model in Times of Crisis*. Geneva: International Labour Office, Sustainable Enterprise Programme.

Bolton, P., Freixas, X., Gambacorta, L., & Mistrulli, P. E. (2013). *Relationship and Transaction Lending in a Crisis*. BIS Working Papers, No 417.

Boot, A. W. A. (2000). Relationship Banking: What Do We Know? *Journal of Financial Intermediation, 9*(1), 7–25.

Boscia, V., Carretta, A., & Schwizer, P. (2009). *Cooperative Banking: Innovations and Developments*. London: Palgrave Macmillan.

Boscia, V., Carretta, A., & Schwizer, P. (2010). *Cooperative Banking in Europe: Case Studies*. London: Palgrave Macmillan.

Brunetti, M., Ciciretti, R., & Djordjevic, L. (2016). The Determinants of Household's Bank Switching. *Journal of Financial Stability, 26*, 175–189.

Bülbül, D., Schmidt, R. H., & Schüwer, U. (2013). *Savings Banks and Cooperative Banks in Europe*. White Paper Series No. 5.

Carretta, A. (2011). *Il Credito Cooperativo. Storia, Diritto, Economia, Organizzazione*. Bologna: Il Mulino.

Chiaramonte, L., Poli, F., & Oriani, M. E. (2015). Are Cooperative Banks a Lever for Promoting Bank Stability? Evidence from the Recent Financial Crisis in OECD Countries. *European Financial Management, 21*(3), 491–523.

Choulet, C. (2016). Institutional Protection Systems: Are They Banking Groups? *BNP Economic Research.*

Coccorese, P., & Shaffer, S. (2018). *Cooperative Banks and Local Economic Growth.* CAMA Working Paper No. 11/2018.

Cole, R. A., Goldberg, L. G., & White, J. W. (2004). Cookie Cutter vs. Character: The Micro Structure of Small Business Lending by Large and Small Banks. *Journal of Financial and Quantitative Analysis, 39*(2), 227–250.

Cornée, S. (2014). Soft Information and Default Prediction in Cooperative and Social Banks. *Journal of Organizational and Entrepreneurial Diversity, 3*(1), 89–109.

Cornée, S. (2017). The Relevance of Soft Information for Predicting Small Business Credit Default: Evidence from a Social Bank. *Journal of Small Business Management*, in press.

Cornée, S., Kalmi, P., & Szafarz, A. (2017). *The Business Model of Social Banking.* Unpublished Manuscript.

Cornée, S., Masclet, D., & Thenet, G. (2012). Credit Relationships: Evidence from Experiments with Real Bankers. *Journal of Money, Credit and Banking, 44*(5), 957–980.

D'Auria, C., Foglia, A., & Reedtz, P. (1999). Bank Interest Rates and Credit Relationships in Italy. *Journal of Banking and Finance, 23*(7), 1067–1093.

Degryse, H., & Ongena, S. (2005). Distance, Lending Relationships, and Competition. *Journal of Finance, 60*(1), 231–266.

Degryse, H., & Van Cayseele, P. (2000). Relationship Lending Within a Bank-Based System: Evidence from European Small Business Data. *Journal of Financial Intermediation, 9*(1), 90–109.

Desrochers, M., & Fischer, K. P. (2005). The Power of Networks: Integration and Financial Cooperative Performance. *Annals of Public and Cooperative Economics, 76*(3), 307–354.

DeYoung, R., Hunter, W. C., & Udell, G. F. (2004). The Past, Present and Probable Future of Community Banks. *Journal of Financial Service Research, 25*(2–3), 85–133.

Di Salvo, R. (2002). La gouvernance des systèmes bancaires mutualistes et coopératifs en Europe. *Revued'Economie Financière, 67*, 65–177.

Egarius, D., & Weill, L. (2016). Switching Costs and Market Power in the Banking Industry: The Case of Cooperative Banks. *Journal of International Financial Markets, Institutions and Money, 42*, 155–165.

Elsas, R., & Krahnen, J. P. (1998). Is Relationship Lending Special? Evidence from Credit-File Data in Germany. *Journal of Banking and Finance, 22*(10–11), 1283–1316.

ESBG. (2013). *European Savings Banks Group, Key Figures.*

Fehr, E., Brown, M., & Zehnder, C. (2009). On Reputation: A Microfoundation of Contract Enforcement and Price Rigidity. *Economic Journal, 119*(536), 333–353.

Fehr, E., & Zehnder, C. (2006). *Reputation and Credit Market Formation.* FINRISK Working Paper, University of Zurich.

Ferri, G., Kalmi, P., & Kerola, E. (2014). Does Bank Ownership Affect Lending Behavior? Evidence from the Euro Area. *Journal of Banking and Finance, 48*, 194–209.

Fiordelisi, F., & Mare, D. S. (2014). Competition and Financial Stability in European Cooperative Banks. *Journal of International Money and Finance, 45*, 1–16.

Fonteyne, W. (2007). *Co-operative Banks in Europe – Policy Issues.* IMF Working Paper.

Fulton, M. (1999). Cooperatives and Member Commitment. *Finnish Journal of Business Economics, 4*, 418–437.

Gambacorta, L. (2008). How Do Banks Set Interest Rates? *European Economic Review, 52*(5), 792–819.

Gianfaldoni, P., & Richez-Battesti, N. (2005). *Les Banques Coopératives en France: Entre Spécificités et Banalisation.* Rapport pour la DIIESE.

Gintis, H., Bowles, S., Boyd, R., & Fehr, E. (2004). *Moral Sentiments and Material Interests: The Foundations of Cooperation in Economic Life.* Cambridge: MIT Press.

Groeneveld, J. M. (2017). *A Snapshot of European Co-operative Banking 2017.* Tilburg: TIAS School for Business and Society.

Grunert, J., Norden, L., & Weber, M. (2005). The Role of Non-Financial Factors in Internal Credit Ratings. *Journal of Banking and Finance, 29*(2), 509–531.

Guille, M. (1994). Savoir bancaire spécifique, marché du crédit et intermédiation financière. *Economie Appliquée, 67*, 49–77.

Hansmann, H. (1997). *The Ownership of Enterprise.* Cambridge, MA: Harvard University Press.

Harari, Y. N. (2012). *From Animals into Gods: A Brief History of Humankind.* North Charleston, SC: CreateSpace Independent Publishing Platform.

Hesse, H., & Cihac, M. (2007). *Cooperative Banks and Financial Stability.* Working Paper No. 07/02, International Monetary Fund.

Iannotta, G., Nocera, G., & Sironi, A. (2007). Ownership Structure, Risk and Performance in the European Banking Industry. *Journal of Banking & Finance, 31*(7), 2127–2149.

Karafolas, S. (2016). *Credit Cooperative Institutions in European Countries.* Berlin: Springer.

Kay, J. (2006, April 26). The Mutual Interest in Building Trust Still Remains. *Financial Times.*

Köhler, M. (2015). Which Banks Are More Risky? The Impact of Business Models on Bank Stability. *Journal of Financial Stability, 16*, 195–212.

La "governance" des systèmes bancaires mutualistes et coopératifs en Europe
Labye, A., Lagoutte, C., & Renversez, F. (2002). Banques Mutualistes et Systèmes Financiers: une Analyse Comparative. Allemagne, Grande-Bretagne, France. *Revue d'Economie Financière, 67*, 85–109.
Lang, F., Signore, S., & Gvetadze, S. (2016). *The Role of Cooperative Banks and Smaller Institutions for the Financing of SMEs and Small Midcaps in Europe*. EIF Working Paper 2016/36, Luxembourg.
Lehmann, E., & Neuberger, D. (2001). Do Lending Relationships Matter? Evidence from Bank Survey Data in Germany. *Journal of Economic Behavior and Organization, 45*(4), 339–359.
Leyshon, A., & Thrift, N. (1999). Lists Come Alive: Electronic Systems of Knowledge and the Rise of Credit-Scoring in Retail Banking. *Economy and Society, 28*(3), 434–466.
Liberti, J. M., & Mian, A. R. (2009). Estimating the Effect of Hierarchies on Information Use. *Review of Financial Studies, 22*(10), 4057–4090.
Machauer, A., & Weber, M. (1998). Bank Behavior Based on Internal Credit Ratings of Borrowers. *Journal of Banking and Finance, 22*(10–11), 1355–1383.
Mercieca, S., Schaeck, K., & Wolfe, S. (2007). Small European Banks: Benefits from Diversification? *Journal of Banking and Finance, 31*, 1975–1998.
Meriläinen, J. M. (2016). Lending Growth During the Financial Crisis and the Sovereign Debt Crisis: The Role of Bank Ownership Type. *Journal of International Financial Markets, Institutions and Money, 41*, 68–182.
Meriläinen, J. M. (2017). Western European Stakeholder Banks' Loan Loss Accounting. *Journal of Financial Services Research*, in press.
Migliorelli, M., & Brunelli, S. (2016). The Transmission of the Monetary Policy in the Euro Area: The Role of the Banks' Business Model. *Annals of Public and Cooperative Economics, 88*(3), 303–322.
Migliorelli, M., & Dessertine, P. (2017). Time for New Financing Instruments? A Market-Oriented Framework to Finance Environmentally Friendly Practices in EU Agriculture. *Journal of Sustainable Finance and Investment, 8*(1), 1–25.
Orléan, A. (1999). *Le Pouvoir de la Finance*. Paris: Odile Jacob.
Ory, J.-N., Jaeger, M., & Gurtner, E. (2006). La Banque à Forme Coopérative Peut-elle Soutenir Durablement la Compétition avec la Banque SA? *Finance Contrôle Stratégie, 9*(2), 121–157.
Ory, J.-N., & Lemzeri, Y. (2012). Efficiency and Hybridization in Cooperative Banking: The French Case. *Annals of Public and Cooperative Economics, 83*(2), 215–250.
Pennisi, E. (2005). How Did Cooperative Behavior Evolve? *Science, 309*, 93.
Petersen, M. A., & Rajan, R. G. (1994). The Benefits of Lending Relationships: Evidence from Small Business Data. *Journal of Finance, 49*(1), 3–37.
Petersen, M. A., & Rajan, R. G. (1995). The Effect of Credit Market Competition on Lending Relationships. *Quarterly Journal of Economics, 110*(2), 407–443.

Pirvu, D., & Banica, L. (2016). The Credit Cooperative System in Romania. In B. Casu & A. Gall (Eds.), *Building Societies in the Financial Services Industry*. London: Palgrave Macmillan.

Raiffeisen, F. W. (1866). *Le Associazioni Casse di Prestito*. ristampa Ecra 2010.

Rilling, J. K., Gutman, D. A., Zeh, T. R., Pagnoni, G., Berns, G. S., & Kilts, C. D. (2002). A Neural Basis for Social Cooperation. *Neuron, 35*(2), 395–405.

Rivaud-Danset, D. (1996). Les contrats de crédit dans une relation de long terme. De la main invisible à la poignée de main. *Revue Economique, 27*(4), 937–962.

Scott, J. A. (2004). Small Businesses and the Value of Community Banks. *Journal of Financial Service Research, 25*(2–3), 207–230.

Sharpe, S. A. (1990). Asymmetric Information, Bank Lending, and Implicit Contracts: A Stylized Model of Customer Relationships. *Journal of Finance, 45*(4), 1069–1087.

Standard and Poor. (2017, April). *The World's 100 Largest Banks*.

Stein, J. C. (2002). Information Production and Capital Allocation: Decentralized Versus Hierarchical Firms. *Journal of Finance, 57*(5), 1891–1921.

Tamagnini, G. (1960). *Appunti di Storia della Cooperazione*. Le Cooperative di Credito, Rivista della cooperazione.

Uzzi, B. (1999). Embeddedness in the Making of Financial Capital: How Social Relations and Networks Benefit Firms Seeking Financing. *American Sociological Review, 64*(4), 481–505.

Uzzi, B., & Lancaster, R. (2003). Relational Embeddedness and Learning: The Case of Bank Loan Managers and Their Clients. *Management Science, 49*(4), 383–399.

Von Thadden, E. (1995). Long-Term Contracts, Short-Term Investments and Monitoring. *Review of Economic Studies, 62*(4), 557–575.

CHAPTER 2

The New Economic Scenario and Its Impact on the Cooperative Banking Business Model

Eric Meyer

2.1 Introduction

Cooperative banks proved to be quite resilient during the financial crisis started in Europe in 2008 and were able to cope fairly well with its challenges. There were only a few cooperative banks that needed government support and most of the cooperative banks and groups remained profitable. The reason for the cooperative banks resilience can partly be found in the nature of the financial crisis. Many shareholders banks engaged in businesses they did not fully understand and acquired assets (like subprime loans) that were then hard to manage. Cooperative banks are locally anchored and they focus on granting loans to the local businesses and therefore they actively take *and* monitor the risk. When cooperative banking groups have been affected by the crisis, the impact usually occurred on a central level, because it is there where the trading activities are concentrated. Hence, it can be affirmed that cooperative banks have been resilient during the financial crisis because they stuck to the "real" and traditional banking model of taking deposits and granting loans and were not involved in risky trading activities they could not manage.

E. Meyer (✉)
University of Münster, Münster, Germany
e-mail: eric.meyer@wiwi.uni-muenster.de

M. Migliorelli (ed.), *New Cooperative Banking in Europe*,
https://doi.org/10.1007/978-3-319-93578-2_2

After the explosion of the crisis, monetary policy and regulation reacted, putting in place a number of measures. Central banks reduced interest rates and started to buy bonds in order to inject liquidity in the market, in this way also trying to encourage the credit activity of the banks. In parallel, regulators assessed the riskiness of banking business and concluded that equity had to be increased over time (especially for large and highly interconnected banks that are systemically relevant). Therefore, monetary authorities and regulators shaped a new economic environment that, on the one hand, supported those banks that have been severely hit by the crisis and, on the other hand, aimed to prevent future financial crises. Nevertheless, in doing that, monetary authorities and regulators probably neglected to consider the impact that the changes proposed might have had on cooperative banks.

In the framework outlined, this chapter analyses how cooperative banks and cooperative banking groups have been affected by the new economic environment, how they could react and which are the implications for the overall cooperative banking model. To do that, Sect. 2.2 describes in more detail the new economic scenario. As some key developments are treated in other chapters of this volume, this chapter only briefly describes the role of regulation and the impact of digitization on cooperative banks since the beginning of the crisis. Instead, the main focus is on the effects of low interest rates. Section 2.3 hence surveys economic evidence on the effects of low interest rates on banks and on cooperative banks and banking groups. Finally, Sect. 2.4 presents some options for cooperative banks to adapt to the new economic environment.

2.2 Key Elements of the New Economic Scenario

2.2.1 Low Interest Rates

During the crisis, central banks all over the world started to reduce the reference interest rates in order to provide liquidity to banks. The inter-banking market had dried up and central banks had to fully assume the function of providing liquidity to the banking market (which up to that point had been carried out efficiently by the inter-bank market). By decreasing the interest rates, central banks aimed to facilitate the refinancing of the banking activities and allow banks to continue their operations, especially as concerns granting loans to the economy. Some central banks started to apply negative interest rates on the banks' deposits to deter the accumulation of funds and to force to hand them out. The European Central Bank (ECB), after reaching the lower-zero bound, started the so-called *quantitative easing* by directly buying bonds and debt in the market and hence significantly expanding its balance sheet. In contrast to central bank interest reference rates, which influence short-term market interest rates, the *quantitative easing* allowed the ECB (by intervening directly on the different maturities of the bond markets) to move downwards long-term interest rates. Consequently, the ECB influenced the entire interest rates' term structure and reduced the differentials in yields between long-term and short-term assets. Since then banks are operating in an environment of very low interest rates and of an interest rate term structure characterized by a very limited slope.

There is a general belief that decreasing interest rates negatively affect the net interest income of banks and therefore lead to lower profits. We will see in Sect. 2.3 that this relationship is much more complex and has to be differentiated according to the banks' business models and strategies. Figure 2.1 shows the development of the banks' net interest income and the interest rates for a period of 60 years for Germany. Three observations are relevant. First, there seems to be a long-run tendency for a reduction of the banks' net interest income. Second, there seems to be no immediate relation between lower interest rates and shrinking net interest income. Finally, the period of extremely low interest rates in the last almost ten years is historically unprecedented.

2.2.2 *Regulatory Burden*

After the crisis, the governments attempted to increase the resilience of the financial system by issuing new regulations addressing the causes of the crisis. Among these new regulations, two have to be emphasized. First, banks have been forced to compile much more detailed reporting to the supervisors and have to carry out much more extensive stress test simulations. Providing data to the supervisors is assumed to put these latter in a better position to detect ailing banks, but it also increases the burden of banks in compiling the data (which results in an increase in the costs for the banks). These costs exhibit a regressive structure. The relative costs are higher for small banks than for larger banks, which is in contradiction to the regulatory target of better monitoring larger and systemically important banks. Second, regulators have introduced higher capital ratios for banks and especially for larger banks. However, this regulation affects different banking models in different ways, because the calculation of the risk-

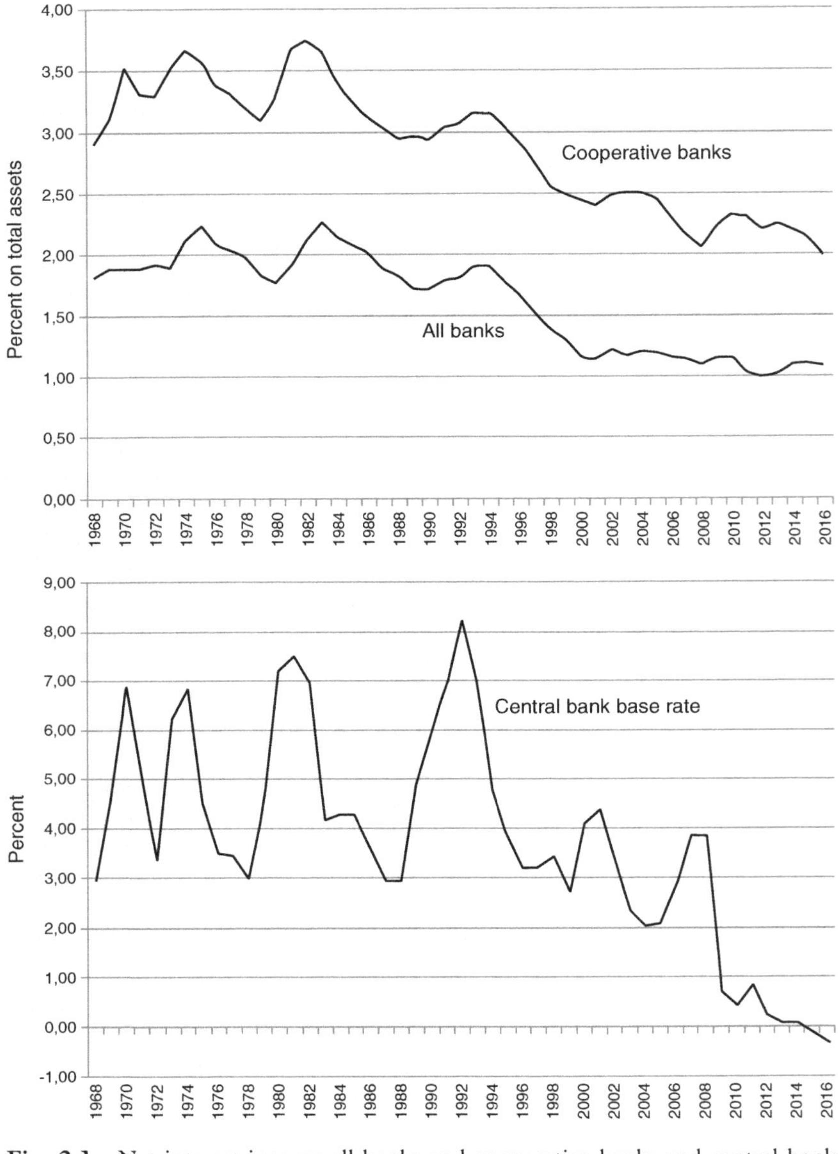

Fig. 2.1 Net interest income all banks and cooperative banks and central bank base rate. Notes: Authors' elaboration on ECB and Bundesbank data

weighted assets normally differs for small banks (like many cooperative banks) and large banks. Small banks usually apply the standardized approach, which is hence the basis for their capital ratio. Increasing their capital ratio means either increasing their capital or reducing their risk-weighted assets by reducing the volume of assets or by shifting into less risky assets. In contrast, larger banks have frequently an internal ratings-based system in use. In addition to the options mentioned above, they may also (within defined limits) change the calculation of their internal ratings, which may result in less risk-weighted assets. Therefore, the leeway for adjusting the capital ratios is usually much bigger for large banks. Moreover, regulations concerning the deposit insurance and bank resolution address the problems caused by large banks during the financial crisis but are somehow inadequate for some cooperative banking systems (and other group systems of smaller banks). In fact, cooperative banks frequently have institutional protection schemes (IPSs) or cross-guarantee schemes within their cooperative banking group, which are able to shield not only limited amounts of deposits but the existence of the whole cooperative. The newly introduced deposit insurance systems lead hence to a double protection in the case of cooperative banks' customers. The existing IPSs or cross-guarantee schemes (that have been established long before the financial crisis) are the first line of defence, to which the deposit insurance is added. Some observers claim that since the whole cooperative bank is protected, a bank resolution can be almost excluded and thus the deposit protection scheme may not be relevant. Nevertheless, cooperative banks were forced to implement separate instruments complying with the European Deposit Insurance regulation and therefore had to incur in additional costs. To sum up, the new regulatory environment correctly targets the causes of the financial crisis, but the effects of these regulations may hit smaller banks (including many cooperative banks) harder than the larger banks. The regulations may result in a disproportionate cost increases for small banks which may reduce profitability and therefore hamper their ability to increase their capital base.

2.2.3 *Digitalization*

The technology for the banking sector is changing. Digitization will have significant impacts on the banking business as a whole and in particular for smaller and locally anchored banks, like cooperative banks. Three developments will have a significant impact. First, the customer interface has changed and will change even more in the future. Digitization offers online solutions for an increasing number of products. Digital offerings started with the introduction of online banking granting easy access to the standardized current accounts, and later on other standardized products like saving products were added. The complexity of products has increased and today consumer credits, mortgage loans and asset management products (robot-advisory) can be offered online. The online channel is increasingly substituting the visit of banks' local branches which have been the basis for cooperative banking. Hence, cooperative banks are more and more forced to adapt their business model to the new online world or they will lose significant parts of their business. Second, the simple standardized products attract new competitors to the banking sector. Fintech companies offer new highly customer-focused products and do not have to take care of an existing highly diversified base of customers as traditional banks. High-tech companies from other sectors (like Amazon or Google) are already offering financial products (e.g. Amazon Pay) and may extend their activities to the banking sector. Both these activities will successively reduce the customer base of banks still focusing on branches and will therefore reduce the income they can generate (while their costs are still connected to their network of branches). Third, digitization exhibits strong economies of scale. Once a product or a process is digitized, it can be scaled up to a large number of additional customers without significant cost increases. Evidently, small banks are not able to reach similar scales like large banks and will therefore experience a disadvantage in comparison to their larger competitors. Within cooperative banking groups, the economies of scale could still be accomplished by moving the digitization activities, or at least the planning and development, on a central level. Small banks will then be able to use efficient digital solutions but also have to cooperate on finding compromises for these solutions. The balance within these groups will shift towards the central level.

2.3 The Impact of Extremely Low Interest Rates on Cooperative Banks[1]

2.3.1 *Interest Rates and Their Impact on Bank Profitability*

If banks are doing "real banking business", they take in deposits in order to grant loans and their earnings from this activity will be determined by

[1] Since the aspects of regulation are analysed in Chap. 4 and the effects of digitization are shown in Chap. 7, in the remainder of this chapter, the focus is on the effects of low interest rates only.

the difference of the interest payments they receive for all of their existing credits and the interests they have to pay for the deposits and other liabilities on their balance sheet.

The effect of low interest rates on the net interest income and subsequently on the profitability of banks has been subject to some research in recent times. For analysing the effects of interest rates, it is necessary to distinguish the *term structure* of interest rates and the *level* of interest rates. Typically, the term structure influences the net interest income, because banks produce a maturity mismatch of their assets and liabilities by holding more short-term liabilities at lower rates and more long-term assets (loans) at higher interest rates. Thus, if the difference between long-term and short-term interest rates increases (if the term structure gets steeper), the banks will be able to increase their net interest income. The impact of interest rate level on the net interest income is more complicated. In theory, if *all* assets and liabilities had flexible rates, the interest rates for loans and deposits could simultaneously adjust to any interest rate level and no effect on the net interest income should be observed. In practice, the reaction of interest income and interest expenses is asymmetrical, because of the maturity transformation assured by the banks (a part of the long-term loans are financed by short-term deposits). Therefore, the interest expenses react much quicker to changes in the interest rates than the interest income from long-term loans. If interest rates start falling, because the loans of the bank have a longer maturity, the income from these loans can be preserved for a longer time (depending on the maturity of these loans). For the deposits, the lower interest rates are applied much quicker (at least for large parts of them), and therefore the interest expenses will decrease. In this case, the net interest income increases. If interest rates increase, the effect will be just the other way around. Interest income will stay low for a longer time, and the interest expenses will increase resulting in a squeezing of the net interest income.

The existing research on the relationship of interest rates and the net interest income or profitability tends to underline the positive relationship of interest rates and the net interest income and profitability. While Samuelson (1945) was among the first who theoretically analysed the relationship of interest rates and bank profits, it took a while until first empirical results appeared. Hancock (1985) confirmed a positive relationship but also analysed the different (asymmetric) effects of interest rates on loans and deposits. Flannery (1981) showed in a study limited to 15 US banks that no relevant relationship between the market rates and their profitability concluding that they had sufficiently hedged against the risks to changing market rates. In a very broad international study, Demirgüc-Kunt and Huizinga (1999) showed a very strong positive relationship between the real interest rates and the banks' net interest margin and profitability. Busch and Memmel (2015) used data for German banks and differentiate the size of banks and the timing of the effects. They observe the positive relationship of interest rates and the net interest margin only in the long run, while in the short run a negative correlation prevails. The positive long-run effect is larger for small banks than for large banks. Borio et al. (2015) assume asymmetries in the demand elasticities of loans and deposits which lead to quantity effects in the net interest income. If demand for loans is more elastic to interest rate increases (or decreases), the volume of new business will be reduced to a larger extent than the supply of new money to the deposits. Borio et al. (2015) also describe possible effects of some price-setting power of banks. In an oligopolistic framework, banks will charge a mark-up on the market rate for the loans and a mark-down on the market rate for their deposits. If interest rates decrease, the leeway for the mark-down will be compressed. This is particularly relevant for the situation of market rates at zero or near zero. Since negative interest rates are hard to implement at least for private customers, the mark-down for deposits will be reduced to zero and therefore the additional income that is generated from this mark-down vanishes, which reduces the net interest income. Similarly, Ennis et al. (2016) describe mechanisms of price-setting power. If banks are able to influence prices, they will use their power in the case of increasing interest rates to keep down the rates on deposits while immediately increasing the rates for loans which will increase the interest margin for the new business of the bank. Thus, the effects of the interest rate level crucially depend on the assumption of some asymmetries or market imperfections: banks may have asymmetric maturity structures in their loans and liabilities, the elasticities for loans and deposits are different or banks dispose of some price-setting power which leads to asymmetric reactions for the assets and liabilities.

Recently, there have been a few additional contributions dealing with the special situation of very low or zero interest rates. Claessens et al. (2017) confirm a positive relationship of interest rates and net interest income, but observe that the effects are larger for lower interest rates. They calculate that for each additional year of "low for long", margins and profitability fall between six and nine basis points. Bikker and Vervliet (2017) also find that low interest rates have a negative impact on the net interest margin, but that banks are able to maintain their profitability by reducing their provisioning. Altavilla et al. (2017) analyse European banks and observe that their profitability is not negatively affected by low interest rates, but they notice changes in the composition of the bank's profits. Net interest income actually decreases, while lower loan loss provisioning and increased commission income compensate this negative effect. As concerns in particular cooperative banks, the papers by Busch and Memmel (2015) and Altavilla et al. (2017) give indications that these banks might be negatively affected by low interest rates, since they are small banks and depend on the net interest income more than other banks.

2.3.2 Cooperative Banks and Cooperative Banking Groups

Due to their historical bottom-up evolution, cooperative banks and banking groups[2] in Europe are rather diverse and exhibit different characteristics concerning size, business focus and internal governance structures. Nevertheless, they also share some common traits. The cooperative banks are owned by their members and their main focus is the provision of financial products and services in their communities. Consequently, their share of loans in their total assets is usually above the average of all European banks and the same applies to the deposits of their customers, as also shown in Fig. 2.2. The values in Fig. 2.2 refer to the ratios of loans and total assets of the cooperative banking groups. If the analysis is restricted to the cooperative banks, the share of loans increases even further for all groups analysed.

Although the share of loans for cooperative banks is well above the European average for all banks (around 40 per cent in 2008 and slightly higher in 2016), there are significant differences between the European cooperative banking groups. The three French cooperative banking groups exhibit rather low shares of loans. This can be explained by the structure of these groups, which are rather centralized and which have allocated significant parts of their business at the groups' central level. The

[2] For a differentiation of cooperative banking groups, see also Chap. 1. The term "group" used in this chapter does not follow their definition. Group in this chapter comprises any group or network of cooperative banks consisting of cooperative banks and their central institutes, which they own.

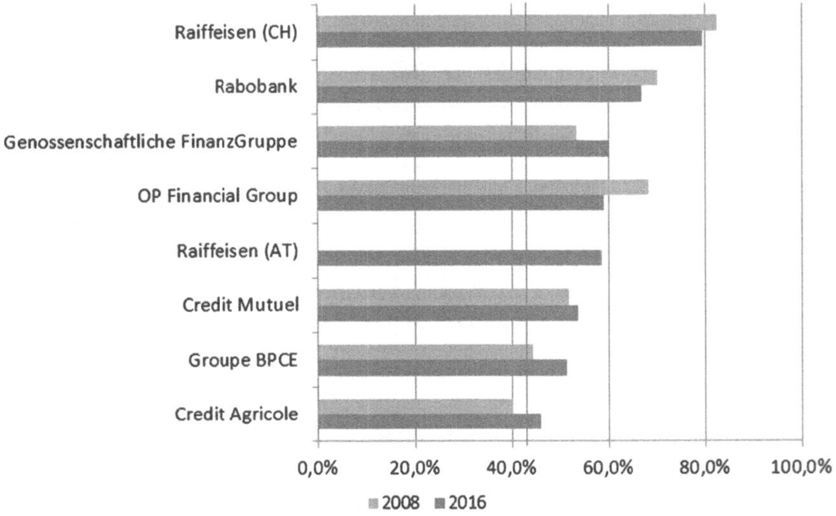

Fig. 2.2 Loans on total assets. Notes: Authors' elaboration balance sheet data

central entity of Crédit Agricole has a strong positioning in investment banking and has invested in activities abroad (e.g. Italy and Greece). BPCE owns Natixis, which also operates in investment banking. In contrast to the French groups, the Dutch Rabobank, which also has a strong centralization level, has a rather high share of loans, in the same way as the highly decentralized German cooperative banking group. Interestingly, the shares of loans for the Crédit Agricole and BPCE cooperative banks taken stand-alone rank at the top of European cooperative banks (as they are focusing on their core business), while the groups as a whole are highly diversified into other activities. The German cooperative banks have all a similar share of loans (about three quarters of their total assets). The Italian banks of Credito Cooperativo, which has been an even more decentralized system (before the ongoing reform[3]), also show a high share of loans in their balance sheets.

On the one hand, these metrics show that cooperative banking groups are mainly "balance sheet banks", that is banks that derive a significant share of their business from granting loans to their customers. But on the

[3] The reform of the cooperative banking sector in Italy is described in Chap. 5.

other hand, there are also significant differences in the relevance of the loans for the cooperative banking groups and how they have distributed the businesses between central banks and the local cooperative banks. The cooperative banks' strong positioning in granting loans is presumed to affect the net interest income and consequently the overall profits of the banks and banking groups.

In the analysis that will follow, the main focus will be on cooperative banking groups. Where necessary and available, information on the cooperative banks is supplemented. There are advantages and disadvantages coming from this restriction. Cooperative banks outsource parts of their business to their central institutions. In order to capture all banking activities of cooperative banks for their customers, it is necessary to take into account the central institutions. Omitting these activities would lead to biased results. Since the purpose of outsourcing these activities is driven by efficiency considerations, it may also bias certain efficiency measures. On the other hand, central institutions have started to initiate and carry out business activities that do not directly link to the primary cooperative banks and therefore they add additional customer relations and business to the group and not all group activities originate at the cooperative banks. Restricting the analysis to cooperative banking groups drastically reduces the number of objects for the analysis, limiting the empirical analysis to descriptive statistics. When considering cooperative banks, the number of objects is sufficient to carry out econometric analyses, but parts of the banking business (which have been transferred to other group institutions) are not covered. These omitted activities may also reallocate the profits between the central institutions and the local cooperative banks and consequently considering only the cooperative banks may skew the result.

2.3.3 Development of Cooperative Banks' Net Interest Income and Profitability

As mentioned at the beginning of this contribution, there has been a general tendency of decreasing interest rates and decreasing net interest income in recent decades. Looking at the development of the past ten years, this development of decreasing net interest income can be confirmed for all cooperative banking groups (see Fig. 2.3). Lower net interest income in 2008 and 2009 for some cooperative banking groups can be derived from higher interest expenses during the financial crisis where refinancing costs in the markets have increased. Starting from 2010 the net

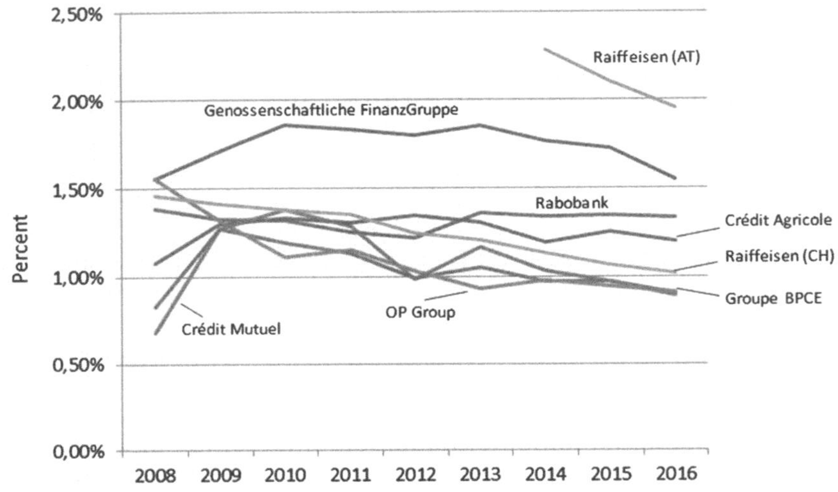

Fig. 2.3 Net interest income on total assets for cooperative banking groups (2008–2016). Notes: Authors' elaboration balance sheet data

interest income has decreased for all cooperative banking groups. Only Rabobank was able to at least stabilize its net interest income. This observation confirms other findings on the impact of decreasing or constantly low interest rates.

For some groups, data is available on the term structure of assets and liabilities. Table 2.1 shows that most groups have slightly increased or stabilized their share of long-term loans (measured as loans of more than five years) and at the same time strongly increased their share of short-term deposits (measured as retail deposits of less than three months). The exception is Germany, where long-term loans show a significant increase. Notice that the German data only refers to local cooperative banks and not to the group as a whole. Therefore, the share of long-term loans is larger probably due to their specialization on granting loans. Increasing the share of short-term deposits may lead to lower interest expenses, and thus banks are using the term structure of interest rates to strengthen their net interest income.

The continuous downward trend in net interest income does not automatically imply a similar development for the operating profits of the cooperative banking groups. In this respect, Fig. 2.4 shows the operating return on total asset for major cooperative banking groups.

Table 2.1 Share of loans (maturity > 5 years) and share of deposits (maturity < 3 months) on total assets

		2017 (%)	*2016 (%)*	*2015 (%)*	*2014 (%)*	*2013 (%)*	*2012 (%)*	*2011 (%)*	*2010 (%)*
German cooperative banks	Loans	55.5	51.8	54.2	53.3	52.6	51.0	50.2	49.4
	Deposits	51.3	50.3	48.2	46.0	44.2	41.7	39.4	38.7
Rabobank	Loans	42.3	38.8	38.3	39.7	41.2			
	Deposits	47.7	44.8	43.9	40.9	42.6	–	–	–
Crédit Agricole	Loans	19.6	18.7	18.0	16.8	17.6	17.1	16.6	
	Deposits	35.6	33.3	31.9	27.9	29.3	26.9	24.8	–
Groupe BPCE	Loans	26.9	26.7	26.8	25.3	26.8			
	Deposits	32.4	30.7	31.5	28.9	31.9	–	–	–
OP Group	Loans	27.2	26.6	27.5	29.6	31.2	30.5	31.6	31.4
	Deposits	45.6	42.6	43.3	42.1	43.3	40.9	41.1	38.2

Notes: Authors' elaboration balance sheet data. There is no data available for the German cooperative banking group. Data is taken from Bundesbank statistics on cooperative banks, deposits include time deposits up to one year and sight deposits, total assets only refer to cooperative banks. Group data will be lower due to different activities on the central level. The given data cannot be compared to the data for groups in Fig. 2.2

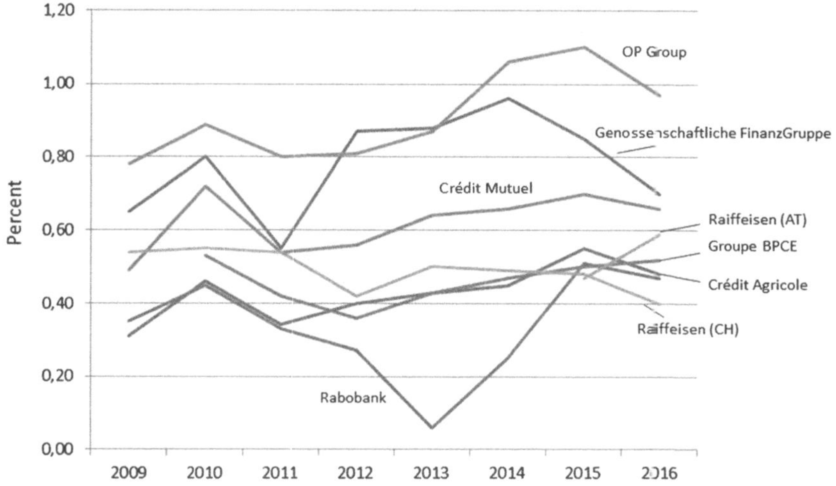

Fig. 2.4 Operating income on total assets for cooperative banking groups (2009–2016). Notes: Authors' elaboration balance sheet data

The operating profits are slightly volatile, but all cooperative banking groups managed to remain profitable. Despite low interest rates and falling net interest income, most of the groups were able to increase their profits from 2011 until 2014–2015 and OP Group, the German cooperative banking group and the French Crédit Mutuel showed quite solid results. Groupe BPCE and Crédit Agricole only slowly increased their profitability. Rabobank experienced some lower profits in the aftermath of the crisis but recovered since 2013 and returned to the profit levels of other cooperative banking groups.[4]

A positive development can be tracked to the cooperative banks within the cooperative banking groups. If banks are assigned to three classes of return on equity (below 8 per cent, between 8 and 10 per cent and above 10 per cent),[5] the cooperative banks in Germany perform better than the other banks in the market (they are more profitable and have a return of equity of above 8 or 10 per cent, respectively). In France, cooperative banks perform only slightly worse than the other banks in the French market, with Crédit Agricole banks being better than the other banks and Banque Populaires and Caisses d'Epargne being below the other banks' performance. Figure 2.5 summarizes the results for Germany and France.

In contrast, cooperative banks in Austria and Italy have performed worse than their non-cooperative competitors, and a majority is below the eight per cent threshold. This changes for Italy if pre-impairment operating profits are considered for calculating the return of equity. Then Italian cooperative banks perform almost exactly like their competitors, and the share of banks below the eight per cent is reduced to half of the cooperative banks. Notice again, that performance measures of cooperative banks may also be influenced by the allocation of activities within the cooperative banking group and therefore any comparison to other banks or between cooperative banks should be considered with great caution.

[4] If profitability is measured as return on equity, the shape of the curves is quite similar to the curves in Fig. 2.4.

[5] The IMF considers a return on equity below eight per cent as weak profitability. All cooperative banking groups have been above this threshold in 2016 except Swiss Raiffeisen which is below but close to the eight per cent threshold. This is remarkable, since cooperative banking groups are well capitalized (the denominator of the ratio is quite large, and therefore cooperative banking groups have to generate even higher profits in order to pass the threshold).

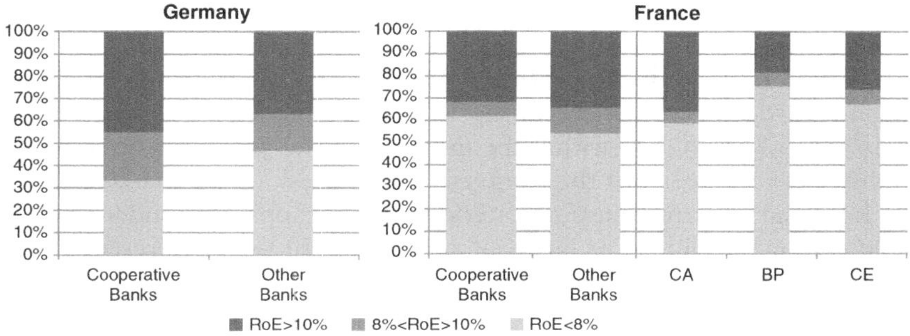

Fig. 2.5 Return on equity classification of cooperative banks in Germany and France in 2016. Notes: Authors' elaboration balance sheet data

2.4 Reacting to the New Economic Scenario

The preceding sections showed that major cooperative banking groups experienced slowly decreasing net interest income, but that they were still able to remain profitable. These were hence quite stable, and only for some banking groups recently declining profit ratios can be attributed to active management decisions to bring risk to the market, to reduce costs and to explore new sources of income.

2.4.1 Bringing Risk to the Market

As described above, the effect of low interest rates on net interest income is slow due to the maturity transformation that banks operate by turning short-term deposits into long-term loans. If interest rates decrease and stay low, interest expenses are reduced while long-term loans are only gradually exchanged with new loans at lower interest levels (the stock of high-yield lows is only slowly depleted and so banks maintain a profitable interest income even at the beginning of low interest rates). Today customers want to fix the low rates for a long period, and as a consequence the banks are accumulating long-run low interest generating loans that could turn the net interest income negative if interest rates start rising again. Because of the very long maturity of these new loans, the reduced low interest income would last for a long time. Therefore, cooperative banks can either sell parts of their long-term loans and reduce their balance sheet or use interest rate swaps to reduce the possible risks of increasing interest rates (and hence transfer the risk to a market counterpart).[6] By using swaps, the cooperative banks would have to manage a new counterparty risk and pay for this service. In many cooperative groups, the first counterpart for banks in the group would be the group's central entity, with the risk remaining within the group until the group's central entity redistribute the risk into the markets. Bringing risk to the market would be hence an effective solution for cooperative groups only under favourable market conditions in terms of swaps rates and in the presence of a structured internal system of management.

2.4.2 *Reducing Costs*

If net interest income decreases, another option to preserve profitability is the reduction of expenses. Cooperative banks have higher net interest income than other banks, which is necessary to cover their higher expenses for their branch network and their staff, which is part of their local anchorage. Thus, cooperative banks have started to react to sluggish profitability by also reducing costs. Besides improving processes and increasing efficiency in the cooperative banks and the cooperative banking groups, banks also started to close branches and reduce the staff (even though at a slower pace than other kind of banks). On the one hand, the withdrawal from regional presence is part of changing consumer behaviour. Customers use online banking services (which are also offered by cooperative banks), and therefore the branches are less frequented than years ago, so that costs per customers in these branches had increased. On the other hand, the reduction of local presence in cities and villages could threaten the local anchorage and weaken one of key characteristics of the cooperative banking business model. Nevertheless, cooperative banks can try to reinvent their local anchorage by using new digital technologies to create new communities with their members.

2.4.3 *New Sources of Income*

Increasing income from other sources than interests is an alternative option for cooperative banks. Moving to services that generate commission income means that cooperative banks have either to develop new

[6] For many, this is in contradiction to the lessons of the financial crisis, that the distribution of risks in markets makes them harder to monitor and to control in times of distress.

services or raise prices for existing products (e. g. current accounts). Nevertheless, this option should be attentively tailored on the specific characteristics and values of cooperative banks. In fact, the increase of prices for basic banking products will have regressive effects (they will weight much more on low income customers than richer customers), which seems against cooperative attitude. Also, changing dramatically the type of services offered may lead cooperative banks to drive away from their traditional business model and to become more and more similar to commercial banks.

References

Altavilla, C., Boucinha, M., & Peydro, J.-L. (2017). *Monetary Policy and Bank Profitability in a Low Interest Rate Environment.* ECB Working Paper, No. 2105.

Bikker, J., & Vervliet, T. (2017). *Bank Profitability and Risk-Taking Under Low Interest Rates.* DNB Working Paper, No. 560.

Borio, C., Gambacorta, L., & Hofmann, B. (2015). *The Influence of Monetary Policy on Bank Profitability.* BIS Working Paper, No. 514.

Busch, R., & Memmel, C. (2015). *Banks' Net Interest Margin and the Level of Interest Rates.* Deutsche Bundesbank Discussion Paper, No. 16/2015.

Claessens, S., Coleman, N., & Donnelly, M. (2017). *"Low-For-Long" Interest Rates and Banks' Interest Margins and Profitability: Cross-Country Evidence.* International Finance Discussion Papers, No. 1197.

Demirgüc-Kunt, A., & Huizinga, H. (1999). Determinants of Commercial Bank Interest Margins and Profitability: Some International Evidence. *The World Bank Economic Review, 13*(2), 379–408.

Ennis, H. M., Fessenden, H., & Walter, J. R. (2016). *Do Net Interest Margins and Interest Rates Move Together?* Economic Brief, 16-05, Federal Reserve of Richmond.

Flannery, M. (1981). Market Interest Rates and Commercial Bank Profitability: An Empirical Investigation. *The Journal of Finance, 36*(5), 1085–1101.

Hancock, D. (1985). Bank Profitability, Interest Rates, and Monetary Policy. *Journal of Money, Credit and Banking, 17*(2), 189–202.

Samuelson, P. A. (1945). The Effect of Interest Rate Increases on the Banking System. *American Economic Review, 35*, 16–27.

CHAPTER 3

Cooperative Banks Lending During and After the Great Crisis

Marco Migliorelli

3.1 Introduction

The financial crisis originated in the United States in 2007 had its first impacts on the real economy in Europe in 2008, where it produced an intense and largely unexpected shock. Few European countries quickly recovered pre-crisis standard of GDP and employment, while others struggled (and in some cases, are still struggling) to adapt their economies to the changed macroeconomic conditions (Fig. 3.1). Given this scenario, this chapter tries to shed some light on whether the Great Crisis has altered the capacity of the cooperative banks to provide credit to the economy. Cooperative banks merit a particular attention as regards lending supply in periods of economic distress as they proved in the past to play a significant countercyclical role. In fact, during economic downturn, cooperative banks have been able in the past to supply credit to their members and clients to a significant higher extent than other kinds of financial institutions (e.g. Bolton et al. 2013; Ferri et al. 2014). Nevertheless, little evidence still exists so far as concerns their lending behaviour during and

M. Migliorelli (✉)
IAE Université Paris 1 Panthéon-Sorbonne (Sorbonne Business School), Paris, France

M. Migliorelli (ed.), *New Cooperative Banking in Europe*,
https://doi.org/10.1007/978-3-319-93578-2_3

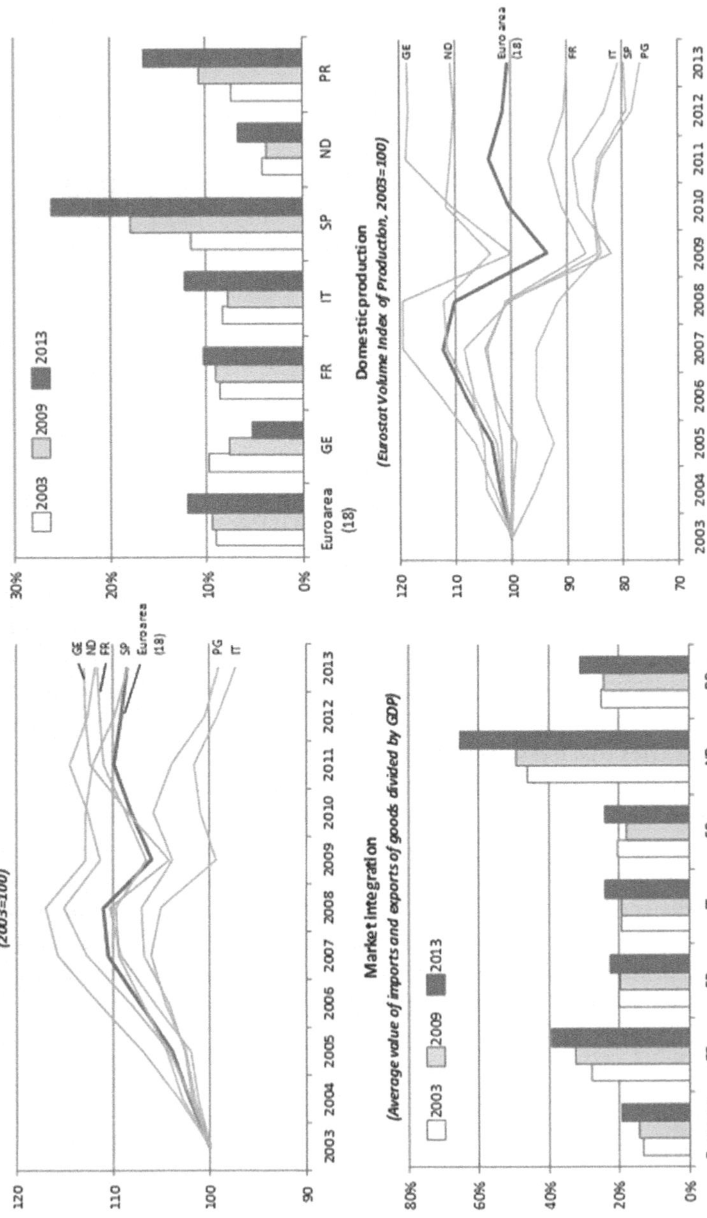

Fig. 3.1 Main macroeconomic indicators for the euro area in the period 2003–2013. Source: Migliorelli and Brunelli (2016). Notes: *GE* Germany, *FR* France, *IT* Italy, *SP* Spain, *ND* The Netherlands, *PR* Portugal

after the Great Crisis. Considering the length and the magnitude of the recession in Europe, an in-depth investigation of the lending behaviour of cooperative banks may contribute to further understand inherent potentialities and limits of this business model.

To do that, this chapter is divided in three parts. First, an empirical analysis is reported to clarify whether cooperative banks have adopted during and after the recession started in Europe in 2008 a specific lending pattern vis-à-vis other kind of banks. This is done by investigating the impact of the different types of banks (in particular commercial banks, savings banks and cooperative banks) on the transmission of the monetary policy in terms of new lending (the so-called *bank lending channel*). Second, for the main market in which no specific lending pattern has emerged in the previous analysis, that is Italy, an investigation is carried out on the role of possible capital shortfalls in cooperative banks' lending behaviour in the attempt to identify possible causes of operational distress (test of the *capital crunch* hypothesis). Finally, in the last part of this chapter, some conclusions on possible limits to the traditional countercyclical role of cooperative banks during and after the Great Crisis are stated.

3.2 Lending Behaviour of Cooperative Banks in the Different Areas of the Continent

3.2.1 *Analysing Lending Behaviour Via the* Bank Lending Channel[1]

One way to analyse the lending behaviour of the different kinds of banks is to investigate the role of the banks' business model in the transmission of the monetary stimulus in terms of lending supply. This strand of literature, which identifies the *bank lending channel*, departs from rejecting the Modigliani-Miller assumption of perfect financial markets and observes that a "black box" usually exists between the central bank's monetary decisions and a (positive or negative) shift in the credit conditions for business and households (e.g. Bernanke and Gertler 1995). This literature demonstrates that structural features of the banking sector, such as size of banks, level of capitalisation, level of liquidity, business models in use, matter while specifying the lending response to policy actions, and for this reason a *bank lending channel* usually exists. To this extent, the most widely adopted investigation method to assess the *bank lending channel*

[1] This section is based on Migliorelli and Brunelli (2016).

consists of the observation of how banks' lending behaviour responds to changes in monetary conditions and other bank-level characteristics, by using data at a single-bank level. A measure of credit response (normally loans) is projected on different possible measures of monetary policy (typically short-term interest rates), as well as on bank-specific characteristics (especially size, capitalisation, liquidity and business model) and other control variables (in particular, demand-side factors). The choice of the inclusion of interaction terms between monetary policy variables and bank-specific variables is also adopted in many empirical specifications (e.g. Ferri et al. 2014; Kashyap and Stein 1995).

The effects of capitalisation on lending are amongst the most studied aspects of the *bank lending channel*. According to a typical deleveraging argument, unexpected capital shortfalls may induce banks to cut back lending in order to restore targeted capital-to-asset positions.[2] In fact, when considering the alternative measures to face capital shortages, banks' managers may consider a reduction in the credit outstanding as a quicker and less costly option than issuing new equity. This issue was first discussed by Bernanke and Lown (1991), who found evidence of the existence of a causal link between low capital-to-asset ratios and low lending growth during the crisis of 1990–1991 in the region of New England, identifying the banks' capital deficits as a triggering cause of a shift in the credit conditions in the market. Other authors (e.g. Hancock et al. 1995) verified that in response to a decline in their own capital, small banks shrank their loan portfolios considerably more than large banks did, hence identifying in size another possible significant component of the *bank lending channel*. As far as it concerns the role of banks' size, some authors (e.g. Kashyap and Stein 2000) argued that larger banks may find it easier to obtain liquidity than smaller banks. In this respect, they demonstrated that the response of bank lending to policy actions is more sensitive in the presence of low levels of liquid assets and hence small banks' lending is usually more sensitive to monetary policy than large banks' lending. With a focus on the relationship between banks' business model and lending, literature (e.g. Bolton et al. 2013; Ferri et al. 2014) has provided evidence that stakeholder banks,[3] backed by the relationship lending paradigm, are

[2] In general, target capital-to-asset ratios are the result of management preferences (risk appetite) and/or regulatory provisions.

[3] Conventionally, the stakeholder banking segment is composed of cooperative and savings banks.

usually more resistant to monetary shocks in terms of lending supply, especially in periods of economic downturn. The empirical literature focused on the euro area has not furnished homogeneous results as concerns the features of the *bank lending channel*. In most of the cases, pre-crisis empirical findings suggest the presence of heterogeneous country-wise reactions. In this regard, De Santis and Surico (2013) analysed the presence of a *bank lending channel* for the first four economies of the euro area separately (namely Germany, France, Italy and Spain) for the period 1999–2011. They found both a high significance and a high heterogeneity in the effects of capital, size and liquidity on the lending behaviours of the banks, especially for Germany and Italy, while smoother effects both in terms of significance and heterogeneity were registered for France and Spain.

3.2.2 Research Method

An analysis of the lending behaviour of cooperative banks during and after the crisis vis-à-vis other types of banks is of the utmost interest. This allows to investigate whether the cooperative banks' countercyclical attitude has been put under pressure as a consequence of the Great Crisis. To do that, it is worth examining the role of the banks' business model in the *bank lending channel* on the basis of specific economic areas within the larger euro area. In fact, and as previously discussed, the Great Crisis impacted asymmetrically the continent. In this respect, an analysis of the role of the banks' business model in terms of lending behaviour in the different areas of the continent (the ones less and the ones more affected by the crisis) represents a well-fitting instrument of investigation for at least three reasons. First, it may provide information as regards the role played in the lending supply during the crisis by the different kinds of banks (in the reminder, the attention is directed specifically on commercial banks, savings banks and cooperative banks). Second, it may give valuable insights on possible divergences in lending behaviour between similar banks operating in different macroeconomic scenarios. Third, and as a by-product, it may provide information to policymakers as regards the effects of a change of the monetary policy on lending in each area of the continent. As this kind of approach is strictly based on the analysis of the transmission of the monetary stimulus, in the analysis that follows the focus of the investigation is restricted to the euro area.

With the aim of analysing the effects of the banks' business model on the monetary policy transmission from this point of view, the investigation has to be carried out in two different phases. The first consists in identifying the main economic areas within the larger euro area. In this respect, countries have to be clustered on the basis of their macroeconomic fundamentals. The second phase previews to run a series of econometric estimations (Arellano-Bond type of GMM estimators) to assess the impact of the various components of the *bank lending channel* for each of the relevant areas identified, with a specific focus on the role of the cooperative business model.

With regard to the first step, a clustering procedure has been performed by taking into account two key macroeconomic indicators: the level of debt and the unemployment rate. These macroeconomic indicators are able to summarise fairly well the financial and economic conditions of a country[4] and are also relevant in shaping the monetary policy (in particular when the primary objective of the stability of prices is reached or not far to be reached[5,6,7]). To form coherent clusters, the hierarchical agglomerative methods of the centroid linkage have to be preferred. Such a procedure infers the creation of groups of units on the basis of the closest distance. Groups, once formed, are represented by their mean values for

[4] Other indicators could be used to group countries in economic areas, for example, the GDP growth or the level of domestic production. In many cases, the clustering procedure would have highlighted the division between the economies of the south of Europe and those of the centre and north of the continent.

[5] In fact, "*Without prejudice to the objective of price stability, the ESCB* [European System of Central Banks] *shall support the general economic policies in the Union with a view to contributing to the achievement of the objectives of the Union*" (Treaty on the Functioning of the European Union, Article 127 (1)). These may include, inter alia, full employment and balanced economic growth.

[6] The objective of the ECB to maintain price stability is defined as "a year-on-year increase in the Harmonized Index of Consumer Prices (HICP) for the euro area of below 2%". The ECB Governing Council clarified in 2003 that in the pursuit of price stability, it aims to maintain inflation rates below, but close to, two per cent over the medium term.

[7] The underlying macroeconomic argument is that countries with high levels of debt and unemployment would be better off with a laxer monetary policy (at least in the short-medium term), while countries with low debt and unemployment would mostly be in favour of a more conservative strategy. An expansionary monetary policy and a higher inflation will allow high-debt high-unemployment countries to reduce the weight of their liabilities in real terms and to give a stimulus to the investments through lower interest rates. On the other hand, low-debt low-unemployment countries may find such a solution to be inefficient if standing close to their production saturation levels.

Country	Unemployment (%)	Debt level (% GDP)
Austria	4.9	74.5
Belgium	8.4	101.2
Cyprus	15.9	111.7
Estonia	8.6	10.0
Finland	8.2	57.0
France	10.3	94.7
Germany	5.2	78.4
Greece	27.5	175.1
Ireland	13.1	123.7
Italy	12.2	132.6
Luxembourg	5.9	23.1
Malta	6.4	72.6
Netherlands	6.7	73.5
Portugal	16.4	128.9
Slovakia	14.2	55.4
Slovenia	10.1	71.1
Spain	26.1	93.9

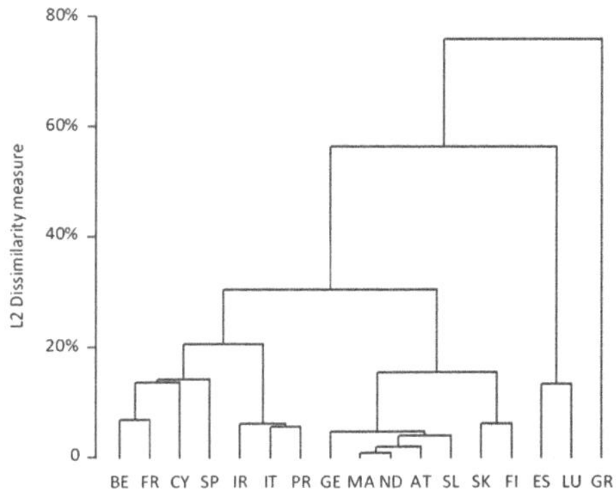

Fig. 3.2 Clustering procedure inputs for European countries and resulting dendogram. Source: Migliorelli and Brunelli (2016). Notes: Data Eurostat, as at Q4 2013. *AT* Austria, *BE* Belgium, *CY* Cyprus, *ES* Estonia, *FI* Finland, *FR* France, *GE* Germany, *GR* Greece, *IR* Ireland, *IT* Italy, *LU* Luxembourg, *MA* Malta, *ND* The Netherlands, *PR* Portugal, *SK* Slovakia, *SL* Slovenia, *SP* Spain

each variable (mean vector), and inter-group distance is defined in terms of length between two mean vectors. The distance dimension used is the Euclidean (L2) dissimilarity measure.[8] The use of this clustering procedure has to be preferred as it allows the use of random starting clusters and deals with the presence of outliers better than other clustering methods.[9,10] Furthermore, the resulting clusters can be directly interpreted as targetable self-standing economic areas, largely independent from the single composing units. Figure 3.2 reports the clustering procedure inputs and the resulting dendogram.

Two main clusters emerge fairly straightforwardly from the dendogram. The first is composed of seven countries (Austria, Finland, Germany, Malta, the Netherlands, Slovakia and Slovenia), mainly belonging to the north-east quadrant of the continent. The second is identified by another seven countries (Belgium, Cyprus, France, Ireland, Italy, Portugal and

[8] In statistical terms, the L2 distance is the square root of the sum of squared differences.

[9] The main drawback of using this procedure is that the same weight is assigned to each country, independently of its relative economic relevance for the euro area. Nevertheless, in the final identification, the two main clusters are similar in terms of total GDP. Hence, the potential bias due to the overweight of the small countries' results being smoothed or absent.

[10] For example, the minimum average sum of squares or Ward's method.

Spain), composing in the majority the south-west quadrant of the euro area. As a matter of fact, and not surprisingly, these positions are those of the countries that animated the political debate surrounding the functioning of the ECB in recent years, in particular as concerns the optimum level of the reference interest rates.[11] Furthermore, two residual clusters are formed by Luxembourg and Estonia together and Greece as a standalone. For the analysis, the first cluster is identified as a Monetary Conservation Targetable Area (MCTA) and the second as a Monetary Expansion Targetable Area (META), on the basis of a qualitative interpretation of the resulting clustering dimensions. The particularly savvy countries (Luxembourg and Estonia) and the specific case of Greece are considered as outliers. Also in consideration of the limited number of observations available for these small economies, outliers are excluded from the analysis. Figure 3.3 gives a geographical overview of the economic areas identified.

The main database used to collect the relevant bank-level accounting information is Bankscope, by Bureau Van Dijk.[12,13] This database contains financial information for a wide number of banks in Europe and worldwide. It is compiled predominantly from the balance sheet and income statement as well as notes from audited annual reports. The analysis has been restricted to commercial banks, savings banks and cooperative banks, in the attempt to focus the scope of the observation on banks carrying out the lending activity as their main core business. For this reason, all other types of financial institutions available in the data set are excluded (investment banks, private banking institutions, government institutions, holding companies, etc.).

[11] Critics to the exceptionally low interest rates were addressed to the ECB by Germany and other north-European countries in particular the period 2011–2016.

[12] In 2016, the contract between Bureau Van Dijk and Fitch (the main provider of financial data included in the Bankscope database) terminated. In 2017, Bankscope was acquired by Moody's Analytics. As a result of these events, this database is no longer available. As Bankscope was one of the reference databases in banking research, some disruption may be expected in the next few years as concerns research based on banks' financial data.

[13] As far as it concerns non-accounting information, the ECB reference interest rate has been taken from the available sources of the ECB, while the GDP growth rates for each country have been taken from Eurostat.

Fig. 3.3 Economic areas within the euro area. Source: Migliorelli and Brunelli (2016). Notes: Elaboration on clustering procedure results

Banks have been analysed at a consolidated level.[14] In this setting, the balance sheet information present in the database is available from 2005 at best. Furthermore, is eliminated from the sample a number of micro-banks, with a cut-off at EUR 50 million in terms of total assets at the end of 2013. The final sample includes 2851 banks based in 14 European countries. Table 3.1 shows its composition by economic area, country and business model. As clearly emerges from the table, German banks widely dominate the MCTA cluster, contributing 81 per cent to the entire sub-sample size. Furthermore, out of these banks, 60 per cent are cooperative banks, underlying the capillary presence of this business model in that country. As far as it concerns the META cluster, Italy reports the highest number of institutions, again as a consequence of the high number of small cooperative banks operating in the peninsula.

Table 3.2 reports some key metrics aimed at describing the banks in the sample, by considering all the banks together and then separately the banks in the MCTA and META. Some significant differences between the two economic areas emerge from the observation of Table 3.2. First and foremost, banks in the MCTA are, on average, smaller than the banks in the META. In fact, the average total assets for the banks in the former is EUR 2.7 billion, against EUR 9.05 billion for the banks in the latter. Nevertheless, the distribution (in terms of size) of the banks in the MCTA is more disperse: the coefficient of variation (calculated as the ratio of standard deviation to mean of total assets) is 5.94 in the MCTA and 3.85 in the META. Furthermore, banks in the MCTA seem to have, on average, a less diversified business than the banks in the MCTA. To this extent, the ratio of the fees to the operating profit is 2.16 in the META and 0.90 in the MCTA.

These features of the sample may be explained by considering the effects on the averaged values of the presence of an extremely large number of small, local cooperative banks operating in central Europe, in particular in Germany and Austria. In this respect, it is important to remind the main peculiarities of the standard cooperative banks' business model

[14] On the basis of the Bankscope classification, we use banks' statements information at the levels C2 (statement of a mother bank integrating the statements of its controlled subsidiaries or branches with an unconsolidated companion present in the Bankscope database), C1 (statement of a mother bank integrating the statements of its controlled subsidiaries or branches with no unconsolidated companion present in the Bankscope database) and U1 (statement not integrating the statements of the possible controlled subsidiaries or branches of the concerned bank with no consolidated companion).

Table 3.1 Number of banks in the sample by economic area, country and business model

	Monetary Conservation Targetable Area (MCTA)							
	AT	*FI*	*GE*	*MA*	*ND*	*SL*	*SK*	*TOT*
	255	*28*	*1551*	*8*	*32*	*17*	*14*	*1905*
Commercial banks	59 *(3.1%)*	22 *(1.2%)*	119 *(6.2%)*	6 *(0.3%)*	30 *(1.6%)*	14 *(0.7%)*	12 *(0.6%)*	262 *(13.8%)*
Savings banks	95 *(5.0%)*	4 *(0.1%)*	501 *(26.3%)*	1 *(0.1%)*	1 *(0.1%)*	1 *(0.1%)*	2 *(0.1%)*	605 *(31.8%)*
Cooperative banks	101 *(5.3%)*	2 *(0.1%)*	931 *(48.9%)*	1 *(0.1%)*	1 *(0.1%)*	2 *(0.1%)*	–	1038 *(54.4%)*
	Monetary Expansion Targetable Area (META)							
	BE	*CY*	*FR*	*IR*	*IT*	*PR*	*SP*	*TOT*
	37	*15*	*210*	*14*	*519*	*27*	*124*	*946*
Commercial banks	25 *(2.6%)*	12 *(1.3%)*	112 *(11.8%)*	14 *(1.5%)*	80 *(8.5%)*	21 *(2.2%)*	43 *(4.5%)*	307 *(32.5%)*
Savings banks	5 *(0.5%)*	1 *(0.1%)*	23 *(2.4%)*	–	37 *(3.9%)*	4 *(0.4%)*	27 *(2.9%)*	97 *(10.3%)*
Cooperative banks	7 *(0.7%)*	2 *(0.2%)*	75 *(7.9%)*	–	402 *(42.5%)*	2 *(0.2%)*	54 *(5.7%)*	542 *(57.3%)*

Source: Migliorelli and Brunelli (2016)

Notes: *AT* Austria, *BE* Belgium, *CY* Cyprus, *ES* Estonia, *FI* Finland, *FR* France, *GE* Germany, *GR* Greece, *IR* Ireland, *IT* Italy, *LU* Luxembourg, *MA* Malta, *ND* The Netherlands, *PR* Portugal, *SK* Slovakia, *SL* Slovenia, *SP* Spain. In parenthesis, percentage with respect to the total sample size for each economic area

that often induces these banks to remain and operate as small independent intermediaries. Primarily, the cooperative bank business model is unique in terms of ownership structure. Cooperative banks cannot exclude new members unless adequately motivating their reasons and, most importantly, the *one-head-one-vote* rule is in use in the decision-making process during the general assembly. Furthermore, cooperative banks have a limited profit-seeking nature. In fact, most of them face constraints in terms of profit distribution. Finally, the link with the territory and the mutualism principle mainly steers their operational scope. Normally, cooperative banks' activity has to be focused first of all towards their members and in

Table 3.2 Selected descriptive statistics of the banks in the sample

	Mean	*SD*	*5th percentile*	*95th percentile*
All banks				
Total assets (€ *bln*)	4.69	23.78	0.09	82.19
Gross loans outstanding (€ *bln*)	2.61	9.54	0.05	50.77
Total equity (€ *bln*)	0.30	1.06	0.01	4.92
K/A ratio (%)	9.27	5.07	4.75	23.20
Fees/operating profit	1.29	6.17	−0.62	14.03
Δ Gross loans outstanding (%)	6.23	9.78	−1.82	43.81
Banks in the Monetary Conservation Targetable Area (MCTA)				
Total assets (€ *bln*)	2.70	16.05	0.09	34.34
Gross loans outstanding (€ *bln*)	1.51	7.16	0.05	20.55
Total equity (€ *bln*)	0.18	0.79	0.01	2.56
K/A ratio (%)	8.96	4.98	5.15	20.64
Fees/operating profit	0.90	2.72	0.06	7.99
Δ Gross loans outstanding (%)	5.90	9.10	−1.29	41.73
Banks in the Monetary Expansion Targetable Area (META)				
Total assets (€ *bln*)	9.05	34.83	0.10	134.06
Gross loans outstanding (€ *bln*)	5.00	13.02	0.05	84.23
Total equity (€ *bln*)	0.59	1.46	0.01	6.97
K/A ratio (%)	9.95	5.20	3.93	30.72
Fees/operating profit	2.16	10.20	−2.44	30.83
Δ Gross loans outstanding (%)	6.96	11.09	−2.34	53.66

Source: Migliorelli and Brunelli (2016)

Notes: Bankscope data. For Total assets, Gross loans outstanding, Total equity and K/A ratio values as at 31/12/2013. For Fees/Operating profit values related to 2013. For Δ Gross Loans Outstanding, average values in the period 2008–2013. The metric Gross loans outstanding does not include loans and advances to banks

the territory where they mainly operate. All these elements have in many countries contributed to limit the size of these banks and their keenness to seek a more differentiated business.

The second main step of the analysis concerns the specification used in order to assess the *bank lending channel* hypothesis. To this extent, it is mainly followed the empirical approach adopted by, among others, Kashyap and Stein (2000) and De Santis and Surico (2013). These authors backed their investigation by the use of an interaction term linking bank-level characteristics to a key parameter of the monetary policy.

In this study, the econometric specification takes the following form[15]:

[15] In the relation 3.1 $\varepsilon_{i,t}$ comprises a fixed error component. In such a specification, to control for a fixed effect is relevant as banks may have fixed strategies concerning loans which may not react to time-varying circumstances.

$$\log(loans_{i,t}) = \varphi \log(loans_{i,t-1}) + \gamma r_t + \lambda_1 (r_t * SIZE_{i,t}) + \lambda_2 (r_t * CAPITAL_{i,t}) + \lambda_3 (r_t * BM_t) + \mu GDP_{i,t} + \theta_t YEAR_t + \varepsilon_{i,t} \quad (3.1)$$

The dependent variable is the logarithm of loans to non-financial institutions issued by bank i in the year of reference. The lagged value of the dependent variable is used as a first control variable. To take into account the monetary stimulus r, the value of the Euro OverNight Index Average (EONIA) is used. In particular, its annual average value is computed on the basis of the daily values. As far as it concerns the possible determinants of the *bank lending channel*, a vector of bank-level features is included in the specification. In particular, it is investigated the role of *SIZE* (log of the total assets), *CAPITAL* (book-based capital-to-asset ratio) and, for the specific interest of our observation, *BM* (business model, dummy variable for commercial, savings and cooperative banks). All these variables are used to form interaction terms with the policy interest rate. Finally, the level of *GDP* of the country in which the bank operates and a vector of dummies indicating the year of reference are further included as control terms (and as proxies of the demand of credit). In principle, a negative coefficient of the monetary policy variable (γ) is expected. As interest rate decreases, the loans issued increase. Furthermore, based on the specification, the assumption of the homogeneity of the policy stimulus transmission would be verified if the coefficients of the interaction terms (λ_n) were to be insignificant. On the other hand, significant coefficients of the interaction terms between the monetary policy variable and the bank characteristics would indicate that the effects of the monetary policy vary depending on bank-level characteristics, and hence that a *bank lending channel* exists. A separate model for each of the two economic areas identified is estimated.

To address the likely endogeneity of certain covariates included in the specification, an Arellano-Bond type of GMM difference estimator is applied (Arellano and Bond 1991). Considering the panel data structure (which is in the form "*small T, large N*"), a serious difficulty linked to the induced correlation between regressor and error term would arise by using a fixed effect model. As Nickell (1981) shows, this is due to the fact that the demeaning process subtracts the individual's mean value from the respective variable.[16] The Arellano-Bond type GMM approach addresses

[16] Note also that this bias is not caused by an autocorrelated error process and it arises even if the error process is independent and identically distributed (iid).

the fixed effect problem by first differentiating the regression equation, in this way removing the unobserved fixed error component. Hence, it exploits the panel data by allowing the use of internal instruments (lagged values of the endogenous variables) as well as by permitting some of the explanatory variables to be considered exogenous. In addition, the Arellano-Bond type GMM approach performs correctly even with unbalanced panel data (Arellano and Bond 1991).

By using such an approach, relation (3.1) is then redefined as:

$$\begin{aligned}\Delta \log\left(loans_{i,t}\right) = \varphi\,\Delta \log\left(loans_{i,t-1}\right) + \gamma\Delta r_t + \lambda_1\Delta\left(r_t * SIZE_{i,t}\right) \\ + \lambda_2\Delta\left(r_t * CAPITAL_{i,t}\right) + \lambda_3\Delta\left(r_t * BM_t\right) \\ + \mu\Delta GDP_{i,t} + \theta_t YEAR_t + \Delta\varepsilon_{i,t}\end{aligned} \tag{3.2}$$

where the error term does not contain the unobserved individual effects u_i:

$$\Delta\varepsilon_{i,t} = \Delta u_i + \Delta v_{i,t} = \left(u_i - u_i\right) + \left(v_{i,t} - v_{i,t-1}\right) = v_{i,t} - v_{i,t-1} \tag{3.3}$$

Lagged and two-lagged values for the independent variables suspected to be endogenous are employed.[17] Three cross sections are hence lost in constructing lags and taking first differences, so that the final estimation period is 2008–2013. In this way, the analysis gets centred on a period including the financial crisis and the years just after. Furthermore, GDP and the policy rate are considered as strictly exogenous variables.[18]

The test for heteroscedasticity is held by using the Breusch-Pagan test (for linear forms of heteroscedasticity) and White's general test. Even in the presence of heteroscedasticity, it can still be assumed that the regression estimates are correct. Nevertheless, their standard errors may be biased and hence the regression estimates are not BLUE. This may severely harm the significance of the regression coefficients and hence their econometric interpretation. In consideration of a certain level of heteroscedasticity in

[17] In more detail, the variables treated as endogenous are r_t*$SIZE_{i,t}$ and r_t*$CAPITAL_{i,t}$ (lagged and two lagged used as instrument) and r_t*BM_i (no lagged values used).

[18] Considering the policy rate (and other macroeconomic indicators) as an exogenous variable is in line with previous studies (e.g. Ashcraft 2006; Ferri et al. 2014). Nevertheless, endogeneity problems could arise by using EONIA to explain changes in banks' loan supply and such a use may represents a potential limitation of the analysis.

the data[19] and to address the above-mentioned issue, heteroscedasticity-consistent and robust standard errors are used.

The Arellano-Bond test is finally run to control for the presence of autocorrelation in the differenced residuals. For consistency, rejection of second-order autocorrelation is sought. The absence of second-order autocorrelation ensures that the lagged instrument of the lagged dependent variable is not correlated with the differenced error term.

3.2.3 Empirical Observation and Discussion of Results

Table 3.3 reports the estimation results for the model formalised in specification (3.2) for the MCTA and for the META, respectively. For both the areas, no second-order serial correlation is found, so the results obtained may be considered consistent. As far as it concerns both the MCTA and the META, the results in Table 3.3 show highly significant coefficients for the lagged dependent variable and for the change in the reference monetary policy rate. The latter is negative (as expected), meaning that a reduction in the policy rate induces an increase of the lending outstanding in the system. From the analysis of the interaction terms intended to verify the presence of a *bank lending channel*, the results obtained provide evidence that size and membership to the cooperative banking business model (the latter only for the MCTA) are bank-level elements able to have an impact on the transmission of the monetary stimulus. Hence, it may be confirmed that a *bank lending channel* today exists in the euro area and the banks' business model is one of its key components.

The interaction term between interest rate and size results to be significant at least at a 95 per cent confidence level in both the specifications, assuming a positive coefficient. A general interpretation of these results, also considering consolidated literature, might be that larger banks are more shielded than smaller banks from the monetary shocks (e.g. Kashyap and Stein 2000). Nevertheless, because of the first difference implied in the Arellano-Bond estimation, this economic explanation of the estimation results may be partially blurred. One may say that even though the estimation results provide proof of the impact of size on the banks' lending behaviour corresponding to a shock in the monetary policy, the direction of this impact cannot be detected straightforwardly.

[19] Both the tests reported large Chi^2 values, rejecting the null hypothesis of constant variance of the residuals (Breusch-Pagan test) and homoscedasticity (White test).

Table 3.3 Estimation results for the two economic areas within the euro area

	Monetary Conservation Targetable Area (MCTA)		*Monetary Expansion Targetable Area (META)*	
	Coefficient	*Robust standard errors*	*Coefficient*	*Robust standard errors*
Δ *log (loans$_{t-1}$)*	0.4037*** (2.95)	0.1368	0.6156*** (4.14)	0.1488
Δ r_t	−0.0191*** (−3.44)	0.0056	−0.0195* (−1.66)	0.0097
Δ (r_t*$SIZE_t$)	0.0038** (2.20)	0.0017	0.0038*** (2.80)	0.0014
Δ (r_t*$CAPITAL_t$)	−0.0344 (−1.35)	0.0359	−0.0054 (−0.16)	0.0343
Δ r_t*COOPER.	−0.0034*** (−3.56)	0.0010	0.0014 (0.51)	0.0028
Δ r_t*COMMER.	0.0051 (0.96)	0.0053	0.0037 (1.39)	0.0031
Δ GDP_t	−0.0044** (−2.14)	0.0021	0.0007 (0.30)	0.0023
Banks	*1761*		*837*	
Observations	*9572*		*4387*	
Year dummies	*YES*		*YES*	
Instruments	*100*		*100*	
Wald X^2	*3869.28*		*2428.55*	
AB test (1)	*0.0000*		*0.0001*	
AB test (2)	*0.6900*		*0.7784*	

Source: Migliorelli and Brunelli (2016)

Notes: The dependent variable is the increase (or decrease) in the log of gross loans outstanding to non-financial corporations for each bank. Arellano-Bond estimation. One-step results. The variables treated as endogenous are r_t*$SIZE_{i,t}$ and r_t*$CAPITAL_{i,t}$ (lagged and two lagged used as instrument) and r_t*BM_i (no lagged values used). Sources of data: Bankscope for banks' balance sheet information, ECB for EONIA daily values and Eurostat for GDP annual growth rates

*** shows significance at 1%, ** 5% and * 10%. *z*-statistics are in parentheses

A more direct interpretation may be given to the role of the banks' business model. To this extent, and only as far as it concerns the MCTA, cooperative banks seem to be able to boost the effects on lending of a reduction in interest rates. In fact, the coefficient of the interaction term between the interest rate and the dummy indicating the association with the cooperative segment is negative and highly significant. This effect is quite relevant, leveraging for about 20 per cent the impact given by the monetary shock taken stand-alone. At the same time, this effect seems not to be present for commercial banks, reinforcing the conclusion that a specific lending outcome linked to the cooperative banking business model is present in the north-eastern half of the continent. These findings concerning the effects of the cooperative banking business model on the transmission of the monetary stimulus are consistent with the most recent evidence focused on the euro area, and in particular for Germany. To this extent, these results confirm the support that these banks have guaranteed to the economy in the period of the economic crisis in Europe (Bolton et al. 2013; De Santis and Surico 2013). A further analysis of the cornerstones of the cooperative banks' business model may explain such a lending behaviour. As cooperative banks are built on relationship lending, they may prefer to keep providing accessible funds to their clients (in particular to their members), largely independently of the money market conditions. In fact, enforcing a long-standing relationship requires an investment in terms of time and costs, as well as it implies a view of the value of the customer based on the long-term. Hence, cooperative banks may avoid laying down existing clients even in period of sluggish financial performance and in case of worsening of their balance sheet positions. On the other hand, banks built on transaction lending, as is the case for commercial banks in particular, may decide their lending strategy prevalently on the basis of the contingent market trends and on their short-medium term evaluation of the value of the customer.

In their work, Ferri et al. (2014) used a similar estimation procedure and obtained (generally) significant but positive coefficients for the interaction term between monetary interest rates and cooperative bank dummy. Commenting those results, they concluded that the positive coefficient could prove the countercyclical role played by cooperative banks in the longer term. This difference with the estimation results reported in this study is most probably due to the different time period analysed.[20] In particular, the sample period (2008–2013) has been characterised by the financial and the economic crisis and by constantly diminishing interest rates. In this setting, a countercyclical attitude seems to be more coherent with a leveraging effect of the reduction of the interest rates (a negative

[20] In Ferri et al. (2014), the authors analysed the period 1999–2011 and the two subperiods 1999–2007 (financial stability) and 2008–2011 (crisis).

coefficient) then vice versa. For this reason, the results of the two studies do not necessarily conflict.[21]

To consolidate these results, and in particular with the aim of investigating possible country-level effects on lending, some additional estimations are run. First, a set of country dummy variables, considered as being exogenous, is included in each specification.[22] Table 3.4 reports the estimation outputs. Overall, the results obtained seem to confirm those of Table 3.3. Amongst the country variables included, only three turn out to be significant. In this respect, a statistically significant negative impact is registered for Ireland, Slovenia and Spain. In particular in Ireland and Spain, the above-mentioned country-level impact may be connected to the deep influence on the banking system of the real estate crash that occurred in these economies after 2008. Furthermore, to take into account the predominant position of Germany and Italy in terms of sample composition of, respectively, the MCTA and the META, an analysis for the two economic areas is run excluding these countries. Table 3.5 reports the estimation results obtained for the two areas. As far as it concerns the MCTA, a slightly lower significance is observed on the lending developments of the cooperative bank business model (which is still significant at 95 per cent confidence level) and the higher impact of the policy rate (in which the coefficient is higher than in Table 3.3 in absolute terms). These results confirm the importance of the cooperative banking business model in supporting the local economy all over the area, and not only in Germany. As regards the META, when excluding Italy from the sample, size becomes insignificant, while cooperative and commercial banks seem to act in a similar way and partially dump the effect of the monetary stimulus. These results may shed some light on the strong influence of small banks in Italy and their potentially distortive role in the monetary policy transmission process during the crisis.

The estimation results provide some interesting evidence with regard to the differences in the *bank lending channel* between the two identified economic areas. In particular, by considering the lower significance of the variables intended to investigate the phenomenon, it may be argued that in the META the incidence of the *bank lending channel* is less pronounced than in

[21] In the same respect and again because of the time period analysed, our results cannot precisely predict the behaviour of cooperative banks in periods of increasing interest rates.

[22] These dummy variables have been considered as "already differenced exogenous variables" in the Arellano-Bond procedure available in STATA.

Table 3.4 Estimation results for the two economic areas, including country dummy variables

	Monetary Conservation Targetable Area (MCTA)		*Monetary Expansion Targetable Area (META)*	
	Coefficient	*Robust standard errors*	*Coefficient*	*Robust standard errors*
Δ *log (loans$_{t-1}$)*	0.4112*** (3.18)	0.1291	0.6164*** (4.19)	0.1469
Δ r_t	−0.0155*** (−2.68)	0.0058	−0.0350* (−1.87)	0.0187
Δ (r_t* *SIZE$_t$*)	0.0037** (2.26)	0.0016	0.0040*** (2.72)	0.0015
Δ (r_t* *CAPITAL$_t$*)	−0.0538 (−1.62)	0.0332	0.0031 (0.09)	0.0346
Δ r_t* *COOPER.*	−0.0028*** (−2.68)	0.0010	0.0017 (0.58)	0.0028
Δ r_t* *COMMER.*	0.0042 (0.82)	0.0051	0.0048* (1.68)	0.0028
Δ *GDP$_t$*	−0.0046** (−2.16)	0.0021	−0.0001 (−0.06)	0.0025
Dummy FI	0.0091 (1.60)	0.0057	–	–
Dummy GE	0.0017 (0.96)	0.0018	–	–
Dummy MA	−0.0247 (−1.20)	0.0206	–	–
Dummy ND	−0.0103 (−0.59)	0.0173	–	–
Dummy SL	−0.0181*** (−3.17)	0.0057	–	–
Dummy SK	0.0009 (0.14)	0.0065	–	–
Dummy BE	–	–	−0.0064 (−0.55)	0.012
Dummy FR	–	–	−0.048 (−0.56)	0.0086
Dummy IR	–	–	−0.0275** (−2.34)	0.0117
Dummy IT	–	–	−0.0091 (−1.11)	0.0082

(*continued*)

Table 3.4 (continued)

	Monetary Conservation Targetable Area (MCTA)		*Monetary Expansion Targetable Area (META)*	
	Coefficient	*Robust standard errors*	*Coefficient*	*Robust standard errors*
Dummy PG	–	–	−0.0250 (−1.61)	0.0156
Dummy SP	–	–	−0.0208** (−2.21)	0.0094
Banks	*1761*		*837*	
Observations	*9572*		*4387*	
Year dummies	*YES*		*YES*	
Instruments	*106*		*106*	
Wald X^2	*468.41*		*391.22*	
AB test (1)	*0.0000*		*0.0001*	
AB test (2)	*0.6722*		*0.8428*	

Source: Migliorelli and Brunelli (2016)

Notes: The dependent variable is the increase (or decrease) in the log of gross loans outstanding to non-financial corporations for each bank. Arellano-Bond estimation. One-step results. The variables treated as endogenous are r_t*$SIZE_{i,t}$ and r_t*$CAPITAL_{i,t}$ (lagged and two lagged used as instrument) and r_t*BM_i (no lagged values used). Sources of data: Bankscope for banks' balance sheet information, ECB for EONIA daily values and Eurostat for GDP annual growth rates. *BE* Belgium, *FI* Finland, *FR* France, *GE* Germany, *IR* Ireland, *IT* Italy, *MA* Malta, *ND* The Netherlands, *PR* Portugal, *SK* Slovakia, *SL* Slovenia, *SP* Spain

*** shows significance at 1%, ** 5% and * 10%. *z*-statistics are in parentheses

the MCTA. Considering the different impact of the financial and sovereign debt crises on the peripheral countries of the continent (mainly composing the META) and on the central countries (mainly composing the MCTA), our findings may also indicate that the ***bank lending channel*** may assume a more pronounced role in areas of economic or financial stability than in areas of turmoil. Namely, banks seem to be more reactive to policymakers' actions when facing distress, while they may partially act independently of the monetary stimulus when standing closer to their operational targets.

Such an argument seems to be particularly relevant for cooperative banks. In fact, while they leveraged the effects of the reduction of the interest rates on lending in the north-east part of the euro area, they were not able to do so in the periphery of the continent. Hence, empirical evidence concerning the south European countries may suggest that the

Table 3.5 Estimation results for the two economic areas, excluding the main countries in terms of sample size

	Monetary Conservation Targetable Area (MCTA), excluding Germany		*Monetary Expansion Targetable Area (META), excluding Italy*	
	Coefficient	*Robust standard errors*	*Coefficient*	*Robust standard errors*
Δ *log (loans*$_{t-1}$*)*	0.4140** (2.25)	0.1844	0.2883 (1.41)	0.2040
Δ r_t	−0.0450*** (−3.20)	0.0140	−0.0376* (−1.87)	0.0202
Δ (r_t* *SIZE*$_t$)	0.0170*** (2.64)	0.0065	0.0009 (0.34)	0.0028
Δ (r_t* *CAPITAL*$_t$)	−0.0768 (−0.82)	0.0935	−0.0722 (−0.98)	0.0733
Δ r_t* *COOPER.*	−0.0052** (−2.09)	0.0025	0.0090* (1.70)	0.0053
Δ r_t* *COMMER.*	−0.0044 (−0.51)	0.0086	0.0087* (1.77)	0.0049
Δ *GDP*$_t$	−0.0054* (−1.94)	0.0028	0.0079* (1.81)	0.0044
Banks	*275*		*438*	
Observations	*1309*		*1686*	
Year dummies	*YES*		*YES*	
Instruments	*90*		*98*	
Wald X^2	*405.28*		*192.07*	
AB test (1)	*0.0069*		*0.1015*	
AB test (2)	*0.5977*		*0.4396*	

Source: Migliorelli and Brunelli (2016)

Notes: The dependent variable is the increase (or decrease) in the log of gross loans outstanding to non-financial corporations for each bank. Arellano-Bond estimation. One-step results. The variables treated as endogenous are r_t*$SIZE_{i,t}$ and r_t*$CAPITAL_{i,t}$ (lagged and two lagged used as instrument) and r_t*BM_i (no lagged values used). Sources of data: Bankscope for banks' balance sheet information, ECB for EONIA daily values and Eurostat for GDP annual growth rates

*** shows significance at 1%, ** 5% and * 10%. *z*-statistics are in parentheses

lending behaviour of cooperative banks tends to converge with those of the other types of banks in the mid-term in economies characterised by prolonged recessions. This may also mean that the traditional anticyclical role of cooperative banks may have encountered limitation due to the exceptional magnitude and length of the downturn.

3.3 Lending Supply, Capitalisation and Non-performing Loans During the Great Crisis: The Italian Case[23]

3.3.1 Credit Crunch *and Levels of Banks' Capitalisation*

The analysis carried out in the previous section suggests, inter alia, that banks' business model may tend to be neutral to the transmission of the monetary policy in economies characterised by prolonged recessions. In Europe, this has been the case in particular for the south-west part of the continent. This implies that cooperative banks in this part of the continent may have had to react to the changed economic scenario and act similarly to commercial banks, in this way questioning (at least in part) the traditional countercyclical role played by these banks during periods of economic crisis. In this respect, it is of great interest to analyse in more detail which elements may have triggered such a phenomenon. To do that, in the reminder of the section the focus is on Italy.[24] This choice depends on two considerations. First, it is one of the European countries in which the cooperative banks' presence assumed a systemic relevance.[25,26] Second, it was one of the countries in Europe in which the crisis had a particularly strong impact on small business and households, which are the key segment of clientele for cooperative banks.

In Italy, cooperative banks used to play an essential macroeconomic role. Even though their weight on the total loan market is lower than 20.0 per cent in terms of volumes, it peaks to almost 40.0 per cent if taking into account the sole small and medium enterprises (SME) segment.[27,28] The relevance of the cooperative banks becomes evident when considering that

[23] This paragraph is based on Migliorelli (2015).

[24] Furthermore, little public intervention has been deployed in the aftermath of the crisis, so that the empirical investigation is less impacted by external factors.

[25] In Italy, the cooperative banking segment is composed of *Banche di Credito Cooperativo* and *Banche Popolari*.

[26] This is still valid during the period analysed. With the reform of the major *Banche Popolari* launched in 2015, which transformed these banks in joint-stock companies, the weight of cooperative banks in Italy has considerably reduced. This reform is discussed in detail in Chap. 5.

[27] These figures concern the situation before the reform of the major *Banche Popolari*.

[28] Source: Credito Cooperativo and European Cooperative Banks Association. Other metrics may be used to underline the importance of the cooperative banking segment in Italy: at 31/03/2014 more than 400 cooperative banks were active in Italy (counting for more than 50 per cent of total Italian banks) with more than 4000 branches and 37,000 employees.

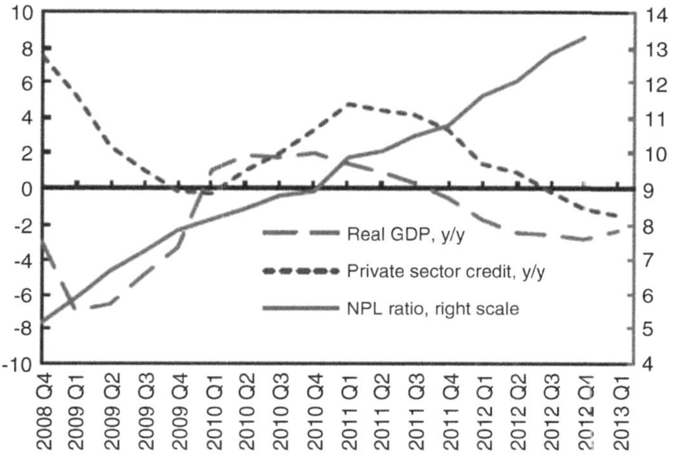

Fig. 3.4 GDP, credit growth and non-performing loans in Italy (in percent). Source: International Monetary Fund (2013)

Italy's SME sector counts for 80.3 per cent in terms of employment and 68.3 per cent in terms of value added, and it is the largest in the European Union by number of firms (3.8 million firms by including enterprises with less than 10 employees).[29] In Italy, GDP went down by 1.2 per cent in 2008 and by 5.5 per cent in 2009. After a partial recovery in 2010 and 2011 (+1.7 per cent and +0.4 per cent), the economy turned again into recession, with a fall of the GDP in 2012 and 2013 of −2.4 per cent and −1.9 per cent, respectively. After these two waves of recession, in the period 2014–2017 the average growth rate was 0.9 per cent per year.[30] In parallel, an unprecedented increase in the level of non-performing loans has been experienced in the market, along with a decline in the credit issued to the private sector (see Fig. 3.4).

[29] Source: European Commission (2012), "*Small Business Act for Europe, Fact Sheet 2012 – Italy*".

[30] Source: Eurostat.

Many observers described the situation depicted in Fig. 3.4 as a *credit crunch*.[31] Relevant literature identifies one of the possible causes of a *credit crunch* in the effects of unexpected levels of non-performing loans on the capital structure of the banks, through asset impairments and economic losses. In this sense, they imply causality between the *credit crunch* and the so-called *capital crunch*. In our analysis, it is hence of interest to analyse whether and in what measure the observed drop in bank lending occurred in Italy in during and after the Great Crisis has been caused by a shortfall in banks capitalisation and to what extent this effect is linked to the cooperative banking segment.

In the analysis of the causes and the implications of a shortfall in bank capital, regulation and management preferences for specific capital targets play an essential role. As far as it concerns regulation, the introduction of risk-based capital-to-asset ratios in the early nineties definitively linked the equity side to the assets sides of the banks' balance sheets. Under a regulatory point of view, undercapitalised banks are the ones which present a capital-to-asset ratio lower than a fixed threshold (as a general rule, under the Basel Accord, regulatory capital must be equal or higher the 8.0 per cent of the risk-weighted assets). In such a framework, when the capital-to-asset ratio falls below the binding minimum requirement, two basic options are available for the bank in order to restore compliancy: issuing new equity (increase the numerator of the ratio) or shifting assets from riskier to less risky classes (decrease the denominator of the ratio). Because of asymmetric information, bank management can find issuing new equity excessively costly, as it involves opening a discussion with the shareholders as well as signalling to the market a state of inadequacy that may be perceived negatively.[32] Undercapitalised banks, in order to quickly adjust their ratios, may prefer cutting back credit and investing in less risky assets classes. To explicit the concept, under the Basel framework loans to real

[31] In their seminal work, Bernanke and Lown (1991) defined the *credit crunch* as "*a significant leftward shift in the supply curve for bank loans, holding constant both the safe real interest rate and the quality of potential borrowers*". In other words, in a situation of *credit crunch* banks may refuse to supply credit at the same conditions they were used to do in previous periods. Whatever the cause, the main drawback of a *credit crunch* lays in the fact that it can hamper the launch of new investments by firms and can impact the consumption of households, leading to a further worsening of the economic cycle.

[32] For example, Stein (1998) concludes that banks issuing new equity may be perceived underperforming by the investors.

estate have in principle a 100.0 per cent weight,[33] against a 0.0 per cent weight for highly rated government bonds. Shifting from real estate lending to government bonds will be then an effective way to push back the capital-to-asset ratio above the regulatory constraint. If this reasoning holds for a sufficiently high number of banks in the same region, the "regulatory" shortfall in capital can lead to a supply-driven cutback in lending, in other words to a *credit crunch*.

In terms of modelling, several variations of the following regression scheme have been adopted in order to assess the variation of bank lending due to capital-driven factors (e.g. Berger and Udell 1994; Peek and Rosengren 1995a):

$$\left(\Delta L / L\right)_{i,t0-t1} = \alpha + \beta_1 \left(K / A\right)_{i,t0} + \beta_2 D_{t0-t1} + \varepsilon_{i,t} \tag{3.4}$$

In the equation, the dependent variable $\Delta L/L$ represents the level of credit growth or retrenchment for the sample unit analysed (either a state, a region or a single bank) in one particular period, K/A is a measure of capital-to-asset ratio at the beginning of the period and D represents a vector of demand-driven variables. Many works have used a lagged measure of the capital-to-asset ratio in order to avoid simultaneity of the lending growth and capital ratio and limit the endogeneity problem. On the other hand, no unanimous consensus exists in literature as far as it concerns the different methods to control for demand-side effects while analysing a *credit crunch*. The factual observation that most of the time shifts in lending demand and supply occur at the same time and with different magnitude on volumes and rates has forced researchers to introduce limitations and adjustments to raw time series and samples. A first way to limit these effects is to restrict the sample to banks operating in the same area and/or to group banks into demand-homogeneous clusters (e.g. Bernanke and Lown 1991; Peek and Rosengren 1995b). In this way, it may be assumed that all the sample units in the same cluster face the same uniform demand of credit. Other authors preferred to approximate the demand of credit with the general economic conditions. In this sense, they included in the regression model a number of key macroeconomic variables, such as employment rate, GDP growth, inflation and so on (e.g. Kashyap and

[33] This may not be the case for banks that adopt the Internal Ratings-Based (IRB) approach to evaluate their credit positions. By using the IRB approach, the weight to assign to each loan varies depending on the borrower's credit standing.

Stein 2000; Ashcraft 2006). Finally, a few researchers used instrumental variables calculated with respect to benchmark periods, in which it may be assumed there were no credit limitations (e.g. Berger and Udell 1994; Watanabe 2007). In any case, none of the methods mentioned assures a complete disentanglement between the supply-side and demand-side effects on credit developments.

3.3.2 Research Method

With the purpose to investigate the effects of capital on lending during the Great Crisis in Italy, the analysis of the market is performed from observations at single bank level. The regression model (OLS) used is in the form:

$$\begin{aligned}(\Delta L / L)_i &= \alpha + \beta_j Capital\ Crunch_i + \gamma_k Substitutions\ Effects_i \\ &+ \delta_l Demand_i + \varepsilon_i\end{aligned} \tag{3.5}$$

The dependent variable $\Delta L/L$ is a measure of incremental loans, mortgages and other financing instruments to non-financial institutions issued by the bank i in the year of reference. To this extent, L represents the gross loans outstanding. Two variables are then used to verify the *capital crunch* hypothesis. The first one is the book-based capital-to-asset ratio, K/A, used in several papers (e.g. Bernanke and Lown 1991; Berger and Udell 1994; Watanabe 2007), calculated at the beginning of the year of the observation of the loans variation. The second one is the variation in equity calculated as the difference between the value at 31 December 2008 and the value at the beginning of the period under analysis, $\Delta K/K$. This variable is used to assess the response in terms of loans to the capital losses that a bank may have experienced from the beginning of the economic crisis, hence analysing the reaction to capital shocks. A vector of behavioural variables is then included in order to try to detect the opportunistic conduct of the banks in terms of substitution effects of loans with other financial instruments available in the market. In particular, during the crisis many observers claimed that banks cut down lending to acquire government bonds (as part of a *carry trade* strategy). In this respect, three variables are used in order to take into account the percentage variation in the levels of government securities, derivatives and loans to banks held by the bank i in the period of reference ($\Delta GNS/GNS$, $\Delta DVT/DVT$ and $\Delta LNB/LNB$). A first demand control variable is used to account for the borrowers' concentration problem that several small banks may have. To this extent, a valuable option is to use the log of the total assets, Log(A) (Peek and Rosengren 1995a). Because of regulatory provisions, banks cannot lend above a certain percentage of their portfolio to a single borrower. In such a framework, small banks may find difficult to lend to big firms as the amount demanded would be relatively too high. Hence, in a situation of economic downturn in which small businesses may suffer the most (as anecdotal observation seems to claim in Italy), small banks may shrink their loans more than bigger banks do in response to the deteriorated balance sheet conditions of the borrowers (i.e. small businesses). A second control variable aims at assessing the impact on lending of the diversification characteristics of the bank. This variable is built as the portion of fee income over the sum of total interest and fee income, *FEE/OI* (Peek and Rosengren 1995a). The underlying consideration is that bank less exposed to the credit business and hence more diversified (with higher *FEE/OI* ratio) may be more insulated in the case of significant shock in the demand of credit in the market. The last demand control variable used is the change in the relevant gross domestic product in the region of activity of the bank in the year of reference (*RGDP*). Such a control variable is used to factor in the impact of the economic conditions in the development of the lending activity. To this extent, each bank has been categorised as national-level bank or as regional bank. For national-level banks, *RGDP* is simply the overall Italian GDP growth rate, while for regional banks it assumes the value of the GDP growth rate of the region of activity. Including demand control variables such as Log(A), *FEE/OI* and *RGDP* should ease the potential bias of the regression coefficients for the K/A and $\Delta K/K$ ratios due to endogeneity. In fact, these variables may predict lending development only as a consequence of demand-side effects. In particular, a prolonged recession can impact both the quantity of credit demanded (hence impacting on the dependent variable) and the capitalisation of the banks, via an increase of non-performing loans. The use of lagged values of $\Delta K/K$ also contributes to limit this problem (Table 3.6).

The model is run separately for the five years of reference of the analysis (from 2009 to 2013). This allows the observation of the evolution of the significance and the magnitude of the regression coefficients over time. The main database used to collect the data for the analysis is Bankscope, by Bureau Van Dijk. At the end of 2013, Bankscope covered 605 active Italian banks and other financial institutions, hence comprising almost the

Table 3.6 Regression variables

Variable	*Symbol*	*Effect side*	*Purpose*	*Reference period*
Δ Loans	$\Delta L/L$	–	Dependent variable	t_0–t_1
Capital-to-asset ratio	K/A	Supply	Capital crunch	t_0
Δ Equity during the crisis	$\Delta K/K$	Supply	Capital crunch	31/Dec/2008–t_0
Δ Government bonds	$\Delta GNS/GNS$	Supply	Substitution effects	t_0–t_1
Δ Derivatives	$\Delta DVT/DVT$	Supply	Substitution effects	t_0–t_1
Δ Loans and advances to banks	$\Delta LNB/LBN$	Supply	Substitution effects	t_0–t_1
Size	$Log(A)$	Demand/supply	Control	t_0
Fees on operating income	FEE/OI	Demand	Control	t_0–t_1
Regional GDP	$RGDP$	Demand	Control	t_0–t_1

Source: Migliorelli (2015)

entire market. The analysis of the market has been again restricted to three types of banks, which carry out the lending activity as their core business: commercial banks, savings banks and cooperative banks. Banks have been analysed at a single level. In this light, consolidated values for baking groups have been taken into account only when more granular information was not available. Furthermore, banks with total assets value lower than EUR 800 million have been excluded. This limitation has been adopted to avoid the presence in the sample of a majority of micro-banks representing a very limited portion of the market. Finally, banks with only partial time series available have been excluded in order to assure the comparability of the regression results over the reference period. The final sample is composed of 138 banks, of which 37 are commercial banks, 24 are savings banks and 77 are cooperative banks. The sample is strongly illustrative of the Italian loan market, as it includes banks representing about 83.0 per cent of the total assets managed by commercial, savings and cooperative banks.[34] In the attempt to closer investigate the trends of the market over the period analysed, Figs. 3.5 and 3.6 show the develop-

[34] Author's estimate on Bankscope data as at 31/12/2013.

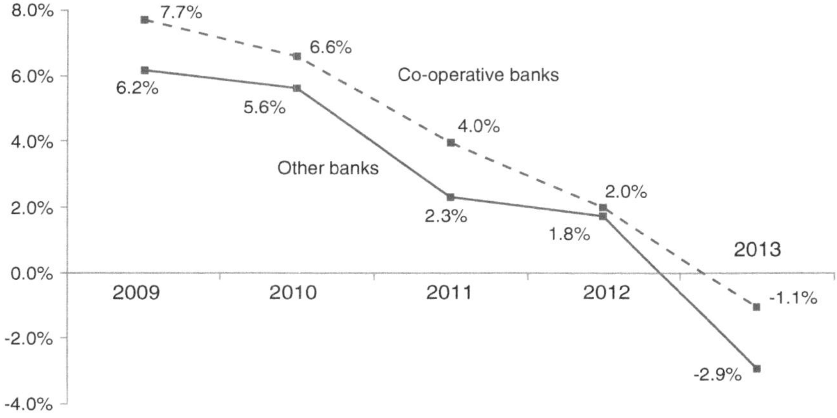

Fig. 3.5 Gross loans increase (decrease) over time in Italy. Source: Migliorelli (2015). Notes: Elaboration on sample data set. Average values calculated on the basis of the sample analysed, outliers excluded

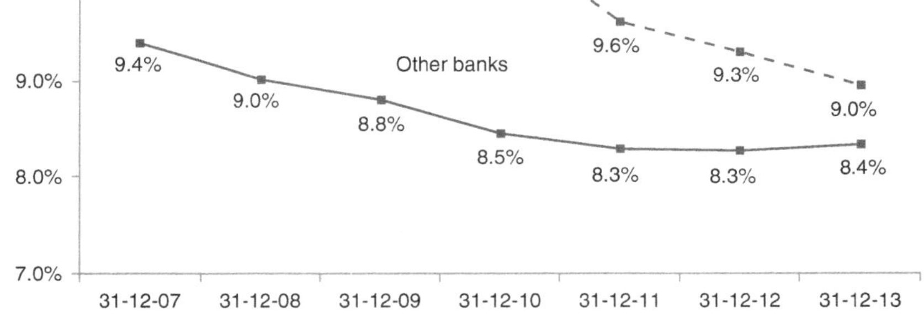

Fig. 3.6 Evolution of the K/A ratio over time for Italian banks. Source: Migliorelli (2015). Notes: Elaboration on sample data set. Average values calculated on the basis of the sample analysed, outliers excluded

ment of the gross loans and the evolution of the capital-to-asset ratio (*K/A*) during the crisis.

Different lines indicate cooperative banks (dotted) and other banks (plain). Some valuable indications can be drawn from the observation of the charts. First of all, Fig. 3.5 shows how the expansion of the credit in the market has continued for all the banks until 2012, even if with progressively decreasing rates over time. The first credit reduction in terms of total volumes outstanding has been experienced in 2013. In this context, cooperative banks have substantially increased over time their exposition with respect to other banks. This highlights the tendency of cooperative banks to support Italian businesses and households all along the crisis, confirming in this way the countercyclical function that has been observed by many authors.[35]

Further indications arise from the analysis of Fig. 3.6. Even if still better capitalised than other banks at the end of 2013, cooperative banks have experienced over time a higher reduction in their relative capitalisation. In particular, the average *K/A* ratio for cooperative banks passed from 11.6 per cent at the end of 2007 to 9.0 per cent at the end of 2013 (−2.6 per cent). In the same period, other banks' average *K/A* ratio mildly worsened from 9.4 per cent to 8.4 per cent (−1.0 per cent). Moreover, savings and commercial banks appear to have succeeded in stabilising their relative capitalisation, at least from 2011 (for these banks, the average *K/A* ratio at the end of 2010 was 8.5 per cent, in line with the value at the end of 2013). On the contrary, cooperative banks have kept reducing their capitalisation over time *vis-à-vis* their assets.

3.3.3 Empirical Observation and Discussion of Results

Tables 3.7 and 3.8 report the regression results for the years covered in the analysis. The results for the full specification provide substantial support to the hypothesis that a *capital crunch* occurred in Italy in 2013. However, this effect was uneven and can be only partially generalised to the entire market. On the one hand, the coefficient of capital-to-asset ratio is positive and significant at 95 per cent confidence level only for cooperative banks, while it is not significant for the entire sample and for other banks. On the other hand, the coefficient of the change in capital since the beginning of the crisis is positive and significant at 95 per cent confidence level for the

[35] See, for example, Di Colli and Girardi (2012) and Zago and Dogili (2014).

Table 3.7 Regression results for 2013

	2013		
	All banks	*Cooperative banks*	*Other banks*
K/A	0.2107	0.8538**	−0.2162
	(0.87)	(2.62)	(−0.60)
ΔK/K	0.0618**	0.1023**	0.0249
	(2.07)	(2.40)	(0.59)
ΔGNS/GNS	0.0085	0.0086	0.0073
	(1.56)	(0.69)	(1.16)
ΔDVT/DVT	−0.0043	−0.0376	0.0108
	(−0.18)	(−1.06)	(0.32)
ΔLNB/LBN	−0.0097*	−0.0085	−0.0102
	(−1.85)	(−0.98)	(−1.56)
Log(A)	0.0123	0.0578***	−0.0091
	(1.06)	(3.36)	(−0.55)
FEE/OI	−0.0498	−0.1963*	0.0711
	(−0.78)	(−1.73)	(0.78)
RGDP	2.2188*	2.4033	1.4048
	(1.67)	(1.22)	(0.76)
Constant term	−0.0378	−0.2302***	0.0274
	(−0.70)	(−2.88)	(0.33)
N	*138*	*77*	*61*
R^2	*0.085*	*0.272*	*0.086*

Source: Migliorelli (2015)

Notes: The dependent variable is the annual percentage change in gross loans outstanding to non-financial corporations for each bank in 2013

*** shows significance at 1%, ** 5% and * 10% respectively. *t*-statistics are in parentheses

entire sample and for cooperative banks, while it remains not significant for other banks. These results suggest that the *capital crunch* hypothesis may be verified for cooperative banks, while the same effect for the rest of the market has been mild or absent. That is, cooperative banks have been forced to shrink loans in 2013 in order to adjust their capital-to-asset ratios. The analysis of the results of the regression for the period spanning from 2012 to 2009 does not provide strong evidences of supply-side effects on the lending developments in these years. In fact, neither the regression coefficient of capital-to-asset ratio nor of the change in capital since the beginning of the recession is significant. The only exception is given by the coefficient of the *K/A* variable for other banks in 2009, which is significant at 95 per cent confidence level. Nevertheless, a low coeffi-

Table 3.8 Regression results for the period 2012–2009

	2012			*2011*		
	All banks	*Cooperative banks*	*Other banks*	*All banks*	*Cooperative banks*	*Other banks*
K/A	0.4762	0.7176	0.1286	0.2832	0.6010	−0.1463
	(1.33)	(1.32)	(0.28)	(0.19)	(0.22)	(−0.45)
ΔK/K	0.352	0.0532	0.0549	0.2066	0.5608	−0.0722
	(0.61)	(0.49)	(0.83)	(0.59)	(0.83)	(−1.10)
ΔGNS/GNS	0.0133*	0.0090	0.0173	−0.0001	−0.0012	−0.0007
	(1.77)	(0.83)	(1.57)	(−0.07)	(−0.69)	(−0.99)
ΔDVT/DVT	−0.0091	−0.0164	−0.0055	0.0204	0.0435	0.0011
	(−0.79)	(−1.03)	(−0.34)	(0.55)	(0.80)	(0.10)
ΔLNB/LBN	−0.0054	−0.0012	0.0060	0.0027	−0.0229	−0.0022
	(−0.57)	(−0.07)	(−0.56)	(0.26)	(−0.42)	(−1.41)
Log(A)	0.0277	0.1023***	−0.0066	0.1886***	0.5340***	−0.0162
	(1.63)	(3.48)	(−0.29)	(2.70)	(4.04)	(−1.14)
FEE/OI	−0.0276	−0.5059**	−0.0388	−1.2583***	−4.1070***	0.0028
	(−0.69)	(−2.17)	(−1.03)	(−2.87)	(−3.99)	(0.04)
RGDP	−0.2301	3.9793	−3.8947*	−3.4099	−2.8920	−0.2998
	(−0.13)	(1.59)	(−1.75)	(−0.52)	(−0.25)	(−0.23)
Constant term	−0.1223	−0.1658	−0.0574	−0.2481	−0.7371	0.1046
	(−1.44)	(−1.29)	(−0.50)	(−0.75)	(−1.18)	(1.52)
N	*138*	*77*	*61*	*138*	*77*	*61*
R^2	*0.200*	*0.222*	*0.152*	*0.115*	*0.337*	*0.094*

	2010			*2009*		
	All banks	*Cooperative banks*	*Other banks*	*All banks*	*Cooperative banks*	*Other banks*
K/A	−0.0682	−0.1909	0.0414	0.2811	−0.0320	0.8161**
	(−0.23)	(−0.36)	(0.13)	(1.47)	(−0.08)	(2.00)
ΔK/K	0.0048	0.0052	−0.0504	–	–	–
	(0.06)	(0.03)	(−0.74)			
ΔGNS/GNS	0.0001	0.0000	0.0023***	−0.0010	−0.0022	−0.0001
	(0.45)	(0.26)	(3.56)	(−0.52)	(−0.51)	(−0.27)
ΔDVT/DVT	−0.0037	−0.0039	−0.0019	0.0071	0.0089	0.0035
	(−0.84)	(−0.55)	(−0.48)	(1.03)	(1.04)	(0.27)
ΔLNB/LBN	0.0046	0.0067	0.0024	0.0001	−0.0025	0.0077
	(0.36)	(0.31)	(0.20)	(0.12)	(−0.25)	(0.39)
Log(*A*)	−0.0251*	−0.0235	−0.0166	−0.0065	−0.0035	−0.0110
	(−1.74)	(−0.87)	(−1.22)	(−0.47)	(−0.14)	(−0.58)

(*continued*)

Table 3.8 (continued)

	2010			*2009*		
	All banks	*Cooperative banks*	*Other banks*	*All banks*	*Cooperative banks*	*Other banks*
FEE/OI	0.0493	0.2134	−0.0399	0.0120	−0.0181	0.0087
	(0.55)	(0.89)	(−0.55)	(0.14)	(−0.08)	(0.09)
RGDP	0.0654	−0.4633	0.2532	0.3914	0.6958	0.1525
	(−0.12)	(−0.49)	(0.48)	(0.92)	(1.18)	(0.23)
Constant term	0.1504**	0.1409	0.1179**	0.0724	0.1325	0.0387
	(2.26)	(1.15)	(1.93)	(1.13)	(1.25)	(0.44)
N	*135*	*76*	*59*	*134*	*75*	*59*
R^2	*0.032*	*0.035*	*0.251*	*0.048*	*0.040*	*0.093*

For 2010, three outlier observations have been dropped out from the sample in order to avoid alteration of the regression results. For 2009, four outlier observations have been dropped out from the sample in order to avoid alteration of the regression results

Source: Migliorelli (2015)

Notes: The dependent variable is the annual percentage change in gross loans outstanding to non-financial corporations for each bank

*** shows significance at 1%, ** 5% and * 10% respectively. *t*-statistics are in parentheses

cient of determination ($R^2 = 0.093$) suggests caution and evidences the risk of overweighting the relevance of this result. The presence of a *capital crunch* in only one year over the period analysed was expected, and it is largely coherent with previous research results both for the US market (e.g. Bernanke and Lown 1991; Peek and Rosengren 1995a) and for the Japanese market (Watanabe 2007; Montgomery 2005). Overall, the results obtained confirm the adjustment effect of a *capital crunch* whenever it occurs. That is, banks tend to operate in an unconstrained manner when they stand close to their target capitalisation, but they are forced to revise their asset composition when they derail excessively from the target. The increase over time of the significance of the regression coefficient of the capital-to-asset ratio in explaining lending is also coherent with a progressive impact of *capital crunch* problem (Fig. 3.7).

The regression results for the *K/A* variable also fit with the developments summarised in Fig. 3.6 and previously described. In particular for cooperative banks, evidence suggests that the continuous reduction in the relative capitalisation that occurred all over the crisis has eventually produced a generalised *capital crunch* in 2013. More specifically, these results for cooperative banks are likely the consequence of the combined effect of

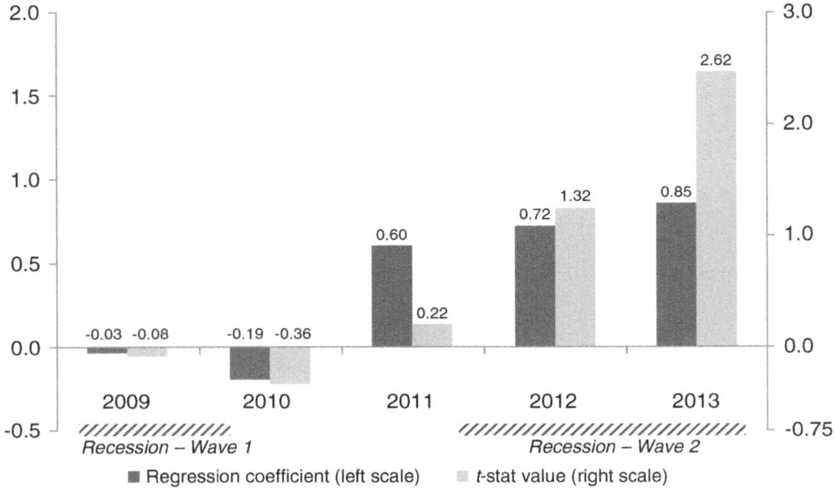

Fig. 3.7 Year-by-year coefficient of the book-based capital-to-asset ratio and related t-statistics for cooperative banks in Italy. Notes: Author's elaboration based on the regression results. Source: Migliorelli (2015)

a sustained lending activity in the period of the crisis and the lack of substantial economic recovery in Italy, in particular in the SME sector. In these conditions, the growth of the credit outstanding registered by these banks has not been paired by a comparable increase of their capitalisation, due in particular to low profitability caused by the largely unexpected explosion of the non-performing loans in the market. In parallel, for other banks the absence of a *capital crunch* is coherent with a more stable capital-to-asset ratio all along the period analysed. This means that commercial and savings banks have been on average more reactive in adjusting their asset and liabilities composition in order not to fall in a situation of capital constraint.[36]

[36] To this extent, the regression results for 2009 for the other banks' cluster, even though they are not particularly strong in terms of overall significance, seem to validate the *capital crunch* hypothesis and the adjustment effect that it carries over. In fact, as it is shown in Fig. 3.6, starting from 2010 these banks have succeeded in stabilising their capital-to-asset ratio, which has been maintained almost unchanged till the end of the reference period (end of 2013). This may signal the attainment of a new capital-to-asset target-level in the market. Hence, the absence of *capital crunch* effects in the period 2010–2013 is coherent with the absence of significant capital stains.

One can argue why cooperative banks may have suffered a ***capital crunch*** in 2013 even though they had, on average, a better capitalisation than other banks. A possible explanation is that cooperative banks' target capitalisation is structurally higher than it is for other kinds of banks. This feature of cooperative banks has to be sought in their ownership structure and in a reduced capability to access the equity market. As far as it concerns the first element, the *one-head one-vote* mechanism and the low profit-seeking nature that shapes the biggest part of the cooperative segment discourage large investors to stably enter the capital of these banks. As a result, the ownership of the cooperative banks remains mainly composed of small economic agents, who may not be in the conditions to infuse additional financial resources in case the bank falls in a situation of financial distress or simply derails from its target capitalisation. This problem is even more relevant in periods of recession, in which small agents are typically short of liquidity. In addition, the reduced size suffered by cooperative banks in Italy substantially made it difficult for these intermediaries to collect new financial resources through the financial market. These elements produce a structural rigidity in the capital of cooperative banks, in particular when compared to other kinds of financial institutions. Such rigidity pushes cooperative managers to preview and maintain higher equity buffers, in order to be able to carry out the activity also in periods of sluggish economic growth and deteriorated performance. Hence, it may not be surprising that a pressure on assets (and in particular on lending) arises for cooperative banks at a higher level of capital-to-asset ratio than for other types of financial institutions.

In addition to the findings connected with the assessment of the *capital crunch* hypothesis, further interesting observations may be drawn by analysing the regression results of the independent variables intended to control for differences in demand. In fact, both the log(A) and the *FEE/OI* ratio have estimated coefficients that are consistently significant for cooperative banks in 2011, 2012 and 2013. The same variables are not significant for the first years of the period analysed and for other banks (in none of the years analysed). These results suggest the presence of specific demand-side factors on the lending developments of cooperative banks all over the economic crisis. Firstly, cooperative banks may have been touched by the borrowers' concentration problem. Serving prevalently small businesses and households, these banks are largely excluded from the market of the big firms. In the case of an asymmetric impact of the crisis on big and small firms, as it has most probably been the case in Italy, cooperative banks' lending activity might have been strongly influenced by the deteriorated balance sheet positions of their target clients, that is small firms. At the same time, they could have been in the impossibility to access the more stable market of the large firms because of the excessively high size of the demanded loans. Overall, this may explain the significance of the log(A) variable for cooperative banks. An alternative explanation to the borrowers' concentration problem to clarify the significance of the log(A) variable may be drawn from a closer analysis of the property structure of cooperative banks in Italy and its implication in terms of target clientele. Members of cooperative banks are prevalently small economic agents operating in a particular area. This has an incidence on the bank size. Furthermore, mutuality and focus in serving members often create a captive market formed prevalently by small businesses and households. Hence, in a period in which small businesses suffer the most, it might be that the log(A) variable has captured the effects of the property structure and the focus towards members more than the borrower's concentration problem. This interpretation is alternative to the one present in the relevant literature. Secondly, the lending activity of cooperative banks may have been influenced by low diversification. In fact, the regression coefficients of *FEE/OI* are significant from 2011 to 2013. In this light, the higher relevance of the lending business might have exposed cooperative banks more than commercial banks to a shock in lending demand. A low *FEE/OI* ratio might again be explained by the presence of a base of clients largely formed by small economic agents, demanding principally traditional banking services.

Finally, these results for the Italian market, which are backed by the observation of the period 2009–2013, seem to support the arguments in favour of a structural reorganisation of the cooperative banking segment in Italy aiming to introduce instruments able, inter alia, to face capital shortfalls at a systemic level. In this respect, two separate reforms were launched in Italy in the period 2015–2016. They are discussed in Chap. 5.

3.4 Limits to the Countercyclical Role of Cooperative Banks

This chapter sheds some light on the lending behaviour of cooperative banks during and after the Great Crisis. In this respect, it aimed at verifying whether the traditional cooperative banks countercyclical role, observed in many studies before the Great Crisis, can be confirmed or has to be questioned. To do that, two specific analyses have been performed. The first investigated the role of the different business models in the *bank lending channel* in two main economic areas within the larger euro area. The second focused on the analysis of the *capital crunch* phenomenon in one leading market for cooperative banks, that is Italy.

On the basis of these analyses, some concluding remarks can be stated. On the one hand, the countercyclical role of cooperative banks can be confirmed for the whole north-east half of the euro area. In fact, the empirical evidence showed that cooperative banks were able to provide credit to business and households to a significantly greater extent than other kinds of banks during and after the crisis period. On the other hand, no evidence of a significant countercyclical role played by cooperative banks emerged as concerns the south-west half of the continent, hit more severely by the crisis. In this respect, the analysis performed demonstrated that in this area the lending behaviour of cooperative banks has mainly converged with that one of other types of banks. The prolonged economic downturn has probably put under pressure the banks' operative margins (in particular trough asset impairments) and pushed cooperative banks to tighten their credit standards as a necessary lever of adjustment. Such an outcome is also supported, for the Italian market, by the evidence that a *capital crunch* has progressively affected the cooperative banking segment since the beginning of the Great Crisis.

Overall, the discussions provided in this chapter highlight once more the inherent attitude of cooperative banks to be financial actors strongly anchored to the real economy at a local level. Nevertheless, in the areas of the continent where the crisis hit more severely and the balance sheet positions of borrowers were put under significant pressure, such an anchoring to the real economy has probably contributed to produce unsustainable credit routines in terms of risk-return.

Finally, the results of the analyses performed in this chapter seem coherent with the idea that profitability should be a central point of attention for cooperative banks in the post-crisis scenario. As a matter of fact, capital adequacy, lending capacity and countercyclical attitude are nested and conditioned to the generation of an adequate level of profits (and irrespectively to any consideration on their retention or possible distribution). For cooperative banks, the capacity in the mid-term to assure satisfactory economic performances appears to be a crucial condition to sustain their unique business model and keep providing a distinctive value to members and the society.

References

Arellano, M., & Bond, S. (1991). Some Test of Specification for Panel Data: Monte Carlo Evidence and an Application to Employment Equations. *Review of Economic Studies, 58*, 277–297.

Ashcraft, A. B. (2006). New Evidence on the Lending Channel. *Journal of Money, Credit and Banking, 38*(3), 751–776.

Berger, A. N., & Udell, G. (1994). Did Risk-Based Capital Allocate Bank Credit and Cause a 'Credit Crunch' in the United States? *Journal of Money, Credit and Banking, 26*, 585–628.

Bernanke, B., & Gertler, M. (1995). Inside the Black Box: The Credit Channel of Monetary Policy Transmission. *The Journal of Economic Perspectives, 9*(4), 27–48.

Bernanke, B., & Lown, C. S. (1991). The Credit Crunch. *Brookings Papers on Economic Activity*, (2), 205–247.

Bolton, P., Freixas, X., Gambacorta, L., & Mistrulli, P. E. (2013). *Relationship and Transaction Lending in a Crisis.* BIS Working Papers, No. 417.

De Santis, A., & Surico, P. (2013). Bank Lending and Monetary Transmission in the Euro Area. *Economic Policy, 28*(75), 423–457.

Di Colli, S., & Girardi, A. (2012). *Restrizione Creditizia durante la Crisi del 2008–2009 e il Ruolo Anticiclico delle Banche di Credito Cooperativo.* Quaderni di Ricerca del Credito Cooperativo, No. 3.

European Commission. (2012). *Small Business Act for Europe, Fact Sheet 2012 – Italy.*

Ferri, G., Kalmi, P., & Kerola, E. (2014). Does Bank Ownership Affect Lending Behavior? Evidence from the Euro Area. *Journal of Banking and Finance, 48*, 194–209.

Hancock, D., Laing, A. J., & Wilcox, J. A. (1995). Bank Capital Shocks: Dynamic Effects on Securities, Loans, and Capital. *Journal of Banking & Finance, 19*(3), 661–677.

International Monetary Fund. (2013, September). *Financial System Stability Assessment – Italy.*

Kashyap, A. N., & Stein, J. C. (1995). The Impact of the Monetary Policy on Bank Balance Sheets. *Carnegie-Rochester Conference Series on Public Policy, 42*, 151–195.

Kashyap, A. N., & Stein, J. C. (2000). What Do a Million Observations on Banks Say About the Transmission of Monetary Policy? *American Economic Review, 90*(3), 407–428.

Migliorelli, M. (2015). Are Italian Cooperative Banks Suffering from Capital Fever? Evidence Over the Lending Crisis. *European Journal of Economics, Finance and Administrative Sciences, 71*, 5–25.

Migliorelli, M., & Brunelli, S. (2016). The Transmission of the Monetary Policy in the Euro Area: The Role of the Banks' Business Model. *Annals of Public and Cooperative Economics, 88*(3), 303–322.

Montgomery, H. (2005). The Effect of the Basel Accord on Bank Portfolios in Japan. *Journal of the Japanese and International Economies, 19*(1), 24–36.

Nickell, S. (1981). Biases in Dynamic Models with Fixed Effects. *Econometrica, 49*(6), 1417–1426.

Peek, J., & Rosengren, E. S. (1995a). The Capital Crunch: Neither a Borrower Nor a Lender Be. *Journal of Money, Credit and Banking, 27*(3), 625–638.

Peek, J., & Rosengren, E. S. (1995b). Bank Regulation and Credit Crunch. *Journal of Banking & Finance, 19*, 679–692.

Stein, J. C. (1998). An Adverse-Selection Model of Bank Asset and Liability Management with Implications for the Transmission of Monetary Policy. *The RAND Journal of Economics, 29*(3), 466.

Watanabe, W. (2007). Prudential Regulation and the Credit Crunch: Evidence from Japan. *Journal of Money, Credit and Banking, 39*(2–3), 639–665.

Zago, A., & Dogili, P. (2014). *Financial Crisis, Business Model and Technical Efficiency of Italian Banche di Credito Cooperativo.* Quaderni di Ricerca del Credito Cooperativo, No. 4.

CHAPTER 4

Cooperative Banks and Banking Regulation in the EU: Key Elements

Marco Migliorelli

4.1 Introduction

The regulatory regime for cooperative banks is not homogeneous in Europe. In each country, national-level legislation defines the cooperative models, including in the financial sector. As a matter of fact, heterogeneity in regulations decisively contributes to a diversified landscape among European countries for financial cooperatives in general and cooperative banks in particular (e.g. Karafolas 2016).

In addition, a number of European-level acts (directives, regulations and related implementing rules) have gradually entered into force, in particular from 2008, with the aim to face the structural imbalances emerged in the financial markets during the Great Crisis. In this respect, the European regulators aimed to foster a stricter supervision of the risks related to banking operations, to strengthen the financial solidity of the market players, to reinforce consumer protection and to foster a *level playing field*. In banking, this body of laws and rules lays today in the framework of the so-called Banking Union and is mainly built around the

M. Migliorelli (✉)
IAE Université Paris 1 Panthéon-Sorbonne (Sorbonne Business School),
Paris, France

M. Migliorelli (ed.), *New Cooperative Banking in Europe*,
https://doi.org/10.1007/978-3-319-93578-2_4

Capital Requirements Directive[1] and Capital Requirements Regulation[2] (CRD IV-CRR package), the Bank Recovery and Resolution Directive[3] (BRRD) and the Deposit Guarantee Schemes Directive[4] (DGSD). In addition, other regulations not specifically focussing on banking have had indeed a significant impact on the sector, as in the case of the Market in Financial Instruments Directives[5] and Market in Financial Instruments Regulation[6] (MiFID I, MiFID II and MiFIR) or the revised Payment Services Directive[7] (PSD II).

Regulation is today a major challenge for cooperative banks in Europe. On the one hand, it represents an increasing administrative burden, which implies an additional effort in terms of compliance as concerns operational processes and organisational structures. On the other hand, and more importantly, regulation often contributes to engendering a reflection on crucial aspects of the cooperative banking business model and pushes for an evolution. In some cases, regulation has also forced cooperative banks to adopt

[1] Directive 2013/36/EU of the European Parliament and of the Council of 26 June 2013 on access to the activity of credit institutions and the prudential supervision of credit institutions and investment firms, amending Directive 2002/87/EC and repealing Directives 2006/48/EC and 2006/49/EC.

[2] Regulation (EU) No 575/2013 of the European Parliament and of the Council of 26 June 2013 on prudential requirements for credit institutions and investment firms and amending Regulation (EU) No 648/2012.

[3] Directive 2014/59/EU of the European Parliament and of the Council of 15 May 2014 establishing a framework for the recovery and resolution of credit institutions and investment firms and amending Council Directive 82/891/EEC, and Directives 2001/24/EC, 2002/47/EC, 2004/25/EC, 2005/56/EC, 2007/36/EC, 2011/35/EU, 2012/30/EU and 2013/36/EU, and Regulations (EU) No 1093/2010 and (EU) No 648/2012, of the European Parliament and of the Council.

[4] Directive 2014/49/EU of the European Parliament and of the Council of 16 April 2014 on deposit guarantee schemes.

[5] Directive 2004/39/EC of the European Parliament and of the Council of 21 April 2004 on markets in financial instruments amending Council Directives 85/611/EEC and 93/6/EEC and Directive 2000/12/EC of the European Parliament and of the Council and repealing Council Directive 93/22/EEC and Directive 2014/65/EU of the European Parliament and of the Council of 15 May 2014 on markets in financial instruments and amending Directive 2002/92/EC and Directive 2011/61/EU.

[6] Regulation No 600/2014 of the European Parliament and of the Council of 15 May 2014 on markets in financial instruments and amending Regulation (EU) No 648/2012.

[7] Directive 2015/2366 of the European Parliament and of the Council of 25 November 2015 on payment services in the internal market, amending Directives 2002/65/EC, 2009/110/EC and 2013/36/EU and Regulation (EU) No 1093/2010, and repealing Directive 2007/64/EC.

completely new organisational models (e.g. in the case of the reforms of the cooperative banking sector in Italy in the period 2015–2016 concerning the major *Banche Popolari* and the *Banche di Credito Cooperativo*). Nonetheless, regulation is not rarely a controversial topic among cooperative banks. Country-level legislation, differences in the governance structures and size as well as different economic scenarios over Europe, may determine mixed impacts (and appreciations) of the same legislative initiative.

In an introductory reading, a thorough analysis of all the possible impacts of regulation on cooperative banks is not possible. Neither would it be a conclusive one when considering that the incidence of regulation is often uneven among cooperative banks. In this respect, the objective of this chapter is twofold. First, it aims to provide a general overview of the cooperative singularity in the framework of the European banking regulation. This is done by discussing the principle of proportionality and by analysing some of the most important adaptations needed to EU banking regulation in order to take into account the inherent characteristics of cooperative banking. Second, it presents an introduction of some of the key elements of the existing regulatory body that have or are likely to have in the near future a significant impact on cooperative banks. Many of these elements are further discussed subject-wise in the reminder of the book.

4.2 The Cooperative Banking Singularity in the EU Regulation

European legislation specifically defines cooperatives. The Regulation on the Statute for a European Cooperative Society (SCE)[8] specifies that "cooperatives are primarily groups of persons or legal entities with particular operating principles that are different from those of other economic agents. These include the principles of democratic structure and control and the distribution of the net profit for the financial year on an equitable basis".[9] The same Regulation also states that "these particular principles include notably the principle of the primacy of the individual which is reflected in the specific rules on membership [...] where the 'one man, one vote' rule is laid down and the right to vote is vested in the individual".[10]

[8] Council Regulation (EC) No 1435/2003 of 22 July 2003 on the Statute for a European Cooperative Society (SCE).

[9] Recital (7).

[10] Recital (8).

Despite that, in banking EU regulation has been traditionally designed on the model of joint-stock companies and cooperative specificities had to be integrated in a more general framework that the one stemming from the typical cooperative banking model. In this respect, two complementary legislative approaches have been adopted to incorporate the cooperative singularity. On the one hand, the use when appropriate of the principle of proportionality. On the other hand, the inclusion of detailed provisions taking into account some of the inherent characteristics of cooperative banks, in particular in relation to the unique rights carried by member shares and the specific organisational structure of cooperative banking groups and networks.

The principle of proportionality is laid down in the Treaty on European Union (Art. 5). The criteria for applying it are set out in the Protocol (No 2) on the application of the principles of subsidiarity and proportionality annexed to the Treaties. Like the principle of subsidiarity, the principle of proportionality regulates the exercise of powers by the EU and it seeks to set actions taken by EU institutions within specified bounds. Under this rule, the action of the EU must be limited to what is necessary to achieve the objectives of the Treaties. In other words, the content and form of the action must be in keeping with the aim pursued.

In banking regulation, the principle of proportionality is widely adopted and it is often included as a guideline for implementing legislation. As an example on how it can be relevant for cooperative banks, the Capital Requirements Regulation (CRR) specifically requires that the Commission and European Banking Authority (EBA), while preparing regulatory technical standards in the areas of mutuals, cooperative societies, savings institutions or similar institutions, should ensure that those standards and requirements can be applied by all institutions concerned in a manner that is proportionate to the nature, scale and complexity of these institutions and their activities.[11] Proportionality is extremely important for small cooperative banks. In fact, for these entities the cost of compliance can be relatively high and usually represents a relevant (and increasing) administrative burden. This is the case in particular for some reporting and disclosure requirements, which would need the deployment of substantial resources (in terms of quantity and skills) and would not add significantly to the supervisory perspective.

As far as it concerns the features of cooperative banks that typically require specific regulatory adaptations, member shares represent a first

[11] Recital (128).

crucial element. These financial instruments carry, in principle, a different set of rights compared to the shares of joint-stock companies. In this respect, two main features of member shares are particularly relevant. First, they are in many cases redeemable to the cooperative. Second, redemption is usually at face value, which implies no participation of members in net assets. Both these features are typically encompassed in national-level legislation. In the current regulatory framework, member shares matter especially in relation to prudential requirements. In this regard, the Basel III defined the criteria to identify common shares for regulatory capital purposes (i.e. the equity instruments with the best quality). Among other conditions, common shares have to represent a principal which is perpetual and never repaid outside of liquidation (setting aside discretionary repurchases or other means of effectively reducing capital in a discretionary manner that is allowable under relevant law) and they have to be instruments entitled to a claim on the residual assets proportionally with their shares of issued capital after all senior claims have been repaid in liquidation (BCBS 2011). These criteria, which apply in principle to all types of banks, cannot be met *as such* by cooperative banks. In this respect, the Basel III regulation left to responsible jurisdictions (as the EU) the specification of the conditions under which member shares can be considered equivalent to common shares for regulatory capital purposes.[12] To this extent, EU regulation identified specific implementing provisions. They are contained in two different legal instruments: the CRR, which previews a number of conditions for common equity recognition for capital instruments of mutuals, cooperative societies, savings institutions or similar entities, especially with regard to permanence of the instrument (including the right to refuse redemption) and loss absorption (Art. 27 and Art. 29), and the delegated regulation of the CRR,[13] which contains further details regarding limitations for the redemption of cooperative shares (Art. 4, Art. 10 and Art. 11).

[12] Basel III provisions only state that implementing regulation should require that capital instruments of non-joint-stock companies are fully equivalent to common shares in terms of their capital quality as regards loss absorption and do not possess features which could cause the condition of the bank to be weakened as a going concern during periods of market stress (BCBS 2011).

[13] Commission Delegated Regulation (EU) 2015/61 of 10 October 2014 to supplement Regulation (EU) No 575/2013 of the European Parliament and the Council with regard to liquidity coverage requirement for Credit Institutions.

Another key feature of cooperative banks that typically requires appropriate regulatory provisions is the particular structure characterising many cooperative banking groups and networks. In regulatory terms, the relevance of these organisational structures is linked to the implementation of several requirements. As an example concerning liquidity, many cooperative groups and networks exist with local banks cooperating and creating a common central institution with no specific role in terms of direct business, but responsible, inter alia, to ensure liquidity to all the concerned entities. The Liquidity Coverage Ratio (LCR) as previewed in the Basel III regulation would create structural difficulty to cooperative groups and networks as local banks usually deposit their excess liquidity at the central institution. Without specific provisions, liquidity transferred to the central institution would have to be treated as a (100 per cent) cash outflow. In addition, the division of tasks between local entities and central institution does not usually foresee the central institution to do any retail business, and therefore it would not take deposits typically characterised by low cash outflows. For these reasons, CRR and delegated regulation of CRR have reflected the possible division of tasks within the groups and networks and allow the treatment of certain deposits in central institutions as stable deposits or liquid assets, if certain conditions are met (e.g. Art. 416(1)(f) CRR, Art. 16 and Art. 27 (1)(b) delegated regulation of CRR).

Despite the use of the principle of proportionality and the inclusion in the key regulations of provisions dealing with the main specificities of cooperative banks, for some observers such an approach conveys the risk to underestimate the potential impact of regulation on the cooperative banking business model and harms diversity in banking (e.g. Ory et al. 2012; Richez-Battesti and Leseul 2016). For these observers, the treatment of cooperative banks (and other banks not built on model of joint-stock companies) as "an exception to the rule" could in the longer term determine a regulatory-driven convergence of the different business models used in banking operations. This might even result in an undesirable macroeconomic outcome as the traditional capacity of relationship lending institutions to supply credit to small companies even in periods of economic downturn observed in many studies (e.g. Bolton et al. 2013; Ferri et al. 2014; Migliorelli and Brunelli 2016) may be weakened.

4.3 Relevant Aspects of Regulation for Cooperative Banks

4.3.1 Capital Requirements

Since the beginning of the Great Crisis, the strengthening of the capital requirements for banks has been considered by policy makers as one of the key instruments in order to assure the stability of the financial sector and reduce systemic risks. In this respect, the relevant European legislation is derived from the Basel III framework and it is mainly contained in the CRD IV-CRR package.

In line with a consolidated approach, the Basel III framework identifies the minimum capital consistencies with respect to the bank's risk-weighted asset. In particular, banks and investment firms need to have a total amount of capital equal to at least 8 per cent of their risk-weighted assets. Nonetheless, the quality of the capital components matters and a number of capital categories are identified in this regard. To this extent, Tier 1 capital is considered to be *going concern* capital and should allow an institution to continue its activities and to prevent insolvency. The purest form of Tier 1 capital is the Common Equity Tier 1 capital (which includes common shares and member shares when meeting the same identification criteria). Tier 2 capital is considered *gone concern* capital and should help ensuring that depositors and senior creditors can be repaid if the institution fails. This category of capital includes hybrid capital and subordinated debt. In addition to Tier 1 and Tier 2 capital requirements, the Basel III framework establishes five different capital buffers: the capital conservation buffer, the counter-cyclical buffer, the systemic risk buffer, the global systemic institutions buffer and the other systemic institutions buffer (see Table 4.1).[14] On top, supervisors may add extra capital to cover for other risks following a supervisory review.

Even without analysing in detail how the CRD IV-CRR is technically implemented, two key aspects can be highlighted as concerns cooperative banks. The first regards the implications in terms of capital absorption of the typical profile of the cooperative banks' clientele. As cooperative banks focus their activity principally toward small and medium enterprises (which are on average riskier than large companies), a risk-weighted assets mechanism to calculate minimum capital requirements may result for cooperative

[14] A detailed categorisation of the different categories of capital is included in the CRR.

Table 4.1 Basel III/CRD IV-CRR basic capital requirements

Requirement	*Ratio (of risk-weighted assets)*
Minimum Common Equity Tier 1 capital	4.5%
Minimum Tier 1 capital (Common Equity Tier 1 plus Additional Tier 1)	6.0%
Minimum Tier 2 capital	2.0%
Minimum total capital	*8.0%*
Capital Conservation Buffer	2.5%
Minimum Common Equity Tier 1 capital plus Capital Conservation Buffer	*7.0%*
Minimum total capital plus Capital Conservation Buffer	*10.5%*

Notes: Adapted from BCBS (2011). The values indicated are mandatory from the end of the phase-in period (1st January 2019)

banks in a structural need to detain higher capital levels (than conventional banks) in order to sustain their orientation in terms of social responsibility and adherence to their values.[15] This need may contribute to explain the observed higher capitalisation levels of cooperative banks with respect in particular to commercial banks. The second main implication for cooperative banks is linked to the modalities to cope with deviations from the minimum regulatory targets. In this respect, in the light of the Basel III provisions, banks can improve their capital ratios in two ways. First, they can increase capital by issuing new shares or not paying dividends to their shareholders to retain profits. Second, they can reduce the risk-weighted assets, by cutting back on lending, selling loan portfolios or making less risky loans and investments. As many cooperative banks (in particular small ones) may find difficult to quickly increase their capitalisation level, as no market capital rising operations are possible and hence a direct contribution from the members would be needed, a risk of a pressure on reducing assets (including loans) can eventually materialise. For some observers, this may give rise to a phenomenon where regulatory principles run broadly counter to the natural orientation of cooperative banks (e.g. Albert and Lamarque 2016).

[15] The relevance of such a phenomenon is even higher considering that cooperative banks use less than commercial banks the Internal ratings-based (IRB) approach previewed in the CRD IV-CRR and that usually allows, with respect to the standardised approach and for the same portfolio of assets, a non-negligible reduction in the capital requirements.

4.3.2 *Governance Requirements*

The issues of governance and the functioning of the management and oversight bodies have taken an important place in the new banking regulatory framework. The provisions included in the CRD IV to this goal have been recently complemented with the guidelines on internal governance issued by EBA in July 2017 and that are applicable starting from 2018 (EBA 2017). This extensive body of regulatory provisions refer to:

- governance of risks, including the risk management roles played by business units, risk management teams, and internal audit and control functions (the three *lines of defence*);
- role of the boards in overseeing the implementation of effective risk management systems (*know your structure*);
- boards' composition (including diversity and independency characteristics) and the personal requisites of the boards' member, with particular emphasis on competence requirements and their evaluation;
- disclosure and reporting requirements, as concerns in particular corporate governance processes and structures;
- compensation systems for administrators;
- more in general, the necessity to foster a sound risk culture to support an effective management of risks.

Some of the requirements included in the relevant regulation can raise specific issues for cooperative banks. This is in particular the case of the evaluation of the competencies of managers and the interpretation of the requisite of independency. In this respect, following the typical cooperative model, many cooperative banks have governance systems that allow clients (including members and hence owners) to be elected to governing bodies. As a matter of fact, in many cases financial expertise is a secondary requisite in the election process with respect to territorial representativeness or the capacity of rising awareness about the interests of the members. As a consequence, for some cooperative banks find candidates who have the required skills to conform to the new principles for competency may be difficult. For these cooperative banks, the governance requirements may hence bring to the need to either review the composition of their governing bodies or to reflect on the possibility to introduce additional mechanisms able to deal with both the specificity of the cooperative model and the necessity to constitute a board that brings together all the skills needed to be considered as collectively efficient.

Another major issue for cooperative banks in terms of governance is represented by the different layers of responsibilities in the management of the risks in case of cooperative banking groups. In this respect, several different models of governance have been observed in the cooperative banking sector (Albert and Lamarque 2016). As regulation requires to further strengthen the role of the governance system in the effective management of risks, a significant impact for cooperative banking groups can be foreseen when it comes to the assessment of the processes and structures in place to this scope. In particular, these processes and structures should guarantee that relevant information is collected and directed to the relevant decision makers within the group, by also assuring adequate reporting at the different levels of the organisation (including top management). As a consequence, the governance requirements will probably play an increasingly important role in the definition and in the implementation of the bank's strategy, including in particular the key aspects of the level of autonomy of the entities of the group and their *risk-appetite*.

4.3.3 The Institutional Protection Schemes

An Institutional Protection Scheme (IPS) is defined in the CRR (Art. 113(7)) as a contractual or statutory liability arrangement which protects its member institutions and in particular ensures that they have the liquidity and solvency needed to avoid bankruptcy where necessary. As a matter of fact, the CRR recognises the status of some networks of cooperative banks in Europe, in which independent entities agree to mutually act as guarantors in case of distress of one or more participants to the network. The difference between IPSs and groups (as defined in the Art. 10 CRR) lays in particular in the degree of independence of the participating banks, which is higher in IPSs (Choulet 2016). In fact, unlike institutions in a consolidated banking group, the members of IPSs are not under the control of a single legal entity, and no specific rules exist governing their ownership links. Currently, IPSs are recognised for regulatory purposes in Austria, Germany and Spain (see Table 4.2). In Italy, discussions on the possibility to establish a new IPS were held before the reform of the *Banche di Credito Cooperativo* in 2016 and then abandoned.[16] The relevance of

[16] The reform of the *Banche di Credito Cooperativo* in Italy previews, inter alia, the possibility for cooperative banks to combine into a single structure with a head holding company, controlled by the banks and tasked with intervening in the event that a governance failure takes place or a bank of the network experiences difficulties. To a large extent, the new structure can be seen as a "reinforced IPS".

Table 4.2 Examples of IPSs in cooperative banking

Austria	*Network of Raiffeisen banks:* • RZB Group: 474 local Raiffeisen banks, 8 regional Raiffeisen banks, 1 parent company (RZB AG), various banks with special functions. Consolidated total assets of EUR 138.4 bn. *Network of Volksbanken:* • Osterreichische Volksbanken-Aktiengesellschaft (VBAG) steered by the OGV: 26 regional Volksbanken, 1 parent company (VBW), various banks with special functions. Consolidated total assets of EUR 27.8 bn.
Germany	*Network of credit cooperatives:* • Genossenschaftliche FinanzGruppe Volksbanken Raiffeisenbanken steered by the BVR: 1.021 local Volksbanken and Raiffeisen banks, 1 central institution (DZ Bank and WGZ Bank), various banks with special functions. Consolidated total assets of EUR 1.163 bn.
Spain	*Networks of savings banks and credit cooperatives:* • Grupo Cooperativo Cajamar: 19 Cajas, 1 parent company (Banco de Crédito Social Cooperativo S.A.). Consolidated total assets of EUR 40.5 bn. • Grupo Cooperativo Solventia: 6 Cajas, 1 parent company (Caja Rural de Almendralejo, SCC). Consolidated total assets of EUR 1.6 bn.

Notes: Adapted from Choulet (2016). Data at the end of 2015. DZ Bank merged with WGZ Bank (previously acting as another parent company) in August 2016

IPSs is also significant in absolute terms, given that about 50 per cent of credit institutions in the euro area are members of an IPS, representing around 10 per cent of the total assets of the euro area banking system (ECB 2016).

The recognition of an IPS, granted by the European Central Bank (ECB), can allow competent authorities, in accordance with the conditions laid down in the CRR, to waive selected prudential requirements or grant certain derogations for IPS member institutions. In particular, the ECB may grant permission to apply a 0 per cent risk weight to exposures to other counterparties which are members of the same IPS (with the significant exception of exposures giving rise to Common Equity Tier 1, Additional Tier 1 and Tier 2 capital items), and the exposures in question may be exempt from the application of the limits on large exposures (Art. 395(1) CRR). Furthermore, the recognition of an IPS is one of the preconditions for granting additional waivers to its members, such as the exemption from the deduction of holdings in own funds (Art. 49(3) CRR), the granting of a liquidity waiver (Art. 8(4) CRR) and the application of lower outflow and higher inflow percentages for LCR calculation (Art. 422(3)(b), 422(8) and Art. 425(4) CRR). The criteria evaluated by the ECB to recognise an IPS include the absence of obstacles to the transfer of funds between units, the rapidity of transfers, the absence of serious difficulties in management matters, the absence of serious problems in corporate governance in connection with members and the decision-making process relative to the support measures that would allow a solution to be found in due course.

Despite the possible advantages, the possibility to participate in a network with a recognised IPS should not be seen for cooperative banks as an opportunity of regulatory arbitrage. On the contrary, the observed existing networks mostly derive their *raison d'être* from a sharing of culture and values between participants. In this respect, networks reflect the mutualistic principle characterising the cooperative model. In operational terms, the establishment of an IPS is often a crucial means of risk management as well as of commercial effectiveness (this latter case in particular when participants share the same brand and products).

4.3.4 *The Opening of the Market of Payment Services to Third Party Providers*

The Payment Services Directive (PSD II), adopted in 2015 and updating and complementing the first directive on payment services[17] (PSD I) issued in 2007, had as main objectives to contribute to further integrate the European payments market, to enhance security for customers and to foster competition in a sector typically featured by high barriers to the entry. The PSD II is operational from January 2018,[18] even though some important requirements will be phased in during a transition period that will last up to 2021.[19]

[17] Directive 2007/64/EC of the European Parliament and of the Council of 13 November 2007 on payment services in the internal market amending Directives 97/7/EC, 2002/65/EC, 2005/60/EC and 2006/48/EC and repealing Directive 97/5/EC.

[18] The deadline for the transposition of the Directive in the EU Member States was set to 13 January 2018.

[19] The adoption by the Council and the European Parliament of the regulatory technical standards (RTS) developed by the European Banking Authority and validated by the European Commission is expected by September 2019. From that date of the adoption, banks will have 18 months to implement the required changes. These include in particular the so-called Strong Customer Authentication (SCA), which in practice will allow third parties to access the customer's payment accounts information.

Among other novelties, the PSD II recognises and regulates new players (FinTech companies) recently emerged in the payment sector and offering innovative internet services spanning from the streamline of the online payment processes to the consolidation of financial information. The Directive identifies these players as Third Party Providers (TPPs) and divides them in two categories: the Payment Initiation Services Providers (PISPs) and the Account Information Services Providers (AISPs). On the one side, the PISPs typically offer services that help consumers to make online payments by means of a link between the payer and the merchant via the payer's online banking module.[20] Thanks to the PIPSs, the transaction can be immediately executed, hence allowing the dispatch of goods or the access to the services purchased online. As the consumer only needs to possess an online payment account to use these services, PISPs can represent an alternative to credit cards and debit cards. On the other side, AISPs typically provide information services that allow customers to have a global view on their financial situation by consolidating in a single platform the information otherwise held in different bank accounts. In addition, AISPs can support customers in analysis-based activities such as budgeting, financial planning and financial data comparison. Both for PISPs and AISPs, the access to the payment account maintained by the customer in a credit institution is essential. For this reason, the PSD II provides specifically that Member States have to ensure that credit institutions do not block or hinder the access to payment accounts and that TTPs have access to credit institutions' payment accounts services in an objective, non-discriminatory and proportionate manner (nonetheless, a formal authorisation from the client is needed).

Even though a complete analysis of the impact of the PSD II on the banking sector is not possible yet, relevant implications can be foreseen for banking institutions. In particular, this is the case for those institutions, such as cooperative banks, which base their business model on the offer of traditional banking services and on a consolidated relationship with the client. In this respect, a first direct impact may be linked to the expected reduction of the stream of revenues from payment services as a consequence of increased competition and the decrease in cost (and pricing) at a single transaction level. Furthermore, and more importantly, the entrance of new intermediaries in the payments sector may represent a factor potentially able to permanently alter the established bank-client relationship.

[20] Examples of these providers are Sofort, Ideal and Trustly.

This may be the consequence of two elements combined. On the one hand, the TPPs platforms will likely become a stable access point for customers in the management of their financials, disintermediating the client from the bank. On the other hand, TPPs will collect a significant amount of information on banks' clients as concerns financial availabilities and spending patterns and will be able to offer an alternative and competitive value proposition. This value proposition will be probably backed by enhanced internet-based customer experience and data-driven offering. As a result, traditional banks may risk experiencing a dilution in the client's relation, following a (technology-driven) tendency that can be observed also in other industries.[21] As far as it concerns cooperative banks in particular, such a possible evolution could be particularly disruptive and should be analysed in the general framework of the impact of digitalisation on their business model. In this respect, the possible implications may be not only linked to the necessary developments of the components of the offering (digital and physical). A reflection on the evolution of the concept of *proximity* may indeed be necessary.

References

Albert, S., & Lamarque, E. (2016). *The Impact of Financial Regulation on Policy and Risk Management in Financial Cooperatives.* Working Paper.

Basel Committee on Banking Supervision (BCBS). (2011). *Basel III: A Global Regulatory Framework for More Resilient Banks and Banking Systems.*

Bolton, P., Freixas, X., Gambacorta, L., & Mistrulli, P. E. (2013). *Relationship and Transaction Lending in a Crisis.* BIS Working Papers, No. 417.

Choulet, C. (2016). Institutional Protection Systems: Are They Banking Groups? *BNP Economic Research.*

European Banking Authority (EBA). (2017, September). *Guidelines on Internal Governance Under Directive 2013/36/EU.*

European Central Bank (ECB). (2016, July). *Guide on the Approach for the Recognition of Institutional Protection Schemes (IPS) for Prudential Purposes.*

Ferri, G., Kalmi, P., & Kerola, E. (2014). Does Bank Ownership Affect Lending Behavior? Evidence from the Euro Area. *Journal of Banking and Finance, 48*, 194–209.

[21] Note here the cases of Airbnb (leader in the short-term real estate renting sector without owning any real estate), Netflix (leader in the home entertainment sector producing only a small share of the contents proposed to its clients) or Uber (leader in the urban transportation sector without owning any car).

Karafolas, S. (2016). *Credit Cooperative Institutions in European Countries*. Berlin: Springer.

Migliorelli, M., & Brunelli, S. (2016). The Transmission of the Monetary Policy in the Euro Area: The Role of the Banks' Business Model. *Annals of Public and Cooperative Economics, 88*(3), 303–322.

Ory, J.-N., De Serres, A., & Jaegger, M. (2012). Comment Résister à l'Effet de Normalisation des Banques Coopératives? *La Revue des Sciences de Gestion, 258*, 69–82.

Richez-Battesti, N., & Leseul, G. (2016). Cooperative Banks in France: Emergence, Mutations and Issues. In S. Karofolas (Ed.), *Credit Cooperative Institutions in European Countries*. Berlin: Springer.

CHAPTER 5

National Initiatives to Drive the Evolution of the Cooperative Banking Sector

Hans Groeneveld, Roberto Di Salvo, Juan Sergio Lopez, and Francesco Di Leo

5.1 Introduction

Although cooperative banks have in general proved to be stable and the least pro-cyclical and risky banks during and after the turmoil started in 2008 in Europe (e.g. Ferri et al. 2014; Henselmann et al. 2016), experi-

H. Groeneveld (✉)
Tilburg University, Tilburg, The Netherlands

Rabobank, Utrecht, The Netherlands
e-mail: hans.groeneveld@rabobank.nl

R. Di Salvo
Federcasse, Rome, Italy

Fondo di Garanzia dei Depositanti del Credito Cooperativo, Rome, Italy

J. S. Lopez
Federcasse, Rome, Italy

F. Di Leo
University of Rome Tor Vergata, Rome, Italy

M. Migliorelli (ed.), *New Cooperative Banking in Europe*,
https://doi.org/10.1007/978-3-319-93578-2_5

ence has been highly heterogeneous in different European countries (Bülbül et al. 2013; Migliorelli and Brunelli 2016). This has depended on a wide range of factors, such as duration of the crisis in the country of activity, governance structure, size, internal competition, internal legislation and even influence of supervision (e.g. Santella 2001; Groeneveld and de Vries 2009; Fiordelisi and Mare 2014; Fiordelisi et al. 2015). Cooperatives in Europe have been shown mostly to develop a culture based on the long term, with cautious risk-taking (Groeneveld and de Vries 2009) because they did not have to maximise profits by, for example, buying exotic financial instruments (Arnold 2014) or stressing their capital adequacy with high levels of lending. Nevertheless, in many cases cooperative banks did not remain shielded from the effects of the crisis and a number of reorganisations in the cooperative sector were undertaken over Europe. This chapter summarises the most relevant ones.

5.2 The Reform of the Cooperative Banking Sector in the Netherlands[1]

5.2.1 Overview

This paragraph portrays the development of the cooperative Rabobank since 2008. This period encompasses turbulent years for all Dutch banks, including Rabobank, but at different moments in time. In the first years of the crisis, Rabobank objectively outperformed other domestic banks in many regards. Rabobank not only excelled from a financial perspective but was also demonstrably perceived by the general public as a beacon of stability amidst great turmoil in Dutch banking (Vogelaar 2012). Up to 2012, annual reports of Rabobank did not convey any need to modify the strategy or governance structure in response to the structural transformation in banking and profound regulatory and economic changes taking place. The urge to change suddenly dawned in 2012–2013 as a result of various events. Rabobank then embarked on restructuring programmes, transformed the governance and tightened up the domestic and international strategy.

[1] This paragraph is authored by Hans Groeneveld, professor of financial services cooperatives at Tilburg University and director of international cooperative affairs at Rabobank. The views in this paragraph are personal and do not necessarily reflect those of Rabobank.

The remainder of this paragraph is structured as follows. Section 5.2.2 briefly discusses changes in the operating environment since 2008. This description helps to interpret Rabobank's internal challenges, discussed in Sect. 5.2.3, and strategic choices, highlighted in Sect. 5.2.4. Section 5.2.5 states some concluding remarks.

5.2.2 External Environment

Since it is impossible to elaborate on all elements of the external environment, we have clustered interconnected factors into three main categories. Each group of factors has exerted and will exercise a substantial impact on Rabobank's strategy, organisation and performance since 2008 and in the near future, respectively.

Macroeconomic Environment

Any examination of retail banking in Europe, including the Netherlands, since 2008 has to start with the observation that economic growth was volatile and sluggish and that financial stability was successively imperilled, rescued and restored. Coming from an era of high growth rates, the Dutch economy dived into several recessions after the Great Crisis and resumed growing at a moderate pace after 2012. As a consequence of increasing bankruptcies of firms, the unemployment rate rose from around 3 per cent to more than 7 per cent in 2012. Central government acted as economic shock absorber during this period. After 2012, the number of business failures declined substantially and the unemployment rate returned to roughly 5 per cent in 2016. In 2015–2016, economic recovery gained firm ground in the Netherlands. This was partly caused by ultra-loose monetary policies of central banks around the globe. At the same time, the expansionary monetary stance has culminated in an unprecedented low interest rate environment which already exists for several years and is expected to persist for some more time. The accommodative monetary stance has steadily impeded the earning capacity of retail banks that are particularly dependent on interest revenues (e.g. Rabobank). Anyway, swings in the economic cycle and monetary policies clearly leave their mark on the performance of banks.

Banking Regulation and Supervision

To prevent a recurrence of the financial crisis, banking regulations have gradually been tightened. The Basel III Accord requires banks to significantly increase both the quantity and quality of capital over the coming years.[2] Furthermore, regulators are contemplating to increase the risk weights for different types of assets on banks' balance sheets. If this really happens, the capital requirements will be pushed up even further, specifically for banks like Rabobank with large volumes of outstanding retail loans. This would also have a dampening influence on the Return on Equity (ROE) (Daniëls and Kamalodin 2016).

In the Eurozone, the evolving debt crisis after the financial crisis underlay the establishment of the Banking Union. Its basic goal is to protect the security and solidity of European banking, thereby minimising the risk that taxpayers have to rescue troubled banks in the future again. In this respect, it is relevant to note that the resolution and deposit guarantee funds have to be filled ex ante by all banks. Given the low profitability environment, the building up of both funds could interfere with a timely fulfilment of higher capital requirements advocated by regulators. Another aspect of the resolution pillar is that banks should have sufficient bail-in financial instruments if they would get into financial difficulties. Some banks will have to pursue wide-ranging adaptations on the liability side of their balance sheet to comply with the new resolution conditions. Apart from the regulatory burdens mentioned above, Dutch banks are subject to a banking tax. This levy puts additional pressure on the reservation capacity of Rabobank to bolster its capital buffers.

Banking Sector Shake Up

In the time span 2008–2013, Dutch government had to deal with exceptional circumstances in Dutch banking. Many banks got into trouble, which seriously threatened financial stability (see for a chronological overview Dutch Central Bank 2015). All in all, 60 per cent of the Dutch banking sector needed some form of government support. Like most European cooperative banks (EACB 2010), Rabobank escaped relatively unscathed from this disruptive period. It did face a cumulative loss in toxic investments of EUR 3.3 billion in 2007–2008, but was able to absorb this amount and even reported a record net profit in 2011.

The longer-term consequences of the turbulences for the Dutch banking market structure in terms of competition, efficiency, diversity, capacity and stability are manifold. First, the reputation and image of all Dutch banks and supervisors were severely damaged and are still rather bleak to

[2] The Basel III Accord is implemented in European legislation through the Capital Requirements Regulation (CRR) and Capital Requirements Directive IV (CRD IV).

date. Second, banking market characteristics have fundamentally changed in the wake of all adverse shocks. The supported banks implemented efficiency programmes geared to shedding jobs, branch network rationalisation and virtualisation. Moreover, these banks reviewed their business models, partly as a result of restructuring requirements specified in the aid programmes. These adjustments have led to a stronger focus on traditional banking activities, a downsizing of investment banking and wholesale lending activities and a reduction in international presence. At the same time, a shift from wholesale funding sources to retail funding occurred. Technological developments have also contributed to the structural transformation in Dutch banking. New and niche players (e.g. fintech) are shaking up the banking industry. Finally, new banking regulations have encouraged the emergence of financing alternatives for small- and medium-sized enterprises (SMEs).

5.2.3 *Internal Challenges*

Paradoxically, its strong financial position and high customer confidence amidst and just after the turmoil in Dutch banking can be considered as the main cause for the challenges Rabobank encountered a few years later. In 2008–2011, Rabobank achieved distinctly superior results in terms of risk and performance (see Groeneveld 2016b). This solid track record was interrupted in 2013. In retrospect, Rabobank refrained from taking decisions to bring its governance, organisation and business model in line with the new realities, that is, the new external, regulatory and competitive environment. In the aftermath of the financial and debt crises, Rabobank was not inclined to make the necessary adaptations. By contrast, other Dutch banks underwent fundamental transformations during the years that they were bounded in their market behaviour and activities by the conditions associated with the received state support. When these limitations no longer applied, Rabobank was "suddenly" faced with agile competitors.

The pressure to pursue fundamental modifications gradually built up. Catalysts to change tack abruptly were the Libor affair[3] and customer due diligence issues with the Dutch supervisor in 2013. These issues hurt the

[3] With regard to the Libor issue, Rabobank Group agreed on financial settlements of EUR 774 million (USD 1 billion) with various authorities in connection with their investigations into Rabobank's historical Libor submission processes in October 2013.

reputation and image of Rabobank. Both the Chief Executive Officer and the executive board member responsible for the international activities resigned following the public announcement of the Libor scandal. Many Local Members' Councils and Supervisory Bodies expressed their discontent and disappointment and demanded an assessment of the governance structure.

It became apparent that its long-applied governance model, strategic focus and activity mix had to be adapted to the changed external configuration. The era of high balance sheet and loan growth was over as a result of new capital requirements and the general trend of deleveraging (see first row in Table 5.1). The earnings and reservation capacity came under pressure because of cyclical and structural developments in banking, among which strengthened competition from non-banks engaging in bank-like activities (EBA 2016).

The establishment of the Banking Union and the associated transfer of banking supervision to the ECB in November 2014 had implications for Rabobank as well. It seems that Rabobank had to streamline its internal administrative processes to be able to comply swiftly with new future reporting requirements.

Table 5.1 Development of total assets, cost-to-income ratio and Common Equity Tier 1 ratio (2008–2016) in the Netherlands

		2008	*2009*	*2010*	*2011*	*2012*	*2013*	*2014*	*2015*	*2016*
Asset growth (%)	Rabobank Group	7.3	−0.1	7.4	12.1	2.6	−10.9	1.8	−0.3	−2.4
	Dutch banking sector	−9.7	−11.6	2.5	4.4	−5.1	−9.5	4.0	−0.0	0.2
CI ratio (%)	Rabobank Group	65.3	64.6	64.5	64.9	66.1	74.9	62.5	62.6	67.1
	Dutch banking sector	186.2	69.2	63.5	60.5	65.8	63.0	63.1	57.6	58.0
Tier 1 ratio (%)	Rabobank Group	12.7	13.8	15.7	17.0	17.1	16.6	16.0	16.4	17.6
	Dutch banking sector	9.7	12.5	11.8	11.8	12.3	12.9	15.4	16.6	17.9

Source: Own calculations based on data from Rabobank and the European Central Bank (ECB)

5.2.4 *Strategic Responses*

In recent years, Rabobank has sought answers to cope with the challenges listed above. As can be distilled from public reports, investors' presentations and the media, Rabobank has pulled up its sleeves to eliminate its backlog and to reshape the organisation thoroughly.

Fundamental Governance Reform[4]
After the turbulent year 2013, an internal Governance Committee was assigned with the task to formulate a future proof governance structure. Its ultimate proposals had to satisfy a number of shared principles and rectify various shortcomings in the previous framework. One of the requirements was that the cooperative nature had to be firmly anchored in the new structure. The revision process lasted about two years. Figure 5.1 summarises the intertwined objectives of the governance transformation: to strengthen both the cooperative and bank in various dimensions.

The Committee's proposals were ultimately approved unanimously by the members' councils of all 106 local Rabobanks on the 2nd of December 2015. One week after this decision at the local level, the local cooperative banks approved this move in the General Meeting of Rabobank Nederland

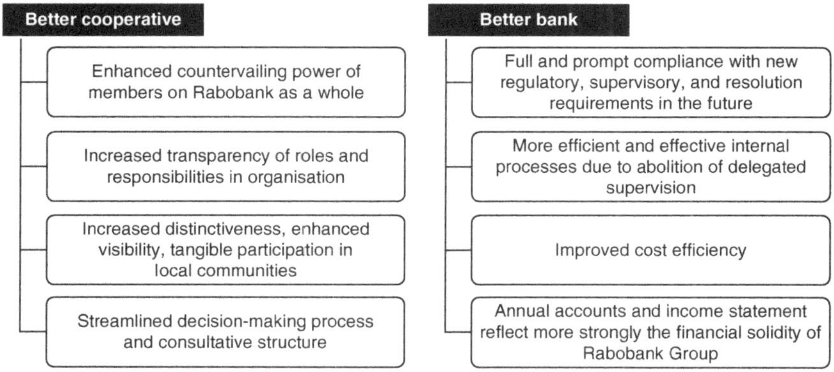

Fig. 5.1 Objectives of governance revision in Rabobank. Source: Groeneveld (2016a)

[4] Part of this sub-section is based on Groeneveld (2016a). This publication details the organisational and governance evolution as well as the backgrounds and main features of the new governance regime of Rabobank.

as well. On 1 January 2016, all local cooperative Rabobanks and Rabobank Nederland merged into one cooperative bank which functions with one banking licence and discloses one consolidated financial statement. At this moment in time, Rabobank is the only cooperative banking group with such a governance structure.

A defining feature of the new governance is that the cooperative part remains linked with the tactical and operational banking business. Bottom-up decision-making entails that member representatives ultimately approve the bank's strategy. The bank is governed by mechanisms and rules connected with its cooperative ownership structure.

The functioning of the new governance is monitored and assessed frequently. Rabobank emphasises that this step means neither a breakdown of local autonomy and orientation (i.e. a key characteristic of every cooperative organisation) nor a centralisation of the organisation. To corroborate these assertions, it refers to the completely redrafted articles of association and other internal rules. Herein, local supervisory bodies and local management teams have been granted authorisations and responsibilities by the executive board of Rabobank to secure the local and decentralised features of the organisation. For instance, the articles stipulate that local banks can develop and execute local policies and member programmes within collectively agreed common principles. Local supervisory bodies as well as local management team chairmen are endowed with the authority and responsibility to deliver satisfactory local banking services and have the opportunity of turning the concept of cooperative identity into reality at the local level.

The most important decision-making body in the governance is the General Members' Council (GMC). The GMC is populated by member representatives, that is, the chairmen of the local supervisory bodies. The GMC determines the strategy of the entire Rabobank Group and safeguards the cooperative identity. It has important formal tasks and responsibilities. The Executive Board and the Supervisory Board of Rabobank are accountable to the GMC.

Cost Reductions, Efficiency Improvements and Capitalisation
The governance transformation appears to have paved the way for substantial cost reductions. As of 2011, its cost-income ratio (CI ratio) significantly exceeds that of all other Dutch banks (see second row in Table 5.1). Since local banks are no longer independent legal entities with an own banking licence, many back-office activities and internal audit, compliance

and risk functions are eliminated at the local level. According to the bank, around 12,000 full time jobs will disappear and the number of local staff will be halved by the end of 2018. Rabobank envisages to open cheaper and smaller offices in residential and suburban areas that will predominantly provide advisory services. The number of local banks diminished from 153 in 2008 to 103 in 2016. During the same period, total domestic branches decreased by 55 per cent to 606.

Increasing difficulties to generate acceptable net earnings from traditional banking activities necessitated efficiency improvements and a revision of the distribution and service concepts. In fact, Dutch banks are currently pursuing quite similar cost reduction strategies and business models. As a matter of fact, A.T. Kearney (2016) states that many EU banks see cost-cutting as the primary tool to improve financial results in the context of tough conditions (higher regulatory burdens/levies, more stringent capital requirements, low interest rates, uncertain economic and geopolitical situation) and tough competition. Like Rabobank, most other Dutch banks intend to realise savings through increasing automatisation and digitalisation. The ultimate goal of these comparable steps is to attain higher profits which are necessary to enhance the quantity and quality of the capital buffer. For a cooperative bank, retained earnings are the main option to solidify its capital base (because it obviously cannot issue equity shares). Regarding the evolution of capitalisation, Table 5.1 illustrates that the Tier 1 capital ratio of Rabobank and the entire Dutch banking sector did not move in sync, which accords with earlier remarks in this section.

Strategic Reorientation

Apart from the cooperative governance reform, the transformation of the business model, efficiency and digitalisation programmes, Rabobank has recently restated its social vision and mission. In the chairman's foreword on page 3 of the annual report 2015, one can read the following: "As a customer-focused cooperative bank, it is our mission to make a substantial contribution to welfare and prosperity in the Netherlands and to feeding the world sustainably. Through the vision set out in Banking for the Netherlands and Banking for Food, we substantiate our position as a social, cooperative bank".

Rabobank further asserts that profit maximisation has never been the overriding purpose. However, it stresses that profits are necessary for meeting capital requirements, continuity and the pursuit of its social goals. It also states that entrepreneurship, cost-effective distribution concepts and innovative financial services at fair prices are prerequisites for every financial cooperative. If these conditions are met, Rabobank is able to hold on to its long-standing "dual-bottom line" approach. Through its "Banking for the Netherlands" and "Banking for Food", Rabobank claims to commit itself to achieving progress in society and in the Sustainable Development Goals defined by the United Nations. "Banking for the Netherlands" is based on its social agenda which was formulated in cooperation with its member representatives. The international strategy centres on "Banking for Food" which is linked to its Dutch agricultural roots.

Evolution of the Rabobank Group

Despite the difficulties and organisational changes, Rabobank's member base increased by 220,000 to around 1.9 million in 2016. The member ratio, that is, the number of members divided by the number of customers of local banks, rose by more than 4 percentage points to 27.1. Although Rabobank lost some domestic loan and deposit market share in recent years, it stayed the largest retail bank in the Netherlands. Furthermore, it consolidated its strong market position in the Dutch Food and Agricultural sector of approximately 85 per cent.

The composition of Rabobank group has notably altered after 2011. In line with the general trend in banking of closing non-profitable business units and selling non-core activities, Rabobank has particularly winded down its insurance, real estate, asset management and international retail banking activities since 2008. The evolution of the number of foreign places of business is also telling. After a fierce increase from 569 in 2008 to 769 in 2013, Rabobank has reduced its foreign presence to around 380 locations in 2016 (Fig. 5.2). In the Netherlands, Rabobank slightly expanded its banking activities via the acquisition and integration of the small Dutch Friesland Bank in 2012. In 1962, the precursor of this bank had actually left the cooperative banking group.

In terms of assets, the share of foreign activities has dropped from around 30 per cent in 2008 to about 20 per cent in 2015 (this ratio stood at 40 per cent in 2006). The decline is a deliberate attempt to cut back foreign credits to free capital for domestic retail activities. Foreign revenues as a percentage of total revenues have on balance risen from 20 to 30 per cent. This shows their important contribution to the reservation capacity of the Group.

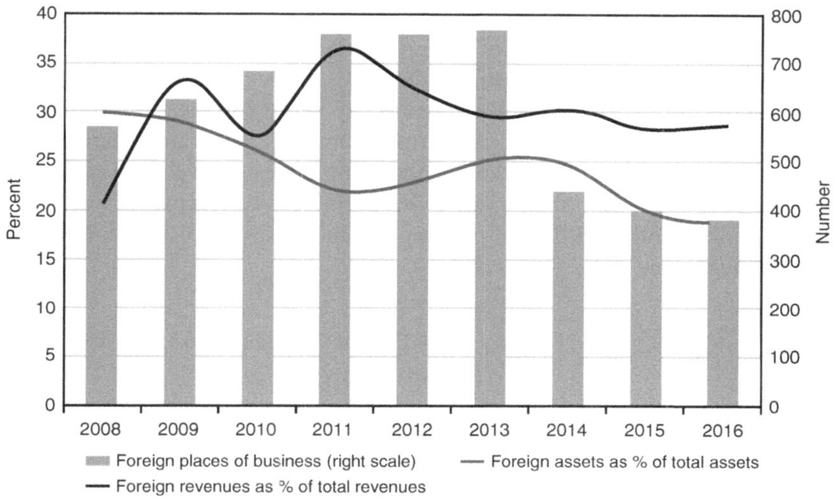

Fig. 5.2 Relative size of foreign activities and number of foreign business locations for Rabobank. Source: Annual Reports of Rabobank

5.2.5 *Concluding Remarks*

In recent years, Rabobank Group has carried out large reforms that have either already positively affected its banking performance, or seem to have created building blocks for positive future—financial—developments. Acknowledging that the viability of every bank rests on trust, reputation and innovative banking services at reasonable and cost-effective charges, the chosen strategic path for the Netherlands gives rise to some concern. Rabobank has opted for more or less identical solutions to interrelated regulatory, cost and profitability challenges in its banking operations and service concepts as other Dutch retail banks (ECB 2016a, b; Dutch Central Bank 2015). In itself, this fact reduces the indispensable diversity in Dutch banking and actually decreases systemic stability. It also poses a "threat" for Rabobank itself. How can it differentiate itself from competitors in the future?

A possible answer to mitigate both risks is to revitalise the cooperative identity and increase the perceived member value. For instance, if Rabobank manages to stimulate the involvement of many members in identifying financial solutions for pressing local economic issues and social needs to be resolved together, this will enhance the legitimacy of and support for its socio-economically driven goals and actions. It would also corroborate its authority in public debates on local and national social matters. In this regard, the internal project to boost the meaningfulness of Rabobank as a cooperative bank seems promising. With an effective and efficient participatory governance and employees actively taking part in local networks, Rabobank can behave and act differently than other Dutch banks. This would yield positive effects for diversity and stability in Dutch banking as well.

5.3 The Reform of the Cooperative Banking Sector in Italy[5]

5.3.1 The Cooperative Banking Industry in Italy and Its Recent Evolution

Cooperative banking has a long history in Italy. The first Banca Popolare (BP) was established in Lodi in 1864, following the example of the German Volksbanken whose model was introduced in Italy through the writings of the economist Luigi Luzzatti. The first Rural Bank (RB) was set up in Loreggia (close to Padua) in 1883 by Leone Wollemborg, who took as a model the German Raiffeisen. Since then, cooperative banking has experienced a long period of growth and strengthening, becoming a relevant part of the Italian banking sector. Both BPs and RBs have been structured as tiered networks with independent banks at the local level and centralised functions and bodies at the upper tiers. RBs were reformed in 1993 to be fully compliant with the universal banking model introduced by the Second Banking Coordination Directive (89/646/EEC). They were also renamed as Banche di Credito Cooperativo (BCCs).[6] Major changes were hence introduced in 2015 (Reform of BPs[7]) and 2016 (Reform of BCCs[8]).

[5] This paragraph is authored by Roberto Di Salvo and Juan Sergio Lopez.

[6] Change of name was not strictly compulsory and the "Rural" and "Raiffeisen" terms were kept respectively in the Province of Trento and in the Province of Bolzano.

[7] Law n. 33/2015, 24 March 2015.

[8] Law n. 49/2016, 8 April 2016.

The Legal Framework

The Italian Consolidated Law on Banking (ICLB)[9] provides for two models of banking institution: joint-stock companies and cooperative banks. Art. 28 ICLB states that "the exercise of banking by cooperative societies is reserved for Banche Popolari and Banche di Credito Cooperativo". Both types of cooperative banks are endowed with the common governance feature which is known as the "one head—one vote" principle, largely shared with many other cooperative banks in Europe. Nevertheless, relevant differences in their legal framework have influenced the organisational structure and evolution of the two cooperative banking segments in Italy.

The Reform in 1993 mainly distinguishes BCCs with reference to the following aspects:

- vote rights: each member has one vote in the general assembly regardless of the number of shares owned;
- share capital: each member may own more than one share, but the overall nominal value of the shares owned may not exceed EUR 100,000;
- members composition: members must have their domicile and/or continuative business within the territory where the bank operates;
- mutualism: at least 51 per cent of the risk activity must be carried out with members;
- territorial ties: 95 per cent of the lending must be in the catchment area (defined by the municipalities where the BCC has a branch and the neighbouring municipalities);
- profit distribution: at least 70 per cent of profits must be put to legal reserve, a further 3 per cent must be paid into a national fund for the development of cooperation and reserves cannot be distributed to members (even in case of liquidation);
- safe business model: derivatives may be used only for hedging purposes.

The BCCs legislative framework is hence clearly aimed at the development of a financial intermediary dedicated to the economic and social development at local level.

BPs are subject only to a small subset of specific rules:

[9] *Testo Unico Bancario*, Decreto legislativo 385/1993, 1 September 1993.

- vote rights: each member has one vote in the general assembly regardless of the number of shares owned;
- profit distribution: at least 10 per cent of net profit must be allocated to legal reserves;
- share capital: each member cannot own more than 0.5 per cent of capital and the majority of shares must be held by members.

No rule binds BPs to work mainly with their members or inside a specific territorial area. With less constraints and catering to the needs of SMEs especially in urban areas (a richer environment compared to the rural areas), they pursued a strategy of individual growth while less attention was given to the development of a mutual network.

The Need for a Reform

The implementation of the Banking Union at European level has certainly urged a reform of cooperative banking in Italy. Policy makers and analysts have recognised the positive role played by cooperative financial institutions in the banking sector.[10] Nevertheless, they have also highlighted some key issues related to weakness and inconsistencies of the cooperative model,[11] mainly concerning governance issues.

In many European countries, cooperative banks have implemented strategies and structural reforms over the past decades, often driven or supported by legislative provisions, alongside a constant increase of their market shares and role in the economy. Centralisation of processes and functions has been finalised with respect to both internal controls and business platforms so as to improve bank management and gain from economies of scale. Some cooperative networks have evolved towards forms of banking groups with a high degree of integration, while other systems have implemented new instruments in order to strengthen the functioning of the network and its safety net.[12] Moreover, after the 2007–2008 global financial crisis, the response of the EU has strongly been redirected to increase the level and quality of bank capital, also assuring a higher degree of regulatory harmonisation. The need for capitalisation

[10] See, for example, Angelini et al. (1998), Fonteyne (2007), Hesse and Čihák (2007), Birchall and Ketilson (2009).

[11] See Gutiérrez (2008).

[12] See Boscia and Di Salvo (2009).

has addressed a new challenge to cooperative banks and has fostered new strategies for group integration.

In Italy, BPs and BCCs have implemented different strategies from those adopted in many European cooperative networks. On the one hand, BPs have lost their network character over time and lessened some cooperative features, by growing individually, in some cases through listing on the stock exchange. On the other hand, BCCs have been engaged in networking policies, mainly aimed at gaining from economies of scale and synergies. The commitment for a stronger safety net and an improvement of local bank management has been relevant, with the enhancement of streamlining processes and stabilisation.[13] Nevertheless, the Italian Government and Supervisory Authority, starting from the launching of the Single Supervisory Mechanism (SSM), have been urged to stabilise the banking industry as a whole and also reform the cooperative sector. Even though the Italian banking sector proved to be resilient during the crisis, Italian and international regulators and supervisors' paramount priority was to implement measures that could, in a relatively short time, reduce the chance of instability and the barriers to recapitalisation of distressed banks. To this end, consolidation strategies[14] and primacy of joint-stock company model were the main guidelines pursued by the Italian authorities, although the cooperative form was still reserved for small-sized banks: "radical changes to the banking sector were inaugurated in 2015: the reform of the popular bank, the self-reform of the banking foundations supported by the government, the reform of the cooperative credit banks, the introduction of the Guarantee on Securitisation of Non-Performing Loans (GACS), and the acceleration of the timing for credit recovery[15]".

[13] The project of establishing an Institutional Protection Scheme (IPS) within the BCC network had been pursued for some years and then abandoned just before the legislative reforms were promoted.

[14] "*Excess capacity and fragmentation along national lines are to some extent hampering the profitability and performance of some euro area banking sectors. Lenders may benefit from further cross-border consolidation*", D. Nouy, Chair of the ECB Supervisory Board at the 2016 Banking Conference Bocconi University. "*Consolidation could help to improve cost-efficiency and profitability*", EU country report Italy 2017.

[15] Ministry of Finance: "Italian Banking Sector: Recent Development and Reform"; Ministry of Finance website.

5.3.2 *The Banche Popolari Experience*

For the BPs' reform lunched in 2015,[16] the Italian authorities choose a dual path:

- banks above the EUR 8 billion threshold in assets were transformed into joint-stock companies (*Società per Azioni, S.p.A.*);
- banks below the EUR 8 billion threshold in asset were maintained as cooperative.

Even though the recent evolution of the BPs system has basically been endowed with the transformation of major Banche Popolari into joint-stock companies, this transformation is the last step of a process started in the 1990s, when some large- and medium-sized banks went for listing on the Italian stock exchange. Indeed, this process was eased by legislative provisions issued in 1992 with this purpose.[17] Since then, the institutional setting of the BPs system has been significantly redesigned, as few banks took the route of open market capitalisation, also incorporating other BPs, while the greater part of medium- and small-sized banks remained close to the original cooperative model. The need for listing (first) and transformation (recently) emerged as a consequence of the expansion of some BPs and the governance problems which arose from the increase of size, also in terms of the number of stakeholders.[18]

On the one hand, the listed status enabled few BPs to tap the capital market, which in turn fostered merging strategies and external growth (see Table 5.2). On the other hand, specific legal provisions regarding limits to individual shareholding restrained the listed banks from take-over actions, in order to preserve the "one head—one vote" cooperative principle. The result of this process has generally been a gradual divergence of the system of Banche Popolari between few large listed banking groups, whose cooperative inspiration declined but ownership could not be

[16] Law n. 33/2015, 24 March 2015.

[17] Law n. 207/1992 and Dlgs n. 481/1992.

[18] The Bank of Italy has urged a change of the governance model since the mid-2000s, when it put under review the functioning of the governance of some Banche Popolari endowed with a large number of stakeholders, which included their employees (see A.M. Tarantola, "Le Banche popolari nel confronto competitivo: vocazione territoriale e profile di governance", paper presented at the Conference promoted by the Istituto Centrale Banche Popolari, Taormina, 27 February 2009 and published on the Bank of Italy web site).

Table 5.2 Listing of the major *Banche Popolari* before transformation into joint-stock companies

Bank (Actual entity)	*Listing history* (Including merged or acquired entities)	*Mergers and acquisition history*
Banca Popolare di Milano	It was listed in 2015.	*Banca Popolare di Milano* was merged with *Banco Popolare* in 2017 and then transformed into S.p.A.
Credito Valtellinese	It was listed in 1994.	It made the following acquisitions in the period 1995–1999: *Credito Artigiano, Banca Popolare di Rho, Banca Popolare di Santa Venera, Cassa di San Giacomo, Banca Artigianato e Industria.* Between 2000 and 2010 it merged with *Banca Regionale di Santangelo, Cassa di Risparmio di Fano, Banca Cattolica, Banca della Ciociaria.*
Banco BPM	*Banca Popolare di Verona e Novara* was listed in 2002 after merging *Banca Popolare di Verona* with *Banca Popolare di Novara.*	*Banca Popolare di Verona e Novara* merged with *Banca Popolare Italiana* in 2007, then *Banco Popolare Group* was formed. *Banco Popolare Group* merged with *Banca Popolare Milano* in 2017, then *Banco BPM* was formed by assuming the S.p.A (joint-stock) status.
UBI Banca	*Banca Popolare di Bergamo* was listed in 1992.	*Banca Popolare di Bergamo* merged with *Banca Popolare di Ancona, Cassa Risparmio di Fano* and *Banca di Brignone* in the mid-1990s. It merged with *Centrobanca* in 2001 and with *Banca Popolare Commercio Industria* in 2003, then the *Banche Popolari Unite (BPU) Group* was formed. The *BPU Group* merged with *Banca Lombarda* in 2007, then the *UBI Banca* group was formed. *UBI Banca* was transformed into S.p.A in 2015. The acquisition of *Banca Popolare dell'Etruria, Banca delle Marche* and *Cassa di Risparmio di Chieti* in liquidation was carried out in 2016.

(*continued*)

Table 5.2 (continued)

Bank (Actual entity)	*Listing history* (Including merged or acquired entities)	*Mergers and acquisition history*
Banca Popolare di Sondrio	It was listed in 1991.	No significant acquisitions of other banks over time. Growth was pursued mainly with internal resources.

Source: Authors' elaboration

contestable, and many small- and medium-sized banks still endowed with the cooperative model.[19]

The Law issued in 2015 in order to force transformation into joint-stock companies was directed at ten BPs which were above the EUR 8 billion.[20] Total assets of those banks represented 90 per cent of the total BPs assets (EUR 530 billion). As of April 2018, four banks out of ten decided to transform into the S.p.A. status, one has merged, two out of the remaining four went into liquidation in June 2017,[21] while the remaining two[22] decided not to transform and wait for the final decision of the Italian Constitutional Court on a case raised by Banca Popolare di Sondrio.[23]

Generally speaking, the evolution of Italian BPs, since the early 1990s, may be summarised as follows:

[19] Banca Popolare di Sondrio is to be considered a different case, since listing on the stock exchange has not fostered external growth through acquisitions of other banks. Banca Popolare di Sondrio is still endowed with a strong regional vocation though some expansion occurred beyond its original business area.

[20] UBI Banca, Banca Popolare di Milano, Banco Popolare, Banca Popolare di Bari, Banca Popolare di Sondrio, Banca Popolare dell'Emilia Romagna, Credito Valtellinese, Banca Popolare dell'Alto Adige, Banca Popolare di Vicenza, Veneto Banca.

[21] Banca Popolare di Vicenza and Veneto Banca were put under national insolvency procedure (LCA) in 2017, after several attempts of implementing recovery plans.

[22] Banca Popolare di Sondrio and Banca Popolare di Bari.

[23] The legal action that Banca Popolare di Sondrio took against the Law n. 33/2015 turned out to be first successful in 2016. Nevertheless, the Italian Constitutional Court confirmed the validity of the Law in March 2018. This will impose the two banks either to transform in joint-stock companies or find alternative solutions (e.g. mergers in other banking groups).

- an important role in financing SMEs and regional economies in Italy has been played both by large-sized, listed BPs and by traditional small- and medium-sized banks, mainly located in towns and operating within industrial districts;
- listed BPs have often been involved in merging operations aimed at rescuing ailing banks, either BPs or joint-stock banks, all over the country;
- the original cooperative governance model has largely been left with smaller BPs, usually located in few regions and provinces;
- large sizing and wide shareholding have driven the governance of a few BPs out of the traditional cooperative model and have also implied a significant extension of their business, also at an international level;
- the Italian experience has progressively diverged from those of other European systems: Banques Populaires in France and Volksbanken in Germany have kept their cooperative status and strong roots in local economies, taking the route of being part of large and well-organised financial networks or cooperative groups rather than increasing size and business scope individually.

At present, 23 BPs still preserve their cooperative status. Their overall size in terms of total assets is around EUR 90 billion and they control a network of 1650 branches all over the country. Nevertheless, their institutional role and market position within the domestic banking industry are to be redefined according to both the new regulatory framework and market challenges. Indeed, small- and medium-sized BPs may play a relevant role also in the new context if they will be able to keep their roots in the "regional dimension" and carry out networking strategies as a response to the need for relevant technological investments (to gain economies of scale) and new instruments of institutional protection (to cope with the crisis management framework at the EU level).

5.3.3 The Role of BCCs in the Italian Economy

BCCs were started as Rural Banks between the late nineteenth and early twentieth century (becoming Rural and Artisan Banks under the 1937 law and Credit Cooperative Banks after the 1993 banking reform), thanks to the efforts of people inspired by the social doctrine of the Catholic Church following the Raiffeisen approach. Their aim was to organise the poorer members of the rural population (especially farmers and artisans), who at that time were particularly vulnerable to defeat poverty and widespread usury. Since then, the BCCs have supported the economic and social growth of their communities becoming a relevant player in financing households as well as small and micro enterprises. The process of consolidation that has affected the Italian banking industry during the last three decades has led to the disappearance of many local banks which were incorporated into medium-large banks.

Today BCCs represent the greatest majority of local banks. In many areas of the country they are the sole local banking reality. Their presence insures a true diversification and competition within the Italian Banking industry. At the end of 2017, there were 300 BCCs with 4256 branches (15.2 per cent of the total banking industry) operating in 2651 municipalities. These are mostly small- and medium-sized urban centres. Members were more than 1.27 million. From the business model perspective, BCCs have a strong expertise in the activity of traditional intermediation, based on the *originate-to-hold* model and on long-lasting fiduciary relationships with customers. Since the mid-1990s, BCCs activity has experienced a steady growth which favoured mostly their typical customers: small enterprises and households. In 2017, 9.5 per cent of the total loans granted to Italian enterprises were issued by a BCC. The percentage rises significantly if referred to small enterprises (Fig. 5.3). The share of financing to households has reached a significant level (8.5 per cent of the total banking industry). Total loans to clients reached EUR 130.7 billion in 2017, while the total funding from clients EUR 157.0 billion.

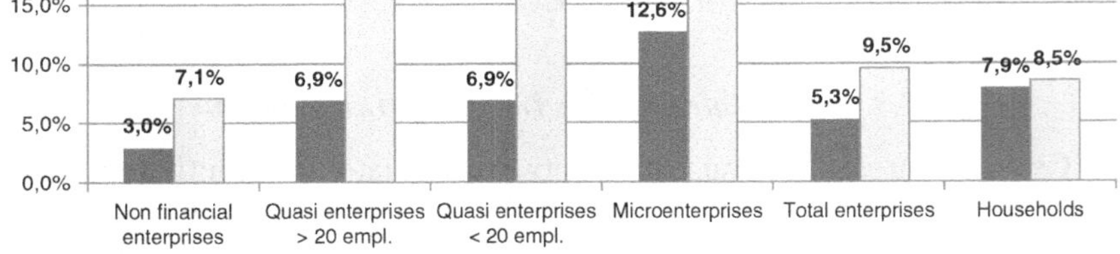

Fig. 5.3 BCCs market share of total loans by sector. Source: Authors' elaboration

5.3.4 *The BCC Network Organisation*[24]

BCCs are local independent banks that have built, over time, a voluntary national horizontal network (also called Credito Cooperativo). This network is structured as a bipolar tiered system, fulfilling different functions:

- an associative side at national and regional levels for strategic coordination, lobbying activities and technical support;
- a corporate side for centralised financial services and products;
- both sides of the network are aimed at ensuring integration, synergy and economies of scale to benefit the single banks of the network.

The associative side is structured on three levels: BCCs join in 15 regional federations that are members of the national association (Federcasse). Federcasse provides for strategic coordination and policy guidelines, as well as developing its safety net, managing external relations, coordinating communication and drawing up the national contract in conjunction with trade unions. Regional federations represent the associated BCCs towards local authorities, managing joint services such as administrative tasks and technical assistance. They also outsource the internal audit function for BCCs. The corporate side is composed by three Central Banking Institutions (CBIs), established as stock companies: Iccrea Group, Cassa Centrale Banca and Raiffeisen Landesbank. The latter provides products and services only to the BCCs located in the South Tyrol province. CBIs (also called second tier banks) provide wide-ranging support to the BCCs in order to increase efficiency and product diversification.

5.3.5 *The BCCs Reform: Context and Background*

The growing relevance of BCCs in the Italian banking industry has been made possible by the progressive strengthening of the network organisation. As in other European experiences,[25] the inefficiencies stemming from the small dimension were addressed and dealt with by cost-sharing strategies and building common structures. A pivotal factor in this suc-

[24] The institutional and organisational setting of BCCs is still based as a network organisation at the time of writing this chapter. However, some changes are expected to take place as long as the reform is being implemented.

[25] For a detailed analysis of the cooperative banks structural evolution, see Di Salvo (2011) and Di Salvo (2003).

cessful growth was the development of a reliable internal safety net: the deposit guarantee scheme (FGD), operating with an extended mandate[26] and complemented by a voluntary bondholder guarantee fund (FGO) and other guarantee schemes. They provide for a broad protection of BCCs customers and are endowed with instruments and financial resources for both bank recovery and crisis management. Indeed, the safety net turned out to be effective during the 2007–2008 global financial crisis, as its initial phase did not bring about either any single BCC default or systemic crisis. However, starting in 2009, the long and hard economic recession had a more serious impact that, within a few years, prompted a 10 per cent decline of GDP and a 25 per cent decrease in fixed investment. Starting from 2010, the BCCs safety net has played an important role for the stabilisation of the network by preventing any single distressed BCCs from going through atomistic liquidation and depositor payout.

In this already dire economic condition, between 2010 and 20115 BCCs had to implement the new and demanding banking regulation that absorbed resources and increased operating costs. At the same time, the large stock of public debt in Italy strongly limited any State support to ailing banks, which other European banks benefited from up to 2013.[27] In 2015, the international institutions started to fear that Italy could become a source of instability and the banking sector was identified as one of the fields needing intervention and reform. Italian banks are traditionally the major providers of finance to the corporate sector (especially SMEs) with the consequent build-up of a large stock of non-performing loans (NPLs) due to the increasing rate of corporate bankruptcy. Moreover, the combination of low demand and low interest rate affected the profitability of the banking sector. Paradoxically, the new rules aimed at managing the banking crisis, introduced by the European Commission, were a major part of the problem, especially concerning small- and medium-sized banks. Until 2015, the Deposit Guarantee Schemes (DGSs) of the Italian banks[28] were able to make a "resolution-like" intervention in order to minimise the impact of a banking crisis employing only private resources. This type of

[26] For a more in-depth analysis of the BCCs' safety net, see Baldi et al. (2015).

[27] In the period between 1 October 2008 and 1 October 2011, the European Commission approved aid to the financial sector for an overall amount of 4.5 trillion euro (36.7% of EU GDP).

[28] There are two DGS in the Italian banking industry: the FGD is the DGS for the BCCs while the FITD is the DGS for all the other banks (e.g. commercial, popular and saving banks).

intervention was used mainly by the BCCs whose FGDs-DGSs could rely on a large range of instruments, from early intervention to the support to insolvency proceedings. The Communication from the Commission on State aid rules[29] and the Decision on the TERCAS case,[30] which assimilated DGS intervention to State aid, significantly restricted this type of operation, depriving the banking sector (and especially the BCCs) of a powerful tool to resolve troubled banks. Moreover, the new regulations on recovery and resolution did not provide viable alternatives for small banks except the atomistic liquidation.[31]

5.3.6 *The BCCs Reform: Principles and Contents*

For the BCCs reform (approved in 2016 following a long dialogue, which lasted more than one year, between the authorities and the BCCs representatives), the Italian authorities decided to set out a model according to the already existing wide range of European experiences. Even though European cooperative banking groups differ on many instances they:

- have many common organisational and governance features;
- are previewed and regulated in the European regulatory and supervisory framework.

As of today, cooperative banking groups in Europe, even with their differences and peculiarities stemming from each national and historical background, generally comply with the Art. 10 of the EU Regulation 575/2013. They meet the following conditions:

- the affiliation (by law or by statute) of the local banks to a central body;
- the central body has the power to issue instructions to the management of the affiliated institutions;
- the central body and affiliated institutions join a cross-guarantee system.

[29] European Commission Communication 2013/C 216/01.

[30] The Commission Decision was issued on the 23rd of December 2015 and stated that the Cassa di Risparmio di Teramo (TERCAS) benefited from a State aid by the Italian interbank DGS (FITD) which was not considered consistent with the European Treaty and the 2013 Communication.

[31] See Di Salvo (2017).

This structure allows the consolidation of the accounts at the group level and the application of the associated supervisory provisions. In selecting and implementing this model the Italian authorities chose a set of specific features that could fulfil their main priorities in term of increasing stability and efficiency. The principal provisions are:

- compulsory affiliation: in order to carry out their banking activity every BCC must join a banking group; each group must have a parent company, incorporated as a joint-stock company, with the majority of its shares held by the BCCs in the group. To avoid excessive fragmentation the law states that the parent company must have net assets of at least EUR 1 billion[32];
- the definition of a cohesion contract that specifies the role and the powers of the parent company;
- the principal powers held by the parent company are:
  - identifying and implementing the strategic orientation and operational objectives of the group;
  - approving (and possibility of removing) of the BCCs' board members;
  - setting up and managing of a cross-guarantee scheme of the obligations assumed by the parent company and the BCCs (according to Art. 10 of the EU Regulation 575/2013);
  - monitoring of BCCs performances;
  - intervening in case the BCCs do not comply with the parent company directives[33];
  - launching early intervention and recovery actions in case of a BCC under distress.
- the cohesion contract must also specify the principal duties of the parent company, which are:
  - safeguarding the cooperative and mutual aims of the BCCs;
  - maintaining a role coherent with the cooperative principles of the group;
  - supporting a business model in line with the BCCs' features;

[32] Specific provisions are included for the small Raiffeisen banks operating in the Italian South Tyrol that can form a provincial group.

[33] Monitoring and intervention should be proportionate to the risks of the affiliated bank.

- safeguarding the stability and safe and prudent management of affiliated banks;
- promoting the competitiveness and efficiency of affiliated banks;
- ensuring a balanced distribution, among the affiliated banks, of the benefits of the common activity.

In this framework, it is worth noting that the Italian authorities limit the parent company's legal form to be a joint-stock company[34] in order to leave the capital partially open to the market. Moreover, the stake of the BCCs can fall below 50 per cent for stability reasons. A central feature of the new cooperative groups is the cross-guarantee scheme that entails the pooling of risks assumed by the group components and makes the excess capital of each bank available to cover liabilities incurred by each affiliated member. This arrangement is a stronger version of an Institutional Protection Scheme (IPS, regulated by Art. 113(7) of the EU Regulation 575/2013). This is the reason for discontinuing the project to set up an IPS for the overall network. Finally, an innovative feature of the reform is the provision that the degree of autonomy of each affiliated bank should be proportional to its risk profile. This rule is intended to provide an incentive to the safe and prudent behaviour in a group characterised by a large number of banks.

The changes being introduced are very deep: after more than 100 years, no credit cooperative bank can operate on its own anymore, unless it is affiliated to a banking group. The parent company has pervasive powers of monitoring, direction and coordination. On the other hand, a major feature of the BCCs was left untouched by the reform, namely their role as cooperative and mutualistic banks, serving local communities. Indeed, the legal provisions mentioned in Sect. 5.3.1 remain unchanged.[35] The BCCs will keep working with a full-fledged banking licence. The cooperative governance is maintained (the members' general assembly elects the board of directors according to the "one head—one vote" rule) and the BCCs remain the (majority) owners of the parent company.

[34] In Finland the central institution of the OP Group is a cooperative as it was in Rabobank (the Netherlands) before the recent reform. In France, the central body of the Crédit Mutuel is the National Association (see the recent sentence in the case Crédit Mutuel Arkéa vs ECB at the European Court of Justice—case T-712/15).

[35] Except the limit of the value of the share owned by a member that lifted from EUR 50,000,000 to EUR 100,000,000.

5.3.7 The Implementation of the Reform: First Results and Main Challenges

The reform does not bind the BCCs to establish one single group. As long as a bank has the requisites in term of capital, organisational structure and pool of perspective affiliates, it can apply to become a parent company. Therefore, right after the approval of the new law a dialogue started between the three central institutions serving BCCs (Iccrea Banca, Cassa Centrale Banca and Raiffeisen Central Bank) in order to explore possible convergences.[36] Ultimately, no agreement could be reached to establish a single banking group. At the time of writing this chapter,[37] three cooperative banking groups are likely to be set up: Iccrea banking group (with 150 banks and around EUR 160 billion in total assets), Cassa Centrale banking group (with 100 banks and around EUR 90 billion in total assets) and Raiffeisen banking group (with 40 banks and around EUR 15 billion in total assets).

The radical transformation of the BCCs from a single voluntary network to three centralised banking groups entails opportunities and challenges. The group structure should help implementing cost rationalisation and better capital allocation. It should also enhance investment capabilities through the pooling of resources. It may support a better diversification of the business model. Last but not least, it may streamline the decision-making process that was quite complex and time-consuming in the network phase. On the other side, the group structure is an organisational challenge too. The complexity of setting up and running such types of groups with a large number of banks of different size and geographical location should not be underestimated. In other countries, the evolution from loose to centralised organisations has developed over a long period of time, often under the benign oversight of the national supervisor. A further challenge is to find the right equilibrium between the joint-stock form of the group and the mutual cooperative aim that should guide the

[36] The three group had quite different dimension and organisational structure in 2016. Iccrea was already a significant institution (with more than EUR 40 billion in assets) and under the ECB supervision. Cassa Centrale Banca was much smaller (EUR 5.5 billion in total assets) and under supervision of the Bank of Italy. Cassa Centrale Raiffeisen, catering only to the Raiffeisen banks located in the Italian South Tyrol region, was even smaller (EUR 3.7 billion in total assets) but in the new law could rely on a special provision to establish a provincial group.

[37] March 2018.

strategies of the group.[38] Reconciling the BCCs vocation to support members and local business with the strategies defined by the parent company (and the constraint stemming from the European supervision) may not be a smooth task. The crucial factor will probably be the concrete governance structure that will be set up in order to manage processes and decisions. If well implemented, the new organisational structure will allow the nascent cooperative banking group to fulfil even more than in the past their role as local bankers in compliance with globalised standards.

5.4 Other Country-Level Developments in Europe from the Beginning of the Great Crisis[39]

5.4.1 Germany

The German cooperative banking model is a mutual, federal and associated one that mainly reflects the federal organisation of the State. At the base of the three-tier model, there are the local cooperative banks, which effectively represent the heart of the cooperative banking network. The second tier of the model is represented by central financial institutions that operate as central and clearing banks, provide services to local banks and define policies related to liquidity management, mutual funds, mortgages and insurances. At the top of this organisation there are the main central financial institutions DZ Bank and WGZ Bank, which started a merger process in August 2016 that should terminate with full integration before the end of 2018.[40]

In Germany, the subprime crisis had a significant impact on the banking system as a whole and some direct effect on tax payers. In fact, in 2008 output losses and fiscal costs were respectively 11.0 per cent and 1.8 per cent of GDP (Laeven and Valencia 2010, 2012). A part recapitalisations, state aid consisted of asset purchase programmes (11.1 per cent of GDP) and asset guarantee programmes (6.1 per cent of GDP). In 2008, *The*

[38] The concept of hybridisation has already entered in the economic literature to describe a condition in which both the joint stock and the cooperative governance model must coexist.

[39] This paragraph is authored by Francesco Di Leo.

[40] In more detail, the two-tier system has a national federation (BVR-Bundesverband der Deutschen Volksbanken and Raiffeisenbanken) which groups together individual cooperatives, regional associations and a system of 11 specialised branches. BVR is not a public limited company and it arranges and manages a deposit guarantee fund.

Guardian observed that "the bail-out marked a change in direction by the German government and amounted to the biggest state intervention in the economy of Germany since the end of the Second World War". It included EUR 400 billion in guarantees for interbank lending to restore liquidity and EUR 100 billion in fresh capital. However, bailouts affected more Sparkassen (savings banks) and their regional Landesbanken than German credit cooperative banks, Raiffeisen and Volksbanken. As a result, the crisis has not overwhelmed the configuration of the model based on the organisation of the members, local roots and long horizon management.[41] Over the last decade, Raiffeisen and Volksbanken have managed to remain stable in their model, size and market share (21.2 per cent in 2016, measured as the mean of domestic market share deposits, domestic market share loans and mortgage market share), showing to be less risky (Beck et al. 2009) and less cyclical (Behr et al. 2013) than other kinds of banks. Today challenges to the German cooperative system are related on the one side to the role of DZ Bank, as one of the most important domestic and European banking players and its diversified business model, and on the other side to the fact that the banking sector is crowded and profit margins are low. For some observers, the actual cooperative network with almost 1000 local and regional banks risk to result too fragmented (e.g. Biasin 2016).

5.4.2 France

In France, the crisis had a significant influence on the banking system, a limited impact on tax payers and no significant consequences on cooperative banks. In 2008, output losses in France were 23.0 per cent of GDP, while fiscal costs were 1.0 per cent of GDP (Laeven and Valencia 2010, 2012). Two recapitalisation packages were arranged in 2008 and a specific asset guarantee programme was launched, but these initiatives did not concern cooperative banks. Crédit Agricole, Crédit Mutuel and BPCE (Groupe des Banques Populaires et des Caisses d'Epargne), the three major cooperative networks in France, resisted to the crisis fairly well and today remain universal and leading actors with a mean domestic market share of 22.9 per cent, 16.3 per cent and 21.1 per cent, respectively.[42]

[41] Nevertheless, in the peak of the crisis, from July 2007 to year-end 2008, DZ Bank experienced write-downs and losses of 0.5 per cent of total assets (or 14.0 per cent of equity) (Groeneveld and de Vries 2009).

[42] EACB (2017). Data are referred to 2016, end of the year.

The French cooperative model is in the form of ***integrated cooperative network***[43] where local and regional banks and the central body are linked by a parent-subsidiary link relationship, characterised by a higher level of control of central institution and where central body is owned by local and/or regional banks. This means three things. First, adherent banks are monitored as a whole. Second, the central body and each bank are subject to the same risk evaluation. Third, own funds or repayment of liabilities can be transferred within the group (Richez-Battesti and Leseul 2016).[44] With reference to the structure and corporate governance of Crédit Agricole and BPCE in particular, some authors observed that their integrated and centralised conglomerates produced a high level of trivialisation (banalisation) of the mutualism form (Richez-Battesti and Leseul 2016). These banks become hybrids (Batac et al. 2008) and today own an increasing number of joint-stock subsidiaries, both within and outside national borders. Differently from Crédit Agricole and BPCE, Crédit Mutuel keeps

[43] See Chap. 1 for an overview on the different cooperative banking models.

[44] At local level, cooperatives are entities held in the form of shares by members; on a regional level, there are the regional savings and loan institutions (Caisses Régionales, Fédérations Régionales); finally the central body (Crédit Agricole S.A. ex Caisse Nationale, Caisses Fédérales), that is, the legal representative, group director and coordinator, grants loans to local banks and guarantees the commitments of regional banks, ensures affiliates operate correctly, manages treasury, organises financial pooling solidarity for regional banks, controls specialised subsidiaries and develops international agreements. Analysing in particular the Crédit Agricole model (MBRES 2017), the local banks have lost their autonomy and banking licence in favour of the regional banks that refer to the parent company called CA Société Anonyme (S.A.) that is an anonymous limited company, listed on the CAC40 Stock Exchange Market and 56.6 per cent controlled by a regional holding company called SAS Rue La Boetie, and CA S.A. itself owns 25.0 per cent of each Caisse Régionale. The Groupe BPCE was founded in 2009 when Groupe Caisse d'Epargne and Groupe Banques Populaires joined. In this way the regional banks (17 savings banks and 15 popular banks) become shareholders of the parent company (BPCE S.A.) which in turn controls branches specialised in the delivery of centralised products and services (leasing, factoring, real estate management, asset management, etc.). A special law of 24 June 2009 settled the competencies of the parent company in terms of arranging the strategy and responsibility concerning solvency, risk management and liquidity. The 2009 law provided that between the Caisses d'Epargne, which became a cooperative bank, and Banque Populaire, a new banking group would be set up (BPCE S.A.). So, the public limited parent company was 66.6 per cent owned by regional savings banks (CNCE) and popular banks (BFBP) and 33.3 per cent by the Caisse des Depots et Consignations. After the 2009 reform, the presence of Fédération Nationale des Caisses d'Epargne had to guarantee the democratic vis-à-vis mutualistic spirit. But over time the balance of power between members has changed and the parent company (BPCE S.A.) has taken definite strategic leadership of the group.

a predominantly national profile and its strategic bodies are the regional federal banks (Fédérations Régionales), which control local banks and offer centralised shared services. In this case, the third tier is represented by the Confédération Nationale du Crédit Mutuel, which has the responsibility of representing the network and ensuring cohesion and control. The federal banks, which are very different one from another in terms of number of adherents and territorial coverage, keep playing a crucial key role in the network thanks to their capacity to remain entrenched in the territory and to retain strategic prerogatives. Hybridisation is then less pronounced.

Since the turmoil cooperative banks in France have displayed a certain level of dynamism and innovative attitude in their retail banking core business, have gained market share and have launched new simple and easy to understand products to boost their business. These actions resulted in an increase in customer deposits (up by 41.1 per cent from 2007 to 2016) and a decline in deposit to lending ratio (down to 0.85 per cent in 2016 from 1.10 per cent in 2007). Recently, all the French cooperative banks have also begun operations of diversification and external growth by creating new finance companies (e.g. Crédit Agricole launched Amundi in a joint venture between with Société Générale to specialise in the asset management), developing trans-border alliance (e.g. Crédit Mutuel launched a commercial agreement with Banco BPM and Banco Popular) and trans-border operations (e.g. starting from 2016 Crédit Agricole-Cariparma, controlled by Crédit Agricole, became the central body for the Italian operations of the bank). These developments may also suggest that membership and democratic governance are keeping losing importance in models featured by large, diversified cooperative banking networks (Richez-Battesti and Leseul 2016). Nevertheless, today French cooperatives are more stable and risk-adverse than before the crisis. Their main challenges refer indeed to their large size and the continue dilution in their cooperative nature (e.g. Batac et al. 2008).

5.4.3 *United Kingdom*

In 2007 the United Kingdom experienced output losses and fiscal costs of 25.0 per cent and 8.8 per cent of GDP, respectively (Laeven and Valencia 2010, 2012). However, bailouts affected only a part of mutual and cooperative banks even if several banks were distressed.[45] In more details, fiscal costs were related to the Dunfermline Building Society takeover (0.1 per cent of GDP) and the loans programme accorded to Bradford & Bingley (in November 2008 the government invested 1.9 per cent of GDP to set up UK Financial Investments to manage together the shareholdings in Northern Rock and Bradford & Bingley). In many cases, private recovery and resolution plans affected distressed cooperatives before insolvency. In fact, many of them were forced into being sold or combining with other mutual entities or accepting venture capital money (Arnold 2014).

The *de facto* system in the United Kingdom sees different cooperative structures, models and experiences. The first form of cooperative entity found all over the United Kingdom are Credit Unions, which are not-for-profit mutual companies, with a penetration rate of 1.9 per cent in the active population aged between 15 and 64. They are owned and controlled by their members and their business model is largely based on the collection of deposits and the offer of lending to the members (Jones 2016). Starting from the 1990s, most Credit Unions faced increasing economic and organisational challenges in developing their business model and governance mechanisms and in expanding membership, assets and liabilities. Reorganisations, started in 2004 and accelerated in 2008, were based on takeovers and integrated system development (Desrochers and Fischer 2005). Moreover, in 2013 the British government announced a GBP 35.6 million investment plan in the sector to support member expansion, improve IT infrastructure, expand products and services, improve efficiency and profitability and ensure that no longer dependence on any public aid was necessary.

The second and maybe most important cooperative model in the United Kingdom is represented by Building Societies. Building Societies specialised in providing mortgages to members. In their heyday, there were hundreds of Building Societies in the United Kingdom, but over the decades the number has sharply decreased (following the so-called ***demutualisation*** process). Today 44 Building Societies are still operating. Transformation and challenges increased with the Building Societies and

[45] In the United Kingdom, many mutuals, which inspired by a more capitalist approach had already significantly reduced their internal presence from the 1980s (Jones 2016), showed their weakness after 2007 because they did not have enough reserves or new depositors/members to supply extra capital funding. From another perspective we observed that they were unable to absorb losses, to attract new deposits and increase lending rates (Arnold 2014).

Mutual Act (2007) and when Nationwide and Yorkshire Building Societies negotiated a temporary change to the terms of the Financial Services Compensation Scheme (FSCS). This pushed for an increasing number of mergers. Overall, their number fell by a quarter in 2008 as a consequence of the subprime crisis. Mergers reduced in 2011 as a result of a new FSCS amendment.[46]

Finally, the Co-operative Bank, a retail and ethical bank that after reported losses of GBP 600 million was subject to a rescue plan in 2013–2014 in order to address a capital shortfall of about GBP 1.9 billion. This was financed by hedge funds (Aurelius Capital Management, Beach Point Capital Management, Silver Point Capital). Problems arose after the 2009 takeover of the Britannia Building Society and the discovery in September 2013 of a GBP 3.6 billion funding gap in its loans portfolio that forced the bank to sell assets and renegotiate the bank's GBP 1.5 billion rescue with the hedge funds. As a result, the holding parent (the Co-operative Group) lost majority control. In May 2014 the bank lost 38,000 customer accounts due to negative publicity but finalised the private GBP 400 million fundraising plan that further shrank the Co-operative Group's ownership. As a consequence, Co-operative Bank reduced losses and improved capital adequacy by selling assets, cutting staff numbers and closing branches. Despite the restructuring, the bank announced a pre-tax loss for 2015 of more than double that of 2014. In April 2017, the Co-operative Group wrote off its stake, and in June 2017 institutional bondholders agreed to convert GBP 426 million of bonds into equity and existing investors agreed to put GBP 250 million of new equity into a new holding company. Lastly, the Co-operative Group, which in the end owned just 1.0 per cent of the bank, sold its stake in September 2017, but a relationship agreement was created, establishing that the bank retains its name and ethical policy until 2020.

[46] Members acquired shares for an amount of GBP 50,000 per individual and per institution. As an example on how the FSCS worked, after the 2007–2008 merger between Nationwide, Cheshire and Derbyshire, a member with GBP 50,000 in each bank at the time of the merger would retain GBP 150,000 of FSCS protection for their funds. But in 2011, mergers drastically reduced as a result of a new single FSCS limit for retail deposits settled at GBP 85,000.

5.4.4 *Austria, Finland and Spain*

Briefly looking at other cooperative experiences since the beginning of the crisis in Europe, the cases of Austria, Finland and Spain are of significant interest. These countries are characterised by different cooperative structures and presence in the territory. In fact, while in Austria and Finland cooperatives represent respectively about 33.5 per cent and 37 per cent of the local retail banking system, in Spain they count for only 7.2 per cent of the domestic market.[47,48]

In Austria there are many Raiffeisen operating mainly in rural areas and smaller Volksbanken with a focus on urban areas. Differently from the German cooperatives, the central institutions (Raiffeisen Zentralbank Osterreich AG and Osterreichische Volksbanken AG) are at the same time central institutions and large commercial banks. Albeit singular cooperatives did not suffer consequences of crisis as a result of their quite conservative business, Osterreichische Volksbanken AG sustained losses related to risky business operations in Eastern Europe (Bülbül et al. 2013) and applied a resolution scheme based on EUR 1 billion state aid and purchasing stakes in associates represented by four banking subsidiaries to the primary level Volksbanken. After an annual loss of more than EUR 1.3 billion in 2011, the Osterreichische Volksbanken AG and controlled Volksbanken connected and realised an integrated system with a joint liability and liquidity scheme and directives coming from Osterreichische Volksbanken AG and directed to associates. In 2015, a step-by-step liquidation process and simplification took place so that the core functions of the Osterreichische Volksbanken AG shifted to the Volksbank Wien-Baden and non-core assets were transferred out of the group (Brazda et al. 2016).

[47] EACB (2017). Data are referred to 2016, end of the year. In 2007 banks in Austria suffered losses of 14.0 per cent of GDP and a total fiscal expenditure of 4.9 per cent of GDP with implication on cooperative central institution Osterreichische Volksbanken-Gruppe (OVAG group). In Spain non-cooperative banks experienced output losses and fiscal costs by 39.0 per cent and 3.8 per cent of GDP in 2007. Lastly, Finnish banks suffered neither crisis nor costs after 2007 (Laeven and Valencia 2010, 2012).

[48] In 2007 banks in Austria suffered losses of 14.0 per cent of GDP and a total fiscal expenditure of 4.9 per cent of GDP with implication on cooperative central institution Osterreichische Volksbanken-Gruppe (OVAG group). In Spain non-cooperative banks experienced output losses and fiscal costs by 39.0 per cent and 3.8 per cent of GDP in 2007. Lastly, Finnish banks suffered neither crisis nor costs after 2007 (Laeven and Valencia 2010, 2012).

In Finland, after a series of mergers, the OP-Pohjola (OP) group appeared in 2014.[49] This group is the most important retail Finnish cooperative group and a case of strategic networks representing today an expression of highest degree of integration in Europe (Kalmi 2016). In fact, local and regional banks are permanently affiliated to the central body, the management of the central body issues instructions to local bank management, there exists a cross-guarantee scheme and solvency and liquidity are monitored on the basis of consolidated accounts. Despite the pronounced role of central organisations within the OP group, local banks retain formal autonomy, there is a supervisor board and a management board elected by members, serving both members and non-members. Recent analysis of OP group development argues that the high level of integration might increase vulnerability due to centrally managed operations (Kalmi 2016).

As concerns the Spanish banking system, during the last decade cooperative banks have been completely restructured even if the financial crisis affected them marginally. The difficult competitive environment in Spain during the financial crisis jeopardised the cooperative movement while the Bank of Spain called for sector concentration, not as consequence of solvency problems but for reasons of sizing and efficiency (Fajardo-Garcia and Soler-Tormo 2016). So, mergers and acquisitions took place under the assumption that greater integration could provide economies of scale. The Spanish transformation concerned mostly local Cajas belonging to the Asociación Nacional de Cajas Rurales but also involved cooperatives belonging to Unión Nacional de Cooperativas de Crédito (UNCC). A peculiarity of the Spanish system, after the recent reform, is that the Bank of Spain is the supervisor and national resolution authority dealing with credit institutions, while the autonomous communities (regions) possess their own prudential supervision powers although in collaboration with the national central bank.

[49] In 2014, Pohjola bank, the central and until that moment listed bank, was fully annexed to the OP group that adopted the joint liability structure. The decision was largely motivated by new regulatory requirements in the group risk management and the operation was financed both by members and launch of investment share, which is a hybrid share instrument.

References

Angelini, P., Di Salvo, R., & Ferri, G. (1998). Availability and Cost of Credit for Small Businesses: Customer Relationship and Credit Cooperative. *Journal of Banking and Finance, 22*(6–8), 925–954.

Arnold, G. (2014). Banking. *Financial Times Guides.*

Baldi, F., Bredice, M., & Di Salvo, R. (2015). Back to the Future: Bank Crisis Management Practices in Italy (1978–2015) and Their Perspectives in the Italian Cooperative Credit Network. *The Journal of European Economic History, 44*, 115–157.

Batac, J., Maymo, V., & Pallas-Saltiel, V. (2008). Entre Mutualisme et Capitalisme: le Modèle de Gouvernance Hybride du Groupe Crédit Agricole. *Revue Internationale de l'Economie Sociale, Recma*, (308), 23–34.

Beck, K. T., Hesse, H., Kick, T., & von Westernhagen, N. (2009). *Bank Ownership and Stability: Evidence from Germany.* CEPR Policy Portal Issues.

Behr, P., Norden, L., & Noth, F. (2013). Financial Constraints of Private Firms and Bank Lending Behavior. *Journal of Banking and Finance, 37*(9), 3472–3485.

Biasin, M. (2016). The German Cooperatives Banks: An Economic Overview. In *Credit Cooperative Institutions in European Countries* (pp. 83–110). Berlin: Springer.

Birchall, J., & Ketilson, L. H. (2009). *Resilience of the Cooperative Business Model in Times of Crisis.* Geneva: International Labour Office, Sustainable Enterprise Programme.

Boscia, V., & Di Salvo, R. (2009). The Theory and Experience of Cooperative Banking. In A. Carretta & P. Schwizer (Eds.), *Cooperative Banking: Innovations and Developments.* Basingstoke and New York: Palgrave Macmillan.

Brazda, J., Blisse, H., & Schedwy, R. (2016). Cooperative Banks in the Austrian Banking System. In *Credit Cooperative Institutions in European Countries* (pp. 3–18). Berlin: Springer.

Bülbül, D., Schmidt, R. H., & Schüwer, U. (2013). *Savings Banks and Cooperative Banks in Europe.* White Paper Series, No. 5.

Co-operative Bank. Annual Report 2015-2016-2017.

Daniëls, T., & Kamalodin, S. (2016). *The Return on Equity of Large Dutch Banks.* DNB Occasional Studies, Vol. 14-5, Amsterdam, The Netherlands.

Desrochers, M., & Fischer, K. P. (2005). The Power of Networks: Integration and Financial Cooperative Performance. *Annals of Public and Cooperative Economics, 76*(3), 307–354.

Di Salvo, R. (2003). *The Governance of Mutual and Cooperative Bank Systems in Europe.* Rome: Cooperative Studies, ECRA.

Di Salvo, R. (2011). *The System of Cooperative Banks in Europe. Governance, Strategic Structures and Evolutionary Trends.* Second Euricse Conference on Cooperative Finance.

Di Salvo, R. (2017). *Recovery and Resolution of Less Significant Banks in the Banking Union Era*. Paper presented at the Fifth FINEST Conference, Trani, September 2017. Italian Version Published on the Quarterly Review Cooperazione di Credito, n. 223, ECRA, Rome.

Dutch Central Bank. (2015). *Perspective on the Structure of the Dutch Banking Sector: Efficiency and Stability Through Competition and Diversity*. Amsterdam, The Netherlands.

European Association of Co-operative Banks (EACB). (2010). *European Cooperative Banks in the Financial and Economic Turmoil: First Assessments*. Research Paper, European Association of Cooperative Banks, Brussels, Belgium.

European Association of Co-operative Banks (EACB). (2017). *Key Statistics – Financial Indicators 2016*.

European Banking Authority (EBA). (2016). *Risk Assessment of the European Banking System*. London, UK.

European Central Bank (ECB). (2016a). *Recent Trends in Euro Area Banks' Business Models and Implications for Banking Sector Stability*. Financial Stability Review: Special Features. Frankfurt am Main, Germany.

European Central Bank (ECB). (2016b). *Report on Financial Structures*. Frankfurt am Main, Germany.

Fajardo-Garcia, G., & Soler-Tormo, F. (2016). The Credit Cooperative System in Spain. In *Credit Cooperative Institutions in European Countries* (pp. 213–232). Springer.

Ferri, G., Kalmi, P., & Kerola, E. (2014). Does Bank Ownership Affect Lending Behavior? Evidence from the Euro Area. *Journal of Banking & Finance, 48*, 194–209.

Fiordelisi, F., & Mare, D. S. (2014). Competition and Financial Stability in European Cooperative Banks. *Journal of International Money and Finance, 45*, 1–16.

Fiordelisi, F., Mare, D. S., & Molyneux, P. (2015, September). *State-Aid, Stability and Competition in European Banking*. MPRA Paper n. 67473.

Fonteyne, W. (2007). *Co-operative Banks in Europe – Policy Issues*. IMF Working Paper.

Groeneveld, H. (2016a). *The Road Towards One Cooperative Rabobank*. Utrecht: Rabobank.

Groeneveld, H. (2016b). Rabobank Before, During and After the Credit Crisis: From Modesty via Complacency to Fundamental Steps. In S. Karofolas (Ed.), *Credit Cooperative Institutions in European Countries*. Berlin: Springer.

Groeneveld, H., & de Vries, B. (2009). European Co-operative Banks: First Lessons of the Subprime Crisis. *The International Journal of Cooperative Management, 4*(2), 8–21.

Gutiérrez, E. (2008). *The Reform of Italian Cooperative Banks: Discussion of Proposals*. IMF Working Paper 74/2008.

Henselmann, K., Ditter, D., & Lupp, P. (2016). *The Effects of the Financial Crisis on Cooperative Banks in Europe. A Critical Comparison.* ZBW Working Papers in Accounting Valuation Auditing, 2016-1.

Hesse, H., & Čihák, M. (2007). *Cooperative Banks and Financial Stability.* IMF Working Paper 2/2007.

Jones, P. A. (2016). British Credit Unions: Transformation and Challenges. In *Credit Cooperative Institutions in European Countries* (pp. 233–249). Berlin: Springer.

Kalmi, P. (2016). Cooperative Banks in Finland. In *Credit Cooperative Institutions in European Countries* (pp. 43–54). Berlin: Springer.

Kearney, A. T. (2016). *The 2016 Retail Banking Radar: The Retail Banking Champions Step Up Their Game.*

Laeven, M. L., & Valencia, F. (2010). *Resolution of Banking Crises: The Good, the Bad, and the Ugly* (pp. 10–146). Washington, DC: International Monetary Fund.

Laeven, L., & Valencia, F. (2012). *Systemic Banking Crises Database: An Update.* Washington, DC: International Monetary Fund.

MedioBanca Ricerca e Sviluppo (MBRES). (2017). *Cumulative Data of the Main International Banks.*

Migliorelli, M., & Brunelli, S. (2016). The Transmission of the Monetary Policy in the Euro Area: The Role of the Banks' Business Model. *Annals of Public and Cooperative Economics, 88*(3), 303–322.

Richez-Battesti, N., & Leseul, G. (2016). Cooperative Banks in France: Emergence, Mutations and Issues. In S. Karofolas (Ed.), *Credit Cooperative Institutions in European Countries.* Berlin: Springer.

Santella, P. (2001). "The Corporate Governance of the Italian Cooperative Banks" (Banche Cooperative o Fondazioni Bancarie? Corporate Governance nelle Banche Di Credito Cooperativo). *Bancaria, 11*(2001), 44–58.

Vogelaar, N. (2012). Rabobank and the Credit Crisis. In J. Mooij & W. W. Boonstra (Eds.), *Raiffeisen's Footprint.* Amsterdam: VU University Press.

CHAPTER 6

The Governance of Cooperative Banks: Main Features and New Challenges

Eric Lamarque

6.1 Introduction[1]

When you ask a member of any cooperative bank what it is that makes the cooperative model unique, the immediate answer is: governance. Members are the owners of the cooperative. Each member has one voting right, independently from the amount of money invested in member shares, making it a model of democracy according to the supporters of

[1] The present chapter is based on the results of several studies conducted over the past five years in one of the Sorbonne Business School research lab (Chair of "Management and Governance of Financial Cooperatives", Université Paris 1 Panthéon-Sorbonne). During this time, we have highlighted the cooperative governance model's main characteristics, how decisions are taken, how risk is managed, and how new regulations impact the existing governance structures. Governance is thus one of the primary topics of our research program. Our contributions have been recognized both from our participation in world summits on cooperatives, and as guests at many cooperative discussion groups with senior management and members on transforming the governance model, while maintaining the fundamental values and principles which have existed now for about 200 years.

E. Lamarque (✉)
IAE Université Paris 1 Panthéon-Sorbonne (Sorbonne Business School), Paris, France
e-mail: eric.lamarque@univ-paris1.fr

M. Migliorelli (ed.), *New Cooperative Banking in Europe*,
https://doi.org/10.1007/978-3-319-93578-2_6

such a system. But only a small group of active members is actually aware of their ability to participate in the various decision-making levels. Many are not so engaged, while some don't even remember they own member shares. Others are just concerned about the return on investment, because it is by using this argument that these particular shares were proposed to them. After the tarnished reputations of banks due to the economic and financial crisis, cooperative banks rediscovered that the main asset they could use to differentiate themselves from traditional shareholder-owned banks is membership. But for such an asset to be valuable, all members need to become aware of their right to participate in the life of their banks.

This chapter focuses on the main features and challenges of governance of cooperative banks. We first expand upon the main parts of the decision-making process in cooperative banks and explain how and at which level members are involved. Dealing with governance means analyzing how decisions are formed and how managers are controlled by members at the various decision-making levels. Next, we identify the main features of the various models of governance in the context of cooperative banking. There is not a single model, but a range of possible structures. Finally, we focus on the definition of risk appetite, which is nowadays a key issue for cooperative banks. In this respect, the responsibilities of boards (and their members) are clearly entrenched in the new regulatory context. As a matter of fact, many cooperative banks view the Basel III requirements as a threat, with the risk of losing their inherent specificity. The main issue here is perhaps to put forward proposals for preserving the model, rather than trying to convince regulators and supervisors to change their mind!

6.2 Features of the Cooperative Banking Model of Governance

Cooperative banks share governance principles that are clearly different from the ones adopted by other kinds of banks. To this extent, a few principles have been identified as standing out and being particularly relevant (Deville and Lamarque 2014). Nonetheless, it is important to underline that these principles are often implemented differently from one cooperative bank to another, thus contributing to the sector's diversity.

6.2.1 Democracy

Customers can join cooperative banks as members. Each member is entitled to one vote regardless of the share of equity s/he holds and how much deposits or loans s/he can count on. At the general assembly meetings members play a role similar to that of shareholders, by voting *inter alia* to determine the returns paid on member shares and by evaluating the performance of general managers at local or regional level. Nevertheless, there are significant differences between traditional shareholder assemblies and cooperative assemblies, due to the "one member, one vote" rule. In this respect, a long-term vision based on social engagement usually takes precedence over short-term financial needs and a large proportion of the economic results usually remains within the cooperative.

6.2.2 Autonomy

Autonomy is another important principle that goes hand in hand with democracy. Nevertheless, it appears to be a concept better adapted to decentralized structures than to highly centralized ones. To this extent, some local branches appear to enjoy real autonomy and discretionary management (as a consequence of a practice rooted in the historical philosophy of the cooperative movement). Usually, local and regional managers mention that the role and importance of local boards constitute a distinctive asset compared to traditional banks. To balance the autonomy that local branches can enjoy, the national and regional levels usually implement tools to foster a common strategic alignment. Certain national levels attempt to influence decision-making or at least coordinate the actions of local entities by focusing in particular on key areas such as marketing, recruitment or risk taking and management. Information and IT systems are often employed for this purpose. Hence, the autonomy that managers have at the local and regional level can vary depending on both the degree and the type of oversight provided by the next authority level.

6.2.3 Accountability

The principle of autonomy, and the freedom of management that comes with it, gives rise to another principle: accountability. Cooperative employees, managers and general managers who enjoy real decision-making authority usually feel genuinely accountable for the results obtained. The principle of accountability applies to cooperative banks at many levels of the organization. As concerns the relationship with customers and members, manager's accountability is exercised first by listening, providing support and cultivating long-term connections. On several occasions the role played by cooperative bank's managers in the local community has been put in evidence, for example, when serving as representative of an association active in the territory in which the bank operates. This active role in the local community is often described as a unique way to build relationships and get to know customers and members.[2] Nevertheless, accountability is also relevant when it comes to employee participation and engagement. It usually translates into low turnover rates, high demand for training and skills improvement and eventually in the interest in internal promotions.

6.2.4 *Non-monetary Compensation and Recognition*

In many cooperative banks, financial incentives are usually not directly tied to results. Bonuses do exist, but they are only paid once the fiscal year is over and are subject to limitations. Elected officers do not receive direct compensation and tend to perform their work on a volunteer basis. Their primary incentives are then the autonomy and freedom to take decisions at the operational level (within limits) and the recognition they have in the local community. Customers and members contribution is also valued and recognition of their efforts is often evident in the decision-making process, in some cases extended to everyone from customer representatives to branch managers. Finally, also employees usually enjoy and value non-financial attributes of their job. In particular, they appreciate the possibility to intervene in the decisions having impact on their daily activity and they feel that it gives meaning to their work.

6.2.5 *Territorial Entrenchment*

Territorial entrenchment is another specific principle of cooperative banks, and it is recognized as guaranteeing proximity to members and customers. In this respect and in line with such a principle, cooperative banks devel-

[2] Nevertheless, such a practice is not without controversy. Local managers are subject to market constraints as well as productivity and profitability needs. For this reason, they normally push to have the highest degree of decision-making authority possible and they feel this is legitimate and necessary due to their role in developing relationships with members and customers.

oped various ways of organizing their structure, according to their size, the territory they cover but also their history.[3] When describing the governance structure of cooperative banks with respect the connection with the territory, the term "inverse pyramid" is often used. The local chairman of the board becomes a member of the board of the regional structure. And the chairman of the board at the regional level could be elected to the board of the national level. Ultimately, any local member could become the chairman of the board of a large cooperative banking group.

6.3 Models of Governance in Europe

A few studies have been conducted on the governance of cooperative banks in recent years.[4] These studies, mainly descriptive, usually analyze the organization and the governance structure of cooperative banking groups or networks by using (at least) one of these three dimensions: the possible levels of decision-making, the interactions between the levels and the capacity of governance bodies (general assembly and board of directors) to influence management decisions.

The first dimension, that is the identification of the possible levels of decision-making, usually allows to give an initial picture of the diversity of the cooperative governance models in banking on the basis of the geographical organization: local-regional-national, local-national and regional-national. Nevertheless, depending on size of the country or the territory in

[3] Three parts of the cooperative banks' structure are usually identified. First, a local structure. Sometimes there is only one branch or a small number of branches in a town or city district. Local customers become hence local members. The range of decisions upon which they have influence is small but is the starting point for constituting boards locally, regionally and nationally from the general assembly of local members. Second, a regional structure. Some cooperative banks have full autonomy to make decisions at regional level. Depending on the size of the branch network (and sometimes following successive mergers between smaller cooperatives), some groups or networks develop a powerful regional level. Others, on the other hand, have no regional decision-making levels. Finally, a national structure. Under the pressure of regulators but also for purposes of internal transformation in order to better control certain decisions and provide greater coherence in the activity of the entire organization, large cooperative banking groups have today centralized many decisions. Not all cooperative banks have all three decision-making levels. Some do not have a local level, but only a regional and a national level. Others do not have the regional level, but only local and national.

[4] One example is the work of Birchall (2017) on cooperative businesses in the United Kingdom, evaluating governance models in several industries including banking. It raises a number of issues and describes the mode of operation of several banks.

which the bank operates, distinguishing between local and regional dimension is not always easy. A methodology for analyzing this diversity of governance levels was proposed by Deville and Lamarque (2014). Following this methodology, it is first important to evaluate the effectiveness of the decision-making power at each level. To this extent, Fig. 6.1 gives an initial overview on the possible arrangements level-wise.

Such an initial layer of analysis allows for a general understanding on how decisions in cooperative groups can be managed, but it is somehow limited in its explanatory power Hence, the authors added a further layer with the aim to understand when it can be considered that a level has a "limited" or a "significant" influence. This analysis is summarized in Table 6.1.

The second dimension to assess the features of governance structure of cooperative banks, which is indeed strictly linked to the first one, concerns the analysis of the interactions between the different decision-making lev-

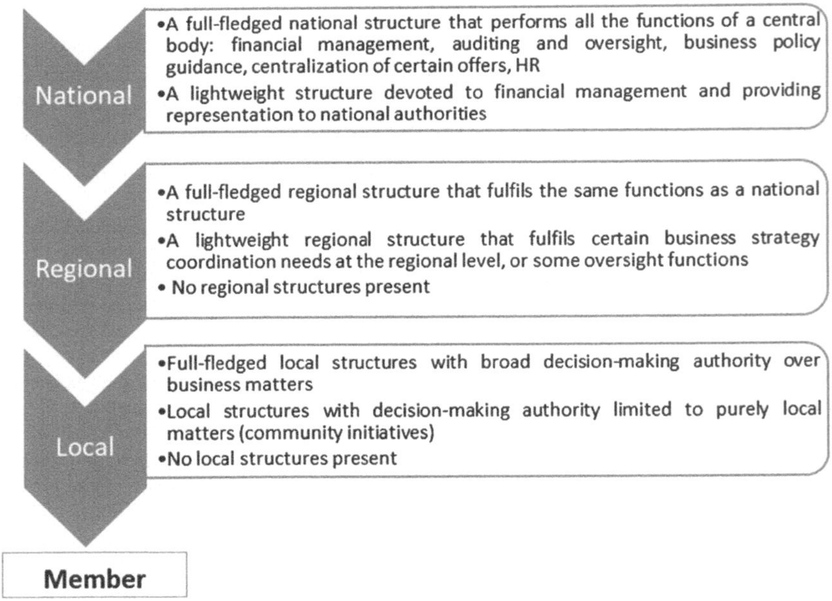

Fig. 6.1 Powers of decision at different levels of governance. Source: Deville and Lamarque (2014)

Table 6.1 Distribution of decision-making authority between levels

	Limited influence	*Significant influence*
National structure	• Only handles oversight of group entities • Organizes the group's solidarity system • Manages liquidity on behalf of branches	In addition to oversight and guaranteeing and managing liquidity: • Defines marketing policy and business objectives for all entities • Names executive managers of regional and local entities and determines the variable share of their compensation • Allocates financial resources to different entities and has full control over the investment policy
Regional or local structure	Cannot take any decisions without approval or outside of the framework established by the national entity	• Defines marketing policy and business objectives for all entities • Names executive managers of regional and local entities and determines the variable share of their compensation • Allocates financial resources to different entities and has full control over the investment policy

Source: Deville and Lamarque (2014)

els. To do that, it is first necessary to identify the type of decisions taken at each level. In this respect, and again following the approach of Deville and Lamarque (2014), four key business areas should be explored: control, human resources, finance and marketing and customer relationship management. In this respect, Table 6.2 shows the type of decisions that may be taken for each business area.

If a level can act only in one area, for example, finance, its authority is hence somehow restricted. If, on the contrary, it can take all the management decisions, its authority has to be considered as relevant. The nature of interactions depends on the degree of real autonomy of regional and local entities with respect to the national structures more than formal arrangements. Even if some local or regional entities may have full autonomy from a legal point of view, things are often more nuanced. The central body usually controls a large number of employees and performs a certain number of functions for the regional entities. For this reason, it tends to exercise a considerable power. As a result, decision-making

Table 6.2 Type and subject of the decisions (excluding risk policy)

	Control	*Human resources*	*Finance*	*Marketing and customer relations management*
Decisions observed	• Formal oversight by a higher authority (audit, inspection) • Oversight by same-level authorities • Reporting to superior levels or other entities from the same level • Comprehensive performance evaluation (customer satisfaction, profitability, productivity, employee turnover) • Existence of benchmarking between local or regional entities	• Recruitment of mid-level managers and employees • Recruitment of senior managers • Financial incentives and bonuses • Disciplinary actions • Definition of individual and group objectives • Training leadership	• Credit risk decisions • Liquidity management • Investment decisions	• Creation of marketing plan • Business decisions (product marketing) • Monitoring customer and member relations

Source: Deville and Lamarque (2014)

authority that sometimes may look relevant (and may often be described as such by those involved at regional and local level), is in reality quite low. As a matter of fact, regional and local entities that truly exercise their decision-making autonomy can do so only if their economic results are solid enough to support their ambitions.[5]

Finally, a third dimension that can be used to analyze the governance of cooperative banks is the capacity of apical governance bodies (general assembly and boards of directors) to influence management decisions. This is a subject of recurring debate in the cooperative sector. The autonomy of managers may be balanced or even overwhelmed by the capacity of governance structures to provide adequate oversight and supervision.

[5] In this respect, the trend among cooperative groups towards centralization and alignment with national structures was visible in a number of countries, including France through the 2000s (Ory et al. 2006).

Nevertheless, consensus is that in cooperative banks the influence of governance and supervisory bodies over managers is relatively weak. Members are elected to the boards more for purposes of political representation than for their skills or knowledge of how banks should be managed. For this reason, they are usually unable to seriously challenge management decisions. This gap in expertise has led elected members to defer decision to managers and avoid too much direct involvement. This is undoubtedly one of the reasons why some cooperative banks have strayed from their roots into financial markets and traditional banking.[6] Recently, however, a growing impact of boards on a number of management decisions can be noted. This increased influence is in particular expected by banking-sector regulators, who want governance structures to not only exercise oversight, but also provide real contributions on major decisions and play an increasingly active role in the definition of risk taking and risk management policies.

By using the three dimensions described to analyze a number of cases in the European cooperative bank sector, three models of governance can be identified[7]: ***centralized governance models***, ***shared decision-making models*** and ***decentralized governance models***. These models are described in Table 6.3.

Such a classification does not cover all the possible existing models, although undoubtedly a large majority. These typologies are in particular helpful in explaining the overall decision-making processes of cooperative banks. In fact, the decision-making influence is not always clearly divided between the levels and final decisions are often the fruit of negotiations and compromises. This phenomenon can be observed in particular in areas such as human resources and marketing. For example, as concerns the implementation of a new approach to customer-relation management, collaboration between the central, local and regional levels has been already observed. In this respect, customer-relation issues are often addressed by forming working groups including branch managers and

[6] Observations have also shown that when elected board members have extensive management experience, they exert a far higher level of influence over managers.

[7] The analytical framework proposed is original and differs from those using legal categories to differentiate between decision-making bodies (such as Di Salvo 2002). To apply it, it is indeed first necessary to analyze decision-making categories more closely and determine how decision-making rights are distributed among the levels.

Table 6.3 Type and subject of the decisions observed (excluding risk policy)

Centralized governance model	A central entity that strongly influences decision-making and is able to exert its authority across all levels over all key group functions (marketing, HR, finance, oversight). In this model, elected members and general assemblies and boards provide assistance in and backing for management decisions made at the regional and local levels.
Shared decision-making model	In this model, decision-making authority appears to be relatively significant at both the national and regional levels. It's a harder model to pin down given that the distribution of decision-making between levels tends to vary from one period to the next. Decisions are often built in common. This model seems to have been more centralized prior to the recession. In recent years regional entities have increased their level of influence on group decisions. Elected assemblies are consulted at the regional and local levels but do not set objectives.
Decentralized governance model	Local and regional entities have significant authority over all key functions. The central body's job is to monitor the performance of local entities, centralize financial data, support implementation of development strategies, and manage liquidity. This model can be broken down into two types, with decision-making authority being concentrated at either the local (large number of small entities) or regional (limited number of regional entities) level. Elected assemblies at the regional and local levels are consulted and may participate in making strategic decisions and defining objectives.

Source: Deville and Lamarque (2014)

representatives from national levels with experience in dealing with these issues. The preferred approach is to develop a unique action plan to be presented to a decision-making authority composed by representatives of all the levels of the organization. The advantage of such approach is that no single entity can impose its vision on the group as a whole. Proposals are structured to appeal to all branches, and the working groups usually avoid designating a single orientation for the entire cooperative group. Even though national entities have an understandable preference for standardized practices, local and regional entities tend to argue that the unique characteristics of the environment in which they operate may justify deviating from standardized proposals. Many observers feel that these working groups spend a considerable amount of time trying to find acceptable solutions that appeal to all branches, while only a handful of proposals end up fully embracing the national framework proposed. National levels understand the futility of trying to impose uniform practices on branches used to a certain degree of autonomy. A great deal of diplomacy is indeed necessary to standardize general practices. In this respect, the challenges encountered by cooperative banks are not so different from those facing major multinationals serving a variety of countries, markets and customers. Nevertheless, the national levels are naturally pushed to enforce a common set of business practices and guidelines to be able to promote a unique identity towards both customers and members. For cooperatives banks, the values inherent to their cooperative status obviously play a key role in the development of these common practices.

6.4 Cooperative Banks and Risk Appetite

Cooperative banks' governance practices often differ according to the nature of the decisions to be taken. Some decisions are taken at local or regional levels with no involvement of national level. Nevertheless, risk-related decisions are largely taken at the national level, with minor adaptations to the local context. This topic is highly regulated and the main tendency is today to centralize the decisions on the level of risk that each entity of a cooperative group can accept. The process of decision-making concerning risk appetite must be clearly defined by the bank and recognized by supervisors. These latter are usually worried about a high degree of autonomy of local branches and have been pushing for many years towards increasing centralization. Hence, the national level will keep playing a crucial role in this area in the next years and it needs to find a complex equilibrium between legal requirements and the ongoing business mainly led by the local branches.

6.4.1 The Specific Place of Risk Governance in Banking

More and more discussions rotate around risk governance in banking, revealing it to be not just a matter for experts in risks analysis and mitigation but a global system and culture that banks must develop and maintain. In particular, the apical governance bodies must adopt a risk appetite framework and define a system of alert with respect to the measures to be taken in case of distress. In this respect, the regulation confers a number of powers to the central organizations of cooperative banks, which stems directly from the applicable directives. In particular, the central organization can:

- Take all necessary steps to ensure the liquidity of the group as well as that of each entity of its network and affiliates and to that effect determine the group's rules of liquidity management (in particular by defining the principles and modalities of the financial management of its constituent entities and the conditions through which the establishments may carry out operations with other credit institutions or investment companies, conduct securitization operations, issue financial instruments or conduct any operation necessary for the management of liquidity).
- Take all necessary steps to ensure the group solvency, especially by implementing mechanisms for internal group solidarity, creating a common guarantee fund and determining its rules of operation (including the modalities of intervention in supplementing funds as well as the contributions of affiliated institutions for its provision and reconstitution).
- Determine the principles and organizational conditions for an internal control mechanism for the group and its network in order to ensure an effective control of the organization as a whole and an effective management of the financial situation of affiliated establishments, particularly by means of on-site controls.
- Determine the policy and principles for risk management as well as the limits for the group and its network and ensure permanent oversight on a consolidated basis.

This predominance of the central level has a clear effect on risk taking and management policies. In general, regulators expect cooperative banks' risk management to be strengthened with a view to improve the decision-making process and ensure effective control over all the entities of the group or network. This implies having an accurate picture of the exposure to risk at the group level.[8] Regulators also expect arrangements for inter-

[8] Several studies link the existence of a risk management arrangement with reduced exposure to risk. See, for example, Aebi et al. (2012), Ellul and Yerramilli (2013).

nal solidarity to be put in place to ensure a proper resolution if one component entity undergoes financial stress. Establishing such mechanisms also has the effect of reinforcing risk governance. In this respect, two principal types of arrangement are currently observable:

- Simple systems of guarantee and solidarity.
- Institutional Protection Schemes (IPS).

A simple system of guarantee and solidarity is in place in some cooperative groups. Its aim is to guarantee the liquidity and solvency of the group and affiliated institutions so as, if need be, to organize the financial solidarity within different groups of entities or brands[9] before looking at overall solidarity between the entities. For example, in the BPCE Group, the central organization is responsible for taking all necessary steps to guarantee solvency for the group as well as for each of the entities or brands. This is done by implementing appropriate internal solidarity mechanisms for the group and creating a guarantee fund common to all the brands (the operational rules, the modalities for releasing supplementary funds, the contributions of affiliated institutions for the provision and reconstitution of the funds are predetermined). All legal entities in a group will come to the aid of beneficiaries in the case of a temporary shortage in liquidity (guarantee of liquidity) or to avoid or manage situations of financial distress (guarantee of solvency). In such a way, the solidarity mechanism is inbuilt in the group and does not constitute a guarantee that can be triggered by a third party (even though supervisory banking authorities might demand the mechanism to be actioned[10]). The main limit of this kind of device is that it cannot benefit from a reduction in prudential requirements, unlike mechanisms such as the Institutional Protection Scheme (IPS).[11] In this respect, it is clear that for the regulator the question ultimately lies in the governance, considering in particular its consequences in terms of reactivity and decision-making in a crisis situation (the organization holding authority).

[9] In many cooperative groups there are several different brands. The entities belonging to the same brand are first solid among themselves before looking for solidarity between the brands and other affiliated entities.

[10] This is in particular the case in France.

[11] For further details on the features of an IPS see Chap. 4.

6.4.2 *Does Risk Appetite Framework Push Really to Centralization?*

In a recent study, Albert and Lamarque (2016) analyzed the effects of the new regulatory context on the governance of large cooperative banking groups in Europe. In more detail, these authors assessed the modalities of definition of the risk appetite and its management at the different levels of the groups. In conformity with prudential regulations, the various groups analyzed had to set up methodologies allowing them to frame their overall appetite for risk. The methodologies were applied on a large scale (all the entities making up the groups) and/or on a consolidated basis. The definition of the appetite for risk was stated according to several leading indicators (LI) covering capitalization and liquidity risk but also, for three of the groups analyzed, profitability risk (earnings volatility). The appetite for risk was thus spread in a granular configuration according to the various kinds of market and credit risks. The operational limits imposed ensured consistency between day-to-day management decisions and management goals. The LI and specific limits constitute, in practice, the risk management strategy. The specific limits apply right up to the consolidated level for three groups, which lead to suppose that they were themselves derived from consolidated leading indicators (CLI). This is in fact the case for three of the groups, which have defined their appetite for risk on a consolidated basis. This supposes a certain degree of centralization or at least of coordination.

In general, the analyses confirmed a growing role for the central body in the definition of the risk appetite; however, its responsibilities can vary enormously from one cooperative group to another. In totally centralized governance models, supervision on a consolidated basis is more than just a starting point for the management cycle and the use of a CLI places the supervision at the heart of a risk management cycle. This management of risk up to group level does not necessarily result in authority over the day-to-day management of local entities. Such authority is observed in one cooperative group only, whose governance is resolutely centralized and whose local units are no longer subject to prudential requirements. Despite the existence of a CLI, a lesser degree of day-to-day authority was also observed in one case. This is also manifested by an absence of hierarchical link between the central unit and the monitoring (and analysis) functions at local level. However, the central unit does have a functional and/or normative authority. The model operated by this kind of groups can be defined as a shared-risk governance model. In one case, the cooperative group maintains clearly more decentralized day-to-day management. Its IPS-type solidarity mechanism explains this finding, with teams that monitor the capitalization of all the units, and a group risk committee. The IPS also ensures the deployment of consistent methodologies at group level. The units are autonomous when it comes to day-to-day strategy and management. This model is effectively decentralized, but not completely because it also implies substantial monitoring from the central body. The role of the IPS can be hence compared to that of a supervisory authority. The existence of an IPS with a defined authority (a capacity for preventive intervention) can be seen as constituting an initial level of centralization, at least for the integration of the management of risks.

6.5 The Governance Bodies of Cooperative Banks

The question of the role of governance, executive directors and executive boards in the internal control system needs to be specifically discussed.[12] This issue is the logical consequence of criticisms made by the authorities about the passivity of governance bodies of cooperative banks when it comes to controlling the risk taking of the banks they supervise. In this respect, in July 2015 the Basel Committee on Banking Supervision (BCBS) published its latest recommendations on the principles of business governance for the banking sector. Among other things, the documents issued by the Basel Committee include a long, non-exhaustive inventory of competencies governance bodies have to cover: capital markets, financial analysis, financial stability, financial reporting, information technologies, strategic planning, risk management, remuneration, regulations, business governance and management. As concerns cooperative banks, cooperative values and social commitment may (should) be added, to name just the most obvious two.[13]

[12] A dissertation of these issues can be found in the work of Karfoul and Lamarque (2009).

[13] In addition to the professionalization of the board members and their collective skills, the functioning of the board is also particularly important. The role of the chairperson is vital to running discussions, organizing members' turns to speak, and respecting everyone's contribution to the debate. Setting up explicit procedures on how things are organized (e.g. agenda, delivery times for the receipt of documents, structure of documents) is naturally part of this work.

The profiling and selection of board members are directly affected by this new regulatory context. This engenders several challenges to the way the board members are recruited. Even the term "recruitment" may seem incongruous, as board members are elected during the shareholders' general meeting (for a bank with share capital) or by members' general assembly (in the case of cooperative banks). Changing the way board members are appointed is not currently under consideration in the cooperative banking sector. However, what clearly appears from these "fit and proper" principles gradually being adopted is that candidates who are proposed for election must fulfill an increasing number of criteria. For cooperative banks, the election of financially experienced board members may be quite problematical. As cooperatives, these banks promote a system that allows clients-members to be elected to governing bodies. In such a system, financial expertise comes second to representation of the members' interests. Therefore, to find candidates who have the required skills and expertise will be an increasing difficult task for cooperative banks. For these banks it is a question of reflecting upon new devices and instruments able to both maintain the specificity of the cooperative model and constitute a board with the required characteristics. All the banks are going to implement training programs for their administrators to maintain and increase the skills base. However, seeing how complex the principles of banking management and associated regulations are, it is not obvious that training will be sufficient.

It is hence not easy for cooperatives to comply with these expectations due to the unique recruitment process of board members, backed by an elective system and not specifically based on individual and collective capabilities. Here again, regulators' concerns may arise about the composition and qualifications of the board members. In regulatory terms, everything converges in the direction of the increase in the level of expertise of the governance bodies, so to enable them to effectively fulfill their function of management decision oversight, challenge them and assume their responsibilities in matters of strategic choices and risk policy. For major cooperative banking groups, recent changes resulted in even stricter supervisory control of the quality of governance and the possible reconsideration of certain administrative appointees. The implementation of the regularly principles has already had consequences, with elected heads of executive boards of cooperative banks that have had to step down from their post.

6.6 The Challenges for the Cooperative Banks' Governance Model Under New Regulatory Provisions

For cooperative banks, a significant evolution in governance principles and methods seems needed to comply with new regulatory requirements. For many supporters of the cooperative model, governance requirements are still considered as threats to the basic principles that shape a cooperative. Our feeling is that the regulators will not modify their policy approach of defining regulations for all banks. In particular, it seems hard to expect a different application of the frequently mentioned principle of proportionality in order to better fit regulation to the cooperatives' unicity in governance. As a result, a strong argument can be made in favor of the idea that without a change in the cooperative banks' governance structures and processes, little room exists for their boards to be fully effective, competent and responsible decision-making bodies.

Leaving aside the issue of gender equality, the question of boards' structure is vital if they are to be in a position to comply with the new obligations and responsibilities. In this respect, it is necessary that the practices of election and appointment of administrators comply with the regulatory provisions and the more specific law governing cooperatives (in addition, the constitution of boards itself is the subject of specific obligations). While the regulators' expectations are logical, they could conflict with cooperative principles. The presence of a "sufficient number" of independent administrators is a first example (in listed companies there is a legal requirement of a minimum of one third of the board members). In this respect, the issue of the effective independence of the administrator is a topic of continuous debate and controversy. Internal codes may already list objective criteria, but they may not be sufficient to ensure the necessary independence of spirit and judgment of board members when it comes to challenge managers. In fact, candidates to board positions are often put forward for election by the executive management during the general assembly, and this can severely harm their independence.[14] As a consequence, the principle of inclusion of independent members in the cooperative banks boards has been substantially rejected by the largest part of the cooperative banks. As cooperative banks boards are composed

[14] Besides, many scientific papers have shown the limits of the independence criterion and there is no obvious relation between the percentage of administrators on a board and the company's level of performance.

of client-members democratically elected at the different levels of their governance structure (local, regional and national),[15] the "genuine" independence of members when selected through democratic process is often used as an argument against the inclusion in the board of members taken from outside the cooperative system. Thus, many cooperative banks consider the status quo perfectly suitable and the renewal of administrators still continues to follow the traditional pattern. Nevertheless, it must be borne in mind that no regulator or expert in governance would consider the board fully independent when observing that all the elected members are customers of the bank. Giving decision-making power to a bank's own clients can of course be seen as a counterweight to manager power, but it may not necessarily reflect the general interest of the cooperative.

The time devoted to tasks and the remuneration of board members are other critical points of attention. These two subjects can be treated together as they are closely linked. Historically speaking, being a board member in a cooperative was akin to volunteering, which presupposes that the concerned individual received no compensation. In the context of cooperative banks, especially those subject to the full regulatory framework because of their size, this voluntary contribution is clearly questionable. The regulations applying to cooperatives often contain specific reminders about the impossibility of offering attendance fees, preferring much lower compensatory allowances. But the involvement in the administration of the bank implies more and more formal consultations, participating to working groups and seminars, as well as reading several hundred pages before meetings. Board members with busy professional lives and skills in different field other than banking can indeed meet the expected regulatory requirements and volunteering. But in such a case, there is a profound contradiction between neutral commitment, the level of expertise requested to board members, their factual involvement and their level of compensation. This is a key dimension in the cooperative model and a sensitive point in terms of governance. The question of board member compensation must be hence raised and must be aligned with the new requirements stemming from regulation.

Finally, a last element of the governance structure of cooperative banks that deserves specific attention is represented by the periodic evaluation of the board members. In this respect, no recognized standards able to take into account the cooperative difference exist. Given the insis-

[15] At times, non-voting members may sit on the board, having been elected by a general assembly (as in the case of Caisses d'Epargne in France).

tence on a proposal for remuneration that effectively matches the time demanded by administration tasks, it can be proposed the implementation of regular evaluation processes rather than waiting for statutory renewal dates before calling the presence of a board member into question. Revocability must not simply be linked to absenteeism or to questions of honorability, but to the reality of an individual's contribution to the work of the board. Defining the profiles and specific skills required will make this evaluation more objective. If we want the chairman of the board to always be considered a responsible leader, if we want boards to be collectively responsible for certain decisions, and if we want to identify the individual responsibility of certain members, a radical change in terms of evaluation should occur.

6.7 Conclusions

The fundamental question cooperative banks must ask themselves is how they want to use their board and governance structure. Are they really strategic for the development and the transformation of the cooperative banking business model? Or are they simply a place to report the feedbacks from customer and members? If the answer to the first question is yes, the governance model must be adapted not only to the requirements of regulators but also to the changes within the banking industry (e.g. digitalization, reputational risk, operational risk) and hence be able to support managers and not just trying to control them. If the answer to the second question is yes, then it is better to leave all decision-making responsibility in the managers' hands and let the boards play a secondary but important role of guarantors of the fundamental principles of a cooperative.

As concluding remark, it is possible to envisage a proposal that aims to guarantee respect for both the basic values of cooperatives and the requirements for the professionalization of the banks' governing bodies. In particular, it can be proposed the creation of a dual governance structure with two types of boards:

- A board of expert members set up along the classic lines of a company in terms of the number of independent members with the profiles and skills required. If ever professional certification for bank administrators became the norm in this sector, there would be no conflict with the rules and principles of its status as a cooperative.

The limits of the board responsibility would be clearly defined in terms of control and the scope of propositions to be made in the domain of strategy, risk management or any other topic defined as its prerogative. It would be necessary to establish clearly the subjects on which it would have definitive decision-making power and those where it would have just a simple power of proposal.

- A cooperative board composed by client-member administrators. This would guarantee that cooperative values and principles are respected before any definitive decisions are made. It would allow client-members' concerns to be taken into account, as boards in their current state already do. The board's role and extent of its powers in decision-making processes would also need to be defined, depending on the topic in question.

Who wrote this contribution believes that such an instrument will ensure respect for both technical demands and cooperative principles and could give governance bodies some genuine weight in decision-making processes, which is the only way to make them really responsible. It cannot be denied that there would be difficulties in the operational implementation of such an instrument, but some experiments implying this double logic and joint participation in decision-making processes already exist. In many cooperative banks there are special committees, besides the board of directors, which are consulted over decisions or associated with them. It has also to be noted that in banks built up around a strong values-based identity, such as Islamic banks, the coexistence of a board of directors and a Sharia board is a reality, with the latter having real controlling powers over the decisions taken. Either way, the time has come to start a real transformation process for governance structure and governance management of cooperative banks.

References

Aebi, V., Sabato, G., & Schmid, M. (2012). Risk Management, Corporate Governance and Bank Performance in the Financial Crisis. *Journal of Banking and Finance, 36*(12), 3213–3226.

Albert, S., & Lamarque, E. (2016). *The Impact of Financial Regulation on Policy and Risk Management in Financial Cooperatives.* Study for the 3rd International Summit on Cooperatives, Quebec.

Birchall, J. (2017). *The Governance of Large Cooperative Businesses.* Manchester, UK: Coop.

Deville, A., & Lamarque, E. (2014). *Identification and Valuation of Cooperative Banking Models*. Study for the 2nd International Summit on Cooperatives, Quebec.

Di Salvo, R. (2002). La Governance des Systèmes Bancaires Mutualistes et Coopératifs en Europe. *Revue d'économie financière, 67*, 165–179.

Ellul, A., & Yerramilli, V. (2013). Stronger Risk Controls, Lower Risk: Evidence from U.S. Bank Holding Companies. *Journal of Finance, 68*(5), 1757–1803.

Karfoul, H., & Lamarque, E. (2009). Gouvernance des Banques et Maîtrise des Risques. *Revue Française de Gouvernance d'Entreprise, 5*.

Ory, J. N., Gurtner, E., & Jaeger, M. (2006). Les Enjeux des Mutations Récentes des Groupes Bancaires Coopératifs Français. *Revue internationale de l'économie, 301*.

CHAPTER 7

The New Paradigm of Digital Proximity for Cooperative Banks

Tiphaine Gorlier, Géraldine Michel, and Valérie Zeitoun

7.1 Introduction: The Banks' Reputation Might Need Working On and Yet a Real Bond Is Actually There

Cooperative banks and proximity: what is at stake? Banking relationships are going digital and characterized by immediacy (remote services, online banking, etc.). In this new relational context, cooperative banks have the ability to stand out in terms of proximity because of their territorial anchorage, unique political model and system of values coming from the social and solidarity economy. However, the attrition of their banking networks, their hybridization and loss of political momentum raise questions: in the digital age, can being cooperative be a strategic relational asset for differentiation with regard to proximity? For this to happen, should cooperative banks move forward a new paradigm of proximity?

T. Gorlier (✉)
IPAG Business School, Paris, France

G. Michel • V. Zeitoun
IAE Université Paris 1 Panthéon-Sorbonne (Sorbonne Business School), Paris, France
e-mail: michel.iae@univ-paris1.fr

M. Migliorelli (ed.), *New Cooperative Banking in Europe*,
https://doi.org/10.1007/978-3-319-93578-2_7

This chapter analyses the interrelations between cooperative bank status and changes in bank client-employee relations in the digital era. In what way and to what extent does digitalizing the client relationship change relations between the client, the bank employee and the bank? How do you build proximity in the digital world? What happens to the very principle of proximity when communication between individuals is interfaced by screens? To answer these questions, we relied on research into proximity in social psychology (Kelley et al. 1983, 2000; Aron et al. 2001) and marketing (Paulssen 2009; Mende and Bolton 2011). Our analysis is also based on the results of two studies. One was conducted using a focus group of ten respondents, clients of French conventional and cooperative banks (Appendix 1). The other was conducted among eight employees of a French cooperative bank through individual interviews (Appendix 2). Based on the above theoretical research and the two empirical studies, we present our conclusions and possible recommendations.

7.2 The Bank-Client Relationship, the Bank's Main Challenge Since Time Immemorial

Banking entails interpersonal relationships. Beyond relational marketing and computing, the bank advisor is the one who provides the service. Proximity is thus first and foremost human (Table 7.1). For cooperative banks, human proximity could be a differentiating factor. Indeed, they have been built on relationships of familiarity, knowledge and trust, with local borrowers. To this end, the advisor must become even more professional, expert and specialized, to provide human added value.

7.2.1 Client Scepticism: Bank Employees Torn on the Fence Between Giving Advice and Financial Objectives

"You've got no choice … All banks are the same …
Either way, you gotta have a bank".
(Bank client)

When addressing the issue of banks among clients or employees, the first thing that stands out is the questions it raises:

Table 7.1 Focus on proximity #1. Definitions

Proximity: what are we talking about?

The concept of proximity is multidimensional: French economists (Gilly and Torre 2000; Rallet and Torre 2004; Bouba-Olga and Grossetti 2008) highlighted two foundational aspects: spatial, reflecting a physical distance, and non-spatial, reflecting a social and economic distance. The non-spatial aspect is essentially relational.

For cooperative banks, the concept of proximity is often used in its spatial aspect. It is geographical in terms of regional development and local anchorage. This aspect is crucial, but just one of many. Moreover, proximity and distance are two different things: proximity is an individual's perception of nearness, according to their own criteria and personal context. Proximity is therefore qualitative and expresses a subjective feeling, whereas distance is quantitative and measured by objective standards (Le Boulch 2001). Proximity is thus both a relational state and a feeling, whose components contribute to building close relationships and processes that lead to assessing the relationship, and thence to a sense of proximity (Laut 1998).

- Clients are very critical of banks. The key factor driving this reputation lies in clients' experience of bank charges as either unjust or unjustified, as well as a sense of no getting around them: "*You've got no choice … All banks are the same … Either way, you gotta have a bank*".
- Employees, on the other hand, find it difficult reconciling the two sides of the job: advice and support on the one hand, and the financial imperative of profitability on the other. So they adopt the rather uneasy stance of justifying their status: "*making people understand that we're not a public service, not free, is complicated*".

And yet, when we examine both stakeholders at greater depth, while the relationship that binds them is indeed contrasted, it is also deep and engaged.

7.2.2 A Rich Relational Context Between Employees and Clients

From as much the client as employee point of view, a bank is seen first of all as a service reflecting a relational dynamic where the human aspect is fully present:

- "*There is a bond, you know, for example I wouldn't say 'I've got an appointment at the bank' but 'with my banker' as if I were talking about my doctor or my boss, so there is a sort of proximity*" (Client).
- "*Sometimes, outside banking, there's life, and I wouldn't wish this on anybody, but in my career I've had to help parents who lost their very young child; mourning like that is terrible, and we have to help out with the forms, the administration … But the human side, the relations, that's very strong*" (Bank employee).

Set alongside a more routine and contemporary context, this relational aspect tends to justify the profession and need for a banker even more (Table 7.2). Since all things change, relations between clients and employees are organized along two axes: rational and emotional. The first refers to the type and content of information exchanged, while the second refers to the proximity felt towards the person spoken to, and how much the other person likes them.

7.2.3 Differentiating Between Banks Is No Longer Solely Relational

From a rational point of view, clients and bank employees have access to information made easy by widely available content. This access, made possible by the arrival of the Internet, has a bilateral impact upon bank client-employee relations:

- On the client side, the information that banks provide allows everybody to be very well informed as to available products and services (particularly interest rates and bank charges). So the factors differen-

Table 7.2 Focus on proximity #2. Human proximity and self-expansion

Human proximity and self-expansion By providing guidance on decisions, the advisor enables their clients to fulfil their goals, strengthening the relationship between them. This is evidenced by the theory of self-expansion (Aron et al. 2001) based on two fundamental premises: (1) individuals are motivated to expand themselves by increasing their potential efficiency and (2) the way to do that is to acquire new and different resources, identities and views within the framework of close relationships (Aron and Aron 1997). An experiment we conducted with 687 respondents indicates that the self-expansion perceived by a client does indeed reinforce his relationships with the bank (Gorlier 2017).

tiating banks are now only a matter of relation. While this may be built up with a manager directly, it can also be the fruit of a pleasant experience with the bank via a digital medium.

- On the employee side, the broadcasting of information tends to generate products and services all more or less aligned with each other: "today, all banks do the same thing". This standardization implies the even greater need to create a relationship with the client to build preference and loyalty.

In today's digital world, the relational aspect has never been so important for consumers. And while it is possible to conduct numerous operations using digital tools, whenever somebody wishes to contact their bank, they expect good quality relations and advice.

> "When the advice you give is more customised,
> the cost that we represent is justified".
> (Bank employee)

From an emotional point of view, the relation with the bank is grasped as one implying a certain degree of mutual familiarity between bank and client. The effect of this entente is to legitimize the transaction, in such a way as the commercial aspect of the communication is acknowledged and seen as normal. Further, it results in mutual recognition of the two stakeholders and enriches the classic banker-client system:

- On the client side, we find them wanting acknowledgement of special situations, of specific needs, conditions and expectations. "*For everyday stuff, we use an online bank, Boursorama, it's great, but I'm not sure whether I could use them for a loan for example ... I think I'd actually need more customized advice*".
- On the employee side, the emphasis is on their capacity to consider a situation in all its complexity. This puts value on the profession and helps them gain professional recognition. And they expect this recognition: "*it's in the relationship that clients come to understand what we provide, our added value*", "*there's no such thing as a good banker who doesn't know his client really well*".

To conclude, the relational challenge is a core issue and seems even more so at a time of information accessible ATAWAD (AnyTime, AnyWhere, AnyDevice) and the emergence of 100 per cent online banks. So the rational difference between banks tends to fade away, and we see products and services aligned upon each other and presumably directly related to this profusion of information which both clients, better informed, and employees, wanting to show that they are competitive, make the most of. At a time of information everywhere, both client and employee seem to tend towards valuing the emotional aspect of their communication, and which thus becomes a bank's prime differentiating factor.

7.3 The Bank-Employee Relationship, a Connection Built on the Individual and Not Institutional Level

7.3.1 *Employees Appreciative of Their Bank*

All the bank employees we interviewed mentioned strong individual relations with their bank. For many, the bank is an institution which trusted them from the start and gave them the means to climb the ladder. So their feedback about the firm was generally positive, highlighting employee involvement within their teams. Nevertheless, although most comments were spontaneously very favourable, we also found that they were more directly related to their experience with the actual teams and branches than the banking institution itself.

- "*I grew up with bank X*".
- "*I'm a bank X baby in the sense that I grew up with them*".
- "*I joined bank X by chance, my mother was a customer and I wanted to work in a bank. I never even thought of bank X, which in my mind wasn't really a bank in those days … My mother spoke about me to her manager, gave him my CV, and a couple of days later I was behind the counter … The older staff trained me and that's where I learned everything … Now, I'm perfectly happy where I am, I could earn more elsewhere, but I'm fine here and I like the place*".
- "*I studied law and wanted to be a lawyer in those days, then when the exams were going on I took over from somebody on maternity leave at bank X and felt good there. I stayed and progressed in the company, I've developed new skills, I've seen some real change, the passage from Franc to Euro … It's a profession that changes every day, and there's real team spirit in this bank, a community, and I've never thought of leaving ever since … It's a bit like a family business …*".

7.3.2 *Contrast Between a Fuzzy Brand Identity and Strong Employee Attachment to Their Cooperative Bank*

There is a deep and genuine appreciation creating an obvious emotional attachment, but when one tries to explore how bank employees perceive the cooperative bank's identity, we come across a distinct difficulty in circumscribing its territory and specifying its character. For example, while there is a relatively clear-cut difference between classic and cooperative banks, pinning down their own identity among the latter is not easy:

- "*Bank X is first and foremost a vanilla bank, a cosy bank, a bit old-fashioned but reassuring, we're reliable*".
- "*Bank X has local roots, that's important … We don't work like international banks, it's a bank that doesn't take big risks, there are no huge ups and downs, that gives us better control and stability*".
- "*When you ask me what difference there is between the various cooperative banks, it's hard … I don't know … Maybe Bank X is more for savers, where other banks might be more 'entrepreneurial' or 'rural'? … But I couldn't really define it for you …*".
- "*There have been changes, growth, but we're still in the process of transforming ourselves, so it's hard to say what Bank X actually is specifically*".

The fuzziness around identity we noted does not make it possible to go beyond personal experience and emotional attachment to a particular branch or professional environment. According to employees, the bank seems to operate according to values similar to those its clients associate with cooperative values (proximity, local engagement), but our observations show that employees found it hard to describe their bank's identity. No matter how much they appreciate their bank, they do not make the connection between their own stories and the bank's own values.

7.4 Digital, a Lever of Competence and Positive Relations

Although online banks are clearly a distinct threat to traditional banks, they are also an opportunity for them to reposition themselves and integrate the digital medium as meaningfully as possible with respect to the market and match their clients' unmet needs as closely as possible. In this

Table 7.3 Focus on proximity #3. Technological proximity and interdependence

Technological proximity and interdependence Technological proximity is all the more important since research in social psychology has shown that frequent, diverse and intense interactions help create a relationship of interdependence. According to the theory of interdependence (Kelley et al. 1983, 2000), the essence of a relationship lies in interaction: two people are close if their interactions reveal they depend on each other for important objectives (Kelley et al. 1983). As part of the experimental study with 687 consumers in the banking sector, research tested the impact of personalized interactivity: the results showed that it increased the perceived interdependence with the bank (Gorlier 2017).

respect, digitality comes over as a platform for heightened competence and generating long-term proximity with its clients (Table 7.3). Across the board, our employee respondents saw three spheres of action and five main areas waiting to be exploited.

7.4.1 *More Streamlined Communication Between Colleagues*

Digitality allows for smoother communication between colleagues, for example, by creating digital client portfolios allowing all the information required to manage them to be entered and kept. This becomes "a living memory", of particular use when transferring portfolios to other parties. Digital platforms make it possible to convey client knowledge from one manager to another, saving time and increasing efficacy but also making it easier to develop client trust in a new manager. On the cooperative bank management level, senior bank executives have supplanted client-members of the bank who were members of the bank board for lacking the relevant legitimate knowledge to assess strategic alternatives in a coordinated way. Technological proximity is a new lever for strengthening the voice and role of these members, and reviewing the political dimension of the cooperative status.

7.4.2 *Greater Efficacy Between Employees and Clients*

Proximity has also become technological. The advanced technological capabilities of banks allow them to meet clients' latest requirements: easy banking, responsiveness, personalized support, bilateral contacts and so on. As physical attendance in bank branches decreases with the increase of remote contact, cooperative banks must incorporate this new proximity into their paradigm.

> "Giving the right answer at the right time is where we score points".
> (Bank employee)

According to employees, digitality enriches client relations in three essential ways:

- Increased responsiveness: digitality is clearly seen as a tool allowing them to deliver fast responses and adapt themselves to their clients' habits and expectations of immediacy. Today's all-round impatience must be satisfied (keeping in tune with the times) and represents an opportunity to valorize service: "*Giving the right answer at the right time is where we score points*".
- Proliferating contacts: digital communication makes client-consultant interaction more regular and thus helps keep the relation more stable and more constant, consolidating the relationship.
- Saving money on low added value communications: the various digital platforms available and particularly the easier management of straightforward transactions save a lot of time allowing employees to optimize their working day for more complex, elaborate and time-consuming issues demanding specific skill sets: "*usually, an ordinary loan today is just an electronic signature on a preformatted form, so it's very simple: all the basic tasks are dealt with, which gives us more time for the trickier questions*". Likewise, digitality frees up time and gives employees more occasions for training and deepening their competence in specific areas, another very good and very useful benefit.

7.4.3 Clients Attributed Greater Value by the Bank

The increased efficacy makes clients more autonomous and allows for better quality communication. Automating routine transactions gives the client "the best of both worlds" halfway between online and traditional banks. Online banking allows for minor transactions where the time saved and smoother transmission of data between employees provides the client with better quality communication with the bank. This results in a richer relationship in terms both rational and emotional and is more positive for both client and employee.

Generally, digitality is perceived as a platform for better quality client contact (proliferation and immediacy of meaningful communication, and automation of low added value interactions) and builds up a more engaging relation of support and partnership (Fig. 7.1, Table 7.4).

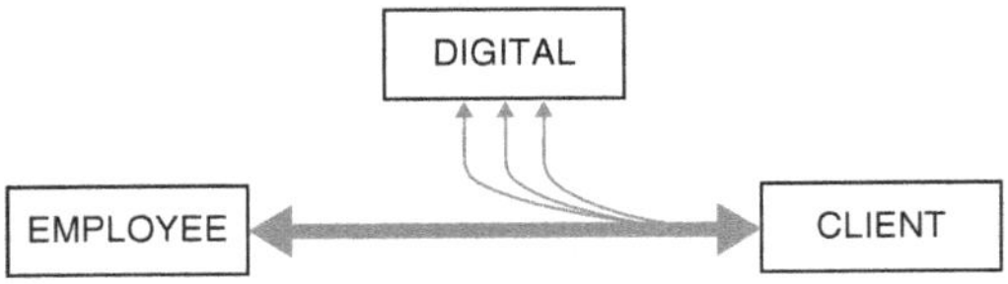

Fig. 7.1 Low added value, automated digital transactions enable better quality relations between clients and employees. Notes: Authors' elaboration

Table 7.4 Focus on proximity #4. Distance by client and attachment styles

Orchestrate the distance by client	Proximity modalities may affect the banking relationships between the cooperative bank and its clients. Technological proximity is a new modality that qualifies time (immediacy in the relationship), reinvents space (connection to location) and transforms transactions (dematerialized flows). Given this, cooperative banks must define a new paradigm of proximity, with their clients' interest at heart. Not all clients have the same expectations in terms of proximity: cooperative banks can be expected to orchestrate the distance according to the real needs of their "members", instead of launching a contact offensive towards all their clients.
Attachment styles and individual preferences for proximity	According to Attachment Theory (Bowlby 1969, 1973, 1980; Ainsworth et al. 1971, 1978), individuals have different relational expectations depending on their particular attachment experiences (Mikulincer and Shaver 2007). These systematic patterns of interpersonal expectations are called attachment styles. Some research has evidenced two main orthogonal dimensions (Brennan et al. 1998; Pierce and Lydon 1998): (1) *Anxiety*, which corresponds to the fear that the partner may not be there in case of need, to an excessive need for approval, to the fear of rejection and abandonment and (2) *Avoidance*, which corresponds to the excessive need to rely on one's self, to the fear of being dependent on others, to the distrust of the partner's caring, to the quest for emotional and cognitive distance. Several marketing studies were conducted in the field of commercial relationships. That by Mende and Bolton in insurance shows that the dimensions of anxiety and avoidance predict preferences for proximity: anxiety correlates positively with the preference for proximity, whereas avoidance correlates negatively with it.

7.5 Cooperative Values, a Similar Vision Between Clients and Employees But Not Rooted in Banks' Own Identities

A cooperative bank's main objective is to be of service to its members, with due respect to the values of accountability, solidarity and democracy. In regard to this main objective, cooperative banks currently suffer from an identity-related vagueness (undifferentiated clientele, similar products and services, risk management like anywhere else, etc.). Their values have been spun-off and often appear as a mere justification or legitimization. Building on a recognized and shared system of values, cooperative banks can create a proximity of values beyond symbolic differentiation. It is not about passing a principle off as reality but providing very tangible evidence: their role in prevention and support, aid in job creation, micro-credit. So the digital medium seems right for strengthening proximity and building positive, lasting relations between clients and employees. Further than this, it represents a major lever in highlighting the specific qualities of banks' cooperative status—a point all the more important in that the notion of "cooperative" has a certain potential, as yet still poorly exploited.

> "You really have to see what's going on,
> so you can actually see that our bank is a cooperative bank".
> (Bank employee)

7.5.1 Cooperative Values Clearly Established in Clients' Minds

From clients' top of mind reactions, the idea of cooperative is immediately associated with cooperative and/or collaborative systems. In this respect, "cooperative" conjures up very positive values: proximity, sharing, solidarity and a form of participatory operation (Fig. 7.2, Table 7.5).

When connected to the banking system, a cooperative seems like an ideal model which partly legitimizes bank costs and, with respect to the banks' reputation, represents a cooperative identity which begs to be rendered credible by concrete, tangible actions.

- "*Part of the idea of the cooperative model is that it's a noble human project. In a sense, it's easier to accept paying if you think it's for the community and that they're not making money off your back!*".

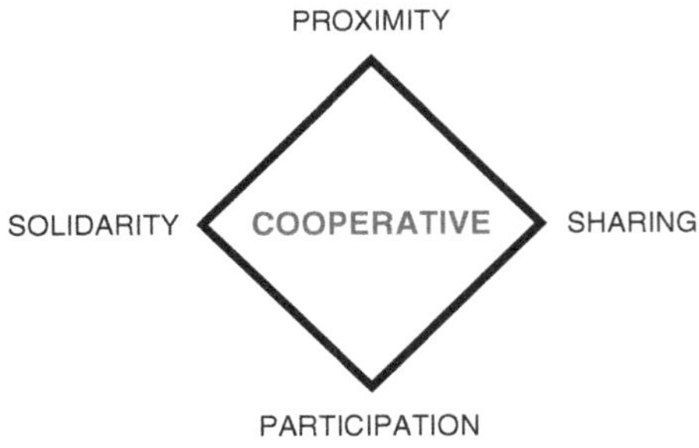

Fig. 7.2 Perceived cooperative values. Notes: Authors' elaboration

Table 7.5 Focus on proximity #5. Proximity of values and similarity

Proximity of values and similarity Studies have shown that a company's social initiatives increase client identification with the company (Marin and Ruiz 2007; Perez 2009). In fact, the identification depends on how much it contributes to self-esteem. In other words, people are more likely to identify with organizations presenting socially desirable qualities because it may help them improve their self-esteem. Getting involved in social initiatives humanizes organizations and allows consumers to identify with them. The perceived parity is a lever for proximity: the similarity-attraction theory (Byrne 1971) and the balance theory (Heider 1958) indicate that people become friends with those who are similar to them. As part of an experimental study with 687 consumers, a study tested the impact of a bank's social and solidarity-based initiatives. The results showed it had a strong influence on the perceived similarity and the strength of the relationship with the bank: when the bank communicated the financial support it provided to social, ecological or cultural projects, clients perceived a greater degree of similarity, reinforcing the bond with the bank (Gorlier 2017).

- *"You must be able to see clearly what is going on, that you have something palpable that tells you that this is a cooperative bank, it mustn't just remain theoretical as it is today … At least, that's what I think!"*.

7.5.2 Employees Not That Convinced by the Meaning of the Word "Cooperative", But Still Proud of the Proximity Established with the Clients

"Cooperative is above all a brand"
"Doesn't mean much to me …"
(Bank employee)

From the employee point of view, while proximity and relationship are core topics to which they are clearly sensitive, astonishingly, the term "cooperative" was mentioned little if at all. Moreover, when put to them, other than territorial anchoring, it conjured up little top-of-mind response.

- "*Cooperative … er … yes … collaborative economy, you mean stuff like that? No, I don't know, doesn't mean much to me …*".
- "*Cooperative is above all a brand*".
- "*For me, it's first and foremost a legal status … yes … Regional anchoring too, which is stronger among cooperative banks like us, it's true we're very much present and active locally, and that's one of our strengths*".

Probing more deeply, although employees do not directly associate it with the idea of cooperative, the cooperative format implies a specific mode of operations and conjures up strong roots from which they derive a certain pride and which they feel resonates directly with their clients.

- "*We're more agile working this way, more flexible, we operate within a smaller perimeter, our action is concentrated in the city … When you support incubators and start-ups, it resonates immediately with your territory, it's a virtuous circle … good for everyone*".
- "*Clients like local action, actions done in the region are meaningful, there's a sort of symmetry of objectives between client and bank*".

7.5.3 A Trilogy: Cooperative-Proximity-Digital

Hence, we observe that proximity, respect, solidarity or even local/regional engagement are values which both clients and employees identify with. At the same time, while clients tend to integrate these values into the notion of cooperative, employees do not. And yet this sense of cooperative is very strong and positive for clients and (if legitimized and made credible by tangible evidence) can represent a genuine factor of differentiation for a bank. It could structure the symbolic space bringing the values of proximity and engagement together for employees and thus form a common, shared rallying point.

It would thus seem that digitality promotes the proximity of employee and client and improves the quality of communication between the two.

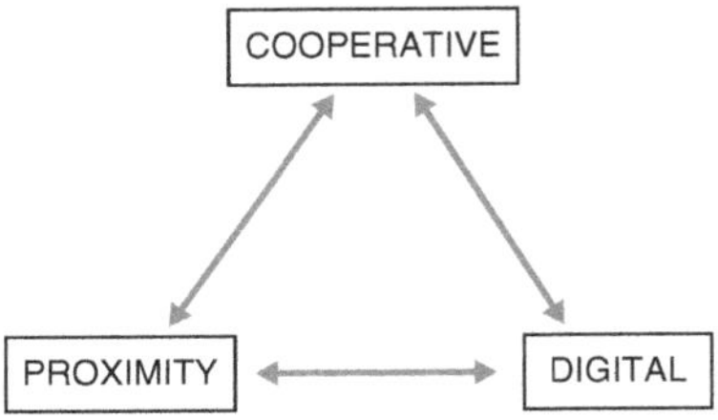

Fig. 7.3 The trilogy. Cooperative, Proximity and Digital. Notes: Authors' elaboration

Moreover, clients picture cooperative values as very much related to proximity, respect, or even local/regional engagement. Although employees do not always make this connection, they still very much share their clients' appeal for these values. It thus transpires quite clearly that, if actually put into practice, a Cooperative, Proximity and Digital trilogy becomes meaningful and has great potential: proximity supported by digitality and both liked and shared by the cooperative identity (Fig. 7.3).

Between the lines of this trilogy, however, there seems to be a weakness. Banks' fuzzy identity does not allow them to get beyond the client-manager relation of proximity and employee-bank recognition. According to employees, the bank clearly acts according to values similar to those its clients associate with cooperative values (proximity, respect, and local engagement), but our empirical studies demonstrate that these values are not part of the brand image but associated with a bank operative or manager. To ensure enduring cooperative values and strong relations between clients and employees, building powerful brands seems to be an essential route for cooperative banks if they wish to differentiate themselves in the consumer's mind.

7.6 Conclusions: Brand, a Lever for Cooperative Banks to Create Enduring Relations with Their Clients

7.6.1 Digitality at the Service of Brand and Cooperative

"I don't need to go anywhere today, I can do ordinary transactions on the internet. Then again, if I'm not sure about anything, or if I need something bigger, I can drop into the bank and talk to my manager".

(Bank client)

Given its advantages from both the client and employee point of view, digitality contributes to proximity by allowing bank employees to concentrate on the clients' needs more and provide them with more customized expertise. So a cooperative bank brand would benefit considerably from what this has to offer, reinforcing its intrinsic values by allowing it to be at the service of each client, customizing as much its relationships as the relevance of its services.

A powerful brand identity is therefore vital:

- For clients so that, over and above their relationship with a manager, they can also engage in a relation with the bank's brand. This client-brand relationship allows for an enduring relationship focused on common values.
- For employees so they feel supported not only by the relationship they build up with their employer over time, but also by the brand values. In-house communication on this would help to create a more objective, more cognitive rather than emotional relationship.

7.6.2 *Brands: Vectors of Meaningful Values*

Branding is a core corporate concern and brands are ubiquitous in our society. They enrich the consumption experience and influence how employees work. Drinking a Coke, taking an Uber, Tweeting, being an IBMer … in a sense, brand is everything! But a brand without value is simply inept. Without values, the meaning it creates trails off, and it loses its distinctive, federating potential (Michel 2017). No values, no brand. Values are essential to rolling out a brand because they are what give sense or meaning, in other words (1) signification, (2) vision and (3) emotion (Berger-Remy and Michel 2015) (Fig. 7.4):

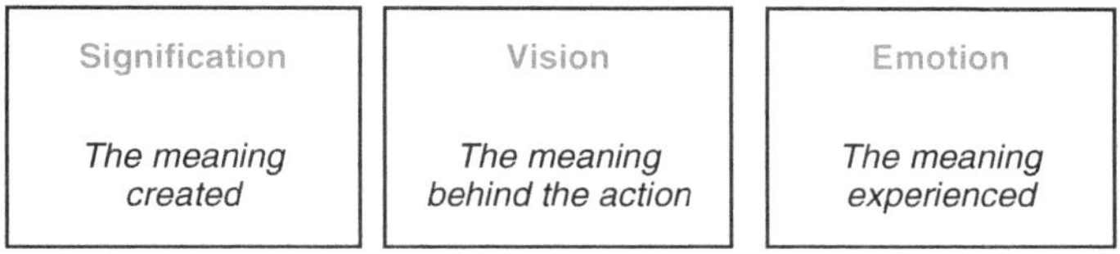

Fig. 7.4 The three aspects of the meaning given by a brand. Notes: Authors' elaboration

1. A brand which conveys values represents a certain ideology and a focal point around which all employees can rally, and contributes to mutual understanding. The brand offering this meaning gives value to both employee and client.
2. The brand provides a meaning to the collective operations and a long-term horizon above and beyond just making a profit. This is all the more true when the brand values are shared by the employees or the clients. It contributes towards company engagement for employees and brand attachment for clients.
3. The brand brings emotion to employees and clients, which could be in the form of brand attachment or identification. When clients ascribe value to the brand, it generates a sense of pride among employees. This explains why it is often easier for a company employee to develop attachment to the commercial brand rather than the corporate brand.

The meaning of brand given to employees and clients is essential to an organization's growth. In banking, cooperative values, which are something both clients and employees appreciate, must be conveyed and expressed by the brands. By adopting cooperative values, a bank brand can create both a difference and uniqueness, and thus federate both clients and employees. We may therefore thus postulate a tetralogy: Cooperative-Digital-Proximity-Brand (Fig. 7.5).

To conclude, both clients and employees project the image of an ideal bank where the efficacy they want hinges directly around the values of honesty and transparency directly related to cooperative values. In this sense, associating cooperative values with a brand can increase clients'

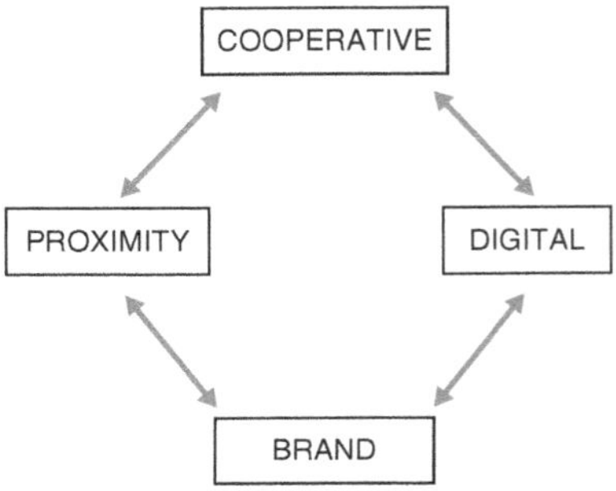

Fig. 7.5 The possible tetralogy. Cooperative-Digital-Proximity-Brand. Notes: Authors' elaboration

perceived value of a bank (driving choice of institution, triggering recognition, and getting away from the impression of having to put up with them). Another result of this is employee pride. At the same time, creating a brand along these lines (strong, unique values) would allow the development of an employer brand which, because of its federating nature and its repercussions on employee rhetoric, could in turn become the rallying signal capable of generating a sense of both engagement and value by its clients.

Appendix 1

Table 7.6 Characteristics of customer sample

Respondents	*Sex*	*Age*	*Occupation*	*Bank*
S1.	Female	37	Architect	Private bank
M1.	Male	28	Engineer	Cooperative bank
J.	Male	44	Fashion retail salesman	Online bank
M2.	Female	41	Secretary	Cooperative bank
C.	Female	29	Nurse	Private bank
L.	Female	33	Legal assistant	Cooperative bank
S2.	Male	37	Sound engineer	Cooperative bank
R.	Male	41	Restaurant manager	Private bank
N.	Female	46	Primary school teacher	Online bank
P.	Male	31	Digital developer	Private bank

Appendix 2

Table 7.7 Characteristics of the employee sample

Respondents	*Sex*	*Professional experience*	*Occupation*
Mr. G	Male	7 years	Financial advisor
Mrs. M	Female	23 years	Branch manager
Mrs. A	Female	30 years	Digital academy director
Mrs. M	Female	18 years	Branch manager
Mr. DM	Male	7 years	Business account manager
Mr. K.	Male	4.5 years	Digital project coordinator
Mr. DH	Male	17 years	Client relation centre
Mr. DM	Male	35 years	Middle office technician

References

Ainsworth, M. D., Bell, S. M., & Stayton, D. J. (1971). Individual Differences in Strange-Situation Behavior of One-Year-Olds. In *The Origins of Human Social Relations* (pp. 17–58). London and New York: Academic Press.

Ainsworth, M. D., Blehar, M. C., Waters, E., & Wall, S. (1978). *Patterns of Attachment: A Psychological Study of the Strange Situation*. Hillsdale, NJ: Erlbaum.

Aron, A., & Aron, E. N. (1997). Self-Expansion Motivation and Including other in the Self. In *Handbook of Personal Relationships* (Vol. 2, pp. 251–270). Hoboken, NJ: John Wiley & Sons Ltd.

Aron, A., Aron, E. N., & Norman, C. (2001). Self-Expansion Model of Motivation and Cognition in Close Relationships and Beyond. In M. Clark & G. Fletcher (Eds.), *Blackwell's Handbook of Social Psychology* (Vol. 2). New York: Wiley.

Berger-Remy, F., & Michel, G. (2015). How Brand Gives Employees Meaning: Towards an Extended View of Brand Equity. *Recherche et Applications en Marketing, 30*(3), 1–25.

Bouba-Olga, O., & Grossetti, M. (2008). Socio-Economie de Proximité. *Revue d'Economie Régionale and Urbaine.*

Bowlby, J. (1969). *Attachment and Loss: Attachment* (Vol. 1). New York: Basic Books.

Bowlby, J. (1973). *Attachment and Loss: Separation* (Vol. 2). New York: Basic Books.

Bowlby, J. (1980). *Attachment and Loss: Loss, Sadness and Depression* (Vol. 3). New York: Basic Books.

Brennan, K. A., Clark, C. L., & Shaver, P. R. (1998). Self-Report Measurement of Adult Romantic Attachment: An Integrative Overview. In *Attachment Theory and Close Relationships* (pp. 46–76). New York: Guilford Press.

Byrne, D. E. (1971). *The Attraction Paradigm*. New York: Academic Press.

Gilly, J.-P., & Torre, A. (2000). *Dynamiques de Proximité*. Paris: L'Harmattan.

Gorlier T. (2017). *Comment Les Marques Créent-Elles de la Proximité? Apport des Théories de l'Expansion de Soi et de l'Attachement*. PhD dissertation, Sorbonne Business School, Université Paris 1 Panthéon-Sorbonne.

Heider, F. (1958). *The Psychology of Interpersonal Relations*. Hove: Psychology Press.

Kelley, H. H., Berscheid, E., Christensen, A., Harvey, J. H., Huston, T. L., & Levinger, G. (1983). *Close Relationships*. New York, NY: Freeman.

Kelley, H. H., Berscheid, E., Christensen, A., Harvey, J. H., Huston, T. L., & Levinger, G. (2000). *Close Relationships*. New York, NY: Percheron.

Le Boulch, G. (2001). *Approche Systémique de la Proximité: Définitions et Discussion*. IIIèmes Journées de la Proximité, Université Paris IX Dauphine.

Laut, J.-L. (1998). Proximité et Commerce: pour l'Eclairage du Concept. *Communication et Langages, 116*, 92–107.
Marin, L., & Ruiz, S. (2007). I Need You Too! Corporate Identity Attractiveness for Consumers and the Role of Social Responsibility. *Journal of Business Ethics, 71*(3), 245–260.
Mende, M., & Bolton, R. N. (2011). Why Attachment Security Matters. *Journal of Service Research, 14*(3), 285–301.
Michel, G. (2017). *Au Cœur de la Marque, les Clés du Management de la Marque* (3rd ed.). Paris: Dunod.
Mikulincer, M., & Shaver, P. R. (2007). *Attachment in Adulthood: Structure, Dynamics, and Change*. New York, NY: Guilford Press.
Paulssen, M. (2009). Attachment Orientations in Business-to-Business Relationships. *Psychology and Marketing, 26*(6), 507–533.
Perez, R. C. (2009). Effects of Perceived Identity Based on Corporate Social Responsibility: The Role of Consumer Identification with the Company. *Corporate Reputation Review, 12*(2), 177–191.
Pierce, T., & Lydon, J. (1998). Priming Relational Schemas: Effects of Contextually Activated and Chronically Accessible Interpersonal Expectations on Responses to a Stressful Event. *Journal of Personality and Social Psychology, 75*, 1441–1448.
Rallet, A., & Torre, A. (2004). Proximité et Localisation. *Economie Rurale, 280*, 25–41.

CHAPTER 8

The Way Forward for Cooperative Banks

Silvio Goglio and Ivana Catturani

8.1 Introduction: Innovation and Cooperative Banks

The cooperative system arises partly as an alternative and partly as a complement to both the private and the public (state and derivative) forms of management. To support its role, the cooperative system should have and propose its own vision of the social and economic structure and of its future evolution. In this perspective, cooperative banks must equip themselves coherently to meet the challenges of global economic and social changes introducing new tools to replace those of the bygone past.

When we mention tools, we do not mean the recent management and financial techniques, initially introduced by financial and banking institutions, both private and public, and simply borrowed by the cooperative world, often under the pressure from national and supranational regulatory authorities. Instead, we refer to the true Schumpeterian innovations, such as new and better solutions (ideas, devices, services or processes) that meet new requirements, unarticulated needs, or existing needs—

S. Goglio (✉) • I. Catturani
University of Trento, Trento, Italy

Euricse, Trento, Italy
e-mail: silvio.goglio@unitn.it

M. Migliorelli (ed.), *New Cooperative Banking in Europe*,
https://doi.org/10.1007/978-3-319-93578-2_8

something original and, as a consequence, new that "breaks into" the market or society. This presupposes having a vision of the capitalist economy, of the dangers and imbalances it creates, of the peculiar role that cooperative finance can play.

In other words, it assumes a clear vision of what the productive and the redistributive orientation and behaviour are and work. Indeed, it is more and more clear that "development" in the capitalistic form, as it has been shaped in recent decades, generates and imposes *stress*, on the natural environment, on the real economy, on society and on the state of knowledge, no longer fully sustainable in a not far away future. In this process, an increasing and distortive role has been played by finance. The problem that the cooperative credit must face is the following: how will cooperative institutions be able to strengthen a finance that favours productive capitalism at the expense of the predatory one, a finance able to protect the nature, the environment, the social and the human capital, the family, and the relational economy from predation?[1]

Innovation should not be confused with simple change. Indeed, innovation is associated with the concept of efficiency, which in turn is linked to a specific objective. For a change to be transformed into innovation, either a product or organization innovation, it needs to affect the existing paradigm. It should be underlined that if the goal is not shared, a change can be innovative only for a group. Cooperative banking introduced a great set of innovations in the beginning of its life at the end of the nineteenth century: not in product, but in principles and social organizations (products were quite simple), and some of them still have a great importance (e.g. the self-help principle and the pyramidal organization). However, some present "innovations", both in products and organizations, look more as cooperative "counter-innovations" that impoverish the original idea. To understand this statement, we should remember that cooperative banks are an alternative in competition with for-profit retail banks not only in product and services development but also as organizations more responsible towards society.

The main innovations (or changes) introduced by cooperative finance in recent years in their organization are exogenous, originating mainly from European and national regulation. The endogenous innovative drive is weak: generalizing, it can be said that today cooperative banks are no longer a driver, but a follower. How many innovators have had the coop-

[1] Predation is the limit case of redistribution.

erative credit after the first two or three decades since its foundation? What substantial changes have been introduced in the cooperative model, from the point of view of governance and of the relationship with the outside world? Lately we are witnessing to the formation of groups, hybrids, and processes of demutualization that have only the purpose of guaranteeing the survival of banks and groups that control them, bringing cooperative banks to the same level as private for-profit banks. If these are the most recent innovations, they are certainly not in the cooperative logic; on the contrary, they are the upsets of this logic and of its *raison d' être*. If this is the direction, the cooperative banks are moving away from the founding principles to homologate either to the private model for profit or to the public/bureaucratic model.

Cooperative finance has therefore slipped from being an innovative solution to a substantially conservative organization of the original model and of its alleged orthodoxy. This process has gone hand in hand with a progressive incapacity to open itself to the outside world, to create areas for connecting ideas (not necessarily orthodox ideas), that is, to create collective and community forms of individual intelligences, which give space to the creation of innovation. Cooperative banking is not a favourable ground to the meeting and the mutual enhancement between different approaches and values, but tends to shut itself into cultural ghettos, when not even territorial ones, opting for a sort of parthenogenesis.

All that has given to organizational structures and governance patterns characterized by a static block of established interests; a corpus of values, assumptions, and norms assimilated and accepted, and no longer challenged, at least formally, although sometimes disregarded; and a thick and rather closed network of personal relationships. The process of questioning such structures has started with the awareness of a part of members and stakeholders, as well of the economic authorities, of the loss of efficiency, due to the difficulty of innovating. This loss of efficiency often goes back to the less recent past but disguised and not evident. It can lead to doubts about the model that is about its assumptions and values, to breakdowns at the level of settled interests, but also to a retrenchment of the leading groups.

In what follows, we will try to read through five issues concerning the cooperative credit by focusing on innovative solutions. The five topics are: (1) members as the centre of the cooperative project, (2) the choice between aggregations and independent small entities, (3) the relationship with the client, (4) digitalization and Fintech, and (5) and the regulation burden.

8.2 Keeping Membership at the Centre of the Project

Cooperative banks can be viewed as financial intermediaries whose main goal is to increase the welfare of their members. According to the so-called "open door" principle, anyone is eligible to become a member, upon the acquisition of at least one share of the cooperative. By becoming a member, an individual establishes a long-term relationship with the bank. This relationship allows on the one hand to acquire the rights deriving from the property of shares and on the other to establish a reciprocal relationship between the bank and the member. The figure of the member is pivotal in a cooperative bank, being the hub of both its governance and its business.

The governance structure of cooperative banks is meant to have members as active players, who should be able to choose the right representatives in the governmental bodies and who should be aware of their power to control it. Property rights influence the governance of the bank through the right to speak and the right to vote at the general meeting. In particular, members vote to elect directors, to set objectives, and to define the strategy of the cooperative bank. In principle, the general assembly, which represents all members as an integrated entity, allows for the collective expression of property rights and ensures fair representation of the interests of all individual members thanks to the principle of "one member–one vote". Differently from shareholders, members are influential for their personal vote and not for the number of shares owned. Despite the democracy guaranteed by this voting mechanism, members may lack inducement to play an active role in the governance. Given their marginal voting power, they may have little incentives to participate in the governance of the cooperative bank, and their incentives even decrease with the number of members. The right to vote incorporates the duty to control the management's work. However, members have little interest in monitoring top managers since they are not individually gaining from their performance. Members may not be aware of the policies adopted or able to understand them. Moreover, the widespread ownership weakens the capacity to make decisions quickly.

Members, therefore, may end up behaving like simple customers, who choose the cooperative bank to obtain personal economic benefits, but who renounce to the involvement deriving from property rights. Moreover, not taking part at the decision process and at the discussion on policies, they disregard the social aspects of being part of a cooperative. More aware of their indirectly controlling power through bank transactions, members disapprove bank's choices by behaving in a similar way to non-member customers. Moreover, they can choose to exercise control through personal contacts with the administrators, trying to influence the chosen policies and consequently the results (Alexopoulos and Goglio 2011). Once again, all this leads to a loss of collegiality in the decisions, the fulcrum of the democratic governance of cooperative banks (Goglio and Catturani 2016).

Also, the business of cooperative banks has members at the core. According to the principle of mutuality, banks as cooperative enterprises are required to carry out their activities mainly in favour of the members, while members as cooperative owners are called to be active as customers in a relationship of reciprocity. The reciprocal knowledge and trust are the base of the so-called relational bank technique, used by cooperative banks to reduce the asymmetry of information to loan money. This is the main source of their differentiation in the banking market. However, as a result of the financial crisis, the new regulation has also imposed cooperative banks to achieve high standards in terms of capitalization and efficiency. The demand for higher performance has in many cases led them to follow similar policies, if not identical, to those of for-profit banks to the detriment of the social structure. As a result, members lose involvement and behave as usual clients, choosing the bank in a utilitarian manner, that is, according to the services offered and their cost. In this way they reduce their level of loyalty, since they do not address exclusively their cooperative bank, whose competitive advantages gets deteriorated. The exclusivity of the mutual relationship between members and cooperative banks is made difficult also by their slowness in shifting to more innovative products. Historically positioned in a more traditional market, while other banks offer the most innovative products, cooperative banks may involuntary push their members towards their competitors: even if not necessarily giving up their membership, members may decide to use their bank only for marginal transactions.

Members are not only bank owners and clients, but also part of a cooperative that is an integral part of the local community. The cooperative bank is regarded by externals as an institution with a social ethic, whose role in the local economy goes beyond the mere credit intermediation. This ethic results in stronger negative reactions once a non-compliant behaviour emerges. In addition to their solidarity within the social structure, both administrators and members should play an active role in spreading the values underlying the cooperative credit among non-members, creating a relationship of trust and reciprocity that strengthens the cooperation among citizens. Mutual knowledge and social bonds, deriving from the network created, would also act as a deterrent in the case of deviation from cooperative behaviour. This is the much-vaunted situation of the peer-to-peer control, which would allow members to activate a form of moral suasion against those who are not paying back the loans. However, due to the increasing corporate size and privacy laws, members cannot have detailed information about the financial status of other members, as they could in the past, and therefore cannot perform this task as controllers. Furthermore, the existence of conflicting interests between members can influence the distortion of this presumed control, negatively affecting the bank's operations.

To conclude, the centrality of the member's role therefore seems to have lost importance as an owner, as core of the business, and as a local co-operator. An innovative push is therefore needed to put the member in the centre again. On the one side, the bank should propose products and services closer to the new needs of clients less traditional and more linked to recent developments, both technological and market, to avoid attracting members only because they are monopolists in a given area. On the other side, it also becomes important to emphasize its role of social mobilizer in the community in which it is established, to create the social fabric that could recreate the humus necessary for the endogenous development of the bank. The member, for his part, as owner of the bank must be able to perform his role as a controller and become aware of his responsibilities.

8.3 Aggregation Versus Many Independent Small Entities

Originally, cooperative banks were born thanks to the initiative of philanthropists influenced by a common ideology. However, the first cooperative banks were single entities, scattered over the territory in a leopard spot, often settled in remote areas, difficultly connected to each other. As soon as they grew in numbers and size, their priority was to create a network that helps them in further developing their business. It was the beginning of the multiplying of various second-level organizations, differently shaped but all intended to sustain the cooperative banks.

In the subsequent evolution, each experience has been articulated in a different way according to the legislation and the historical background of the state. In the same case, cooperative banks centralized the supply of many services and let the single banks with the retailing part—for example, Desjardin. In other cases, cooperative banks joined second-level organizations aimed to promote the cooperative issues as lobby—for example, Italian BCC. A common feature was indeed the need to create networks between banks in order to grow and meet the ever-increasing requests of customers and members, keeping costs competitive. Indeed, one of the thorniest problems that cooperative banks always had to face is the trade-off between efficiency and small size. The incapacity to exceed a minimum organizational structure causes higher operating costs and reduces profit margins: as a consequence, the choice to increase their market power through aggregations or/and the integration in a more articulated system was a forced route.

Aggregations have created slightly larger banks more widespread in the territory and with a more articulated internal structure. This, on the one hand, has allowed the diversification of risks, while on the other it has expanded the social base and the links among members, as expected from a cooperative enterprise. However, even if larger, these banks are still marginal in domestic markets. Aggregations are then a step toward economy of scale and more structured bank allowing the banks to remain independent, but it does not completely solve the problems. To face the competition of commercial banks, a network of second level is required. The integrations can take different forms: (1) horizontal integrations, typically national and regional federations with lobbying tasks, and (2) vertical additions, typically second-tier banks or banking groups.

In a horizontal network, every bank is considered an independent peer. The federations essentially play a policy role and are the privileged interlocutor in central institutions. Cooperative banks, linked by second-level structures, are independent both from the business and the governance point of view. The network should help them in creating a critical mass, which should empower their voice. The strength of this system is the group cohesion, though in reality cooperative banks not always follow logics devoted to mutual cooperation: indeed, often they are in competition with each other on the same local market and the cooperative principle, that would favour cooperation between cooperatives rather than rivalry, gets lost.

In a vertical system, the second-tier bank is more powerful than those at the periphery: it provides services and products that otherwise local banks would not be able to develop efficiently and influences their governance. Moreover, groups are a source of stability for the financial system. However, in most of the cases, the bank at the top does not have a cooperative structure, usually taking the form of a commercial bank, partly owned by affiliated cooperative banks, and decisions are taken according to the "one share-one vote" logic. The affiliated ones therefore waive part of their independence to delegate it at the top. The reduced degree of autonomy is offset by a greater capital availability and more solid guarantees.

The second-level structure has also consequences on the role of members. In particular, vertical integration can create governance problems and disaggregate the social base, since it tends to diminish, or otherwise impoverish, the role of the members in the governance of the bank. Indeed, their rights to property are limited to the first level and they have control only over the financial transactions financed by the cooperative bank. The vote of the members has instead a greater impact on the choice of the local bank's president who might be seated in the board of the top bank. This is ultimately its most impactful governance choice. However, the board of the second-level bank has the power to remove directors in the cooperative banks deemed as non-compliant. A consequence is the reinforcement of the problem of groupthink that is of the pathology of the thought system exhibited by a group that tries to minimize conflicts and reach consensus without an adequate recourse to the analysis, evaluation, and verification of ideas. The groupthink presents itself here in a double role: not only within the board of directors of the second tier but also at the level of individual banks, where the "inconvenient" directors can be replaced.

Can cooperative banking group be still considered cooperative? Do cooperative banks in horizontal networks de facto answer to cooperative principles? Are they administered in a cooperative way? Or is it becoming a mere brand? These questions animate the debate about which the best solutions are nowadays to shape cooperative banks in the banking market.

Currently, in Europe, there are at least 15 "cooperative" banking groups. In choosing between converging in a banking group or remaining independent, an intermediate situation could be configured. Cooperative banks could organize themselves in a network based on collaboration: the network should be aimed to the mutual support and work for the promotion of investments in local development. Those investments should be sustainable at the social, economic, and environmental level. Not just therefore a federation that vehicles lobbying policies, but a cooperative coordination with positive effects on the local economy.

8.4 How to Leverage the Unique Relationship with the Client

Cooperative banks are defined as relationship banks. As often repeated, the relationship represents the major advantage over commercial banks for the lending activity. From a theoretical point of view, the relationship represents a way to reduce the information asymmetry usually present in the relation between clients and members on one side and managers and directors on the other (Alexopoulos et al. 2013). The proximity and the knowledge allow loosening the formal requests for granting loans. The greater the duration and the solidity of this relationship, the greater the possibility of receiving credit using soft information to fill the information gap.

However, lending on the base of a personal link with clients is not just a prerogative of cooperative banks, but it is a characteristic of local banks, of which cooperative banks are just one type. The peculiarity of cooperative banks lies in its ownership structure: besides the direct acquaintance with the bank management due to proximity, the client can also choose to join the ownership of the bank. This choice should define a long-term relationship, more solid and deeper, characterized by reciprocity and mutualism. On the one hand, the member is called on to use the cooperative as its preeminent financial intermediary; on the other hand, bank should devote all its effort to meet member's financial need not having profit as its goal. The uniqueness of this relationship, therefore different from that of other local banks, should increase the comparative advantage in defining the risk profile of members.

By combining the social constraints deriving from localism with the responsibility towards the membership (i.e. the power to vote and control the governance), the ability to further reduce the information asymmetry and to mobilize local savings has enabled cooperative banks to re-establish and even strengthen the trust in the banking system, when this was strongly threatened by the recent crisis. However, the possibility of providing credit on a relational basis is currently challenged by the new techniques for granting loans and by the regulation on privacy that limits the sharing of information. At the same time, cooperative banks are undergoing a standardization process in this field, and credit decisions are made according to undifferentiated techniques, for which cooperative banks do not always have much experience and know-how. Moreover, the expansion of the company structure and its greater diversification worsens the credit risk associated with the weakening of the relationship banking technique.

The credit loan on a relational basis is not detached by dangers in addition to usual risks. The bank runs the risk of being captured by the relationship established with the client, especially when this last has an economic weight in the local area. For example, the bank may decide to keep the credit line open even if the customer is in default because its possible bankruptcy would imply a loss for both the credit institution and the local economy. This situation reshapes the democratic principle: though members have the same voting power, they are differently weighted in lending. A company able to capture the bank will absorb the resources of the cooperative influencing the future investing decisions of the bank.

According to some researchers, among the members of the cooperative bank there would be a further form of relationship, for which mutual knowledge would reduce the risk of insolvency through peer review. The knowledge among members who live in the same territory and who are often included in the same economic and social context should decrease the risk of opportunistic behaviour, while increasing a feeling of fear for the loss of reputation due to non-repayment of the credit. This link among members, based on control and reporting of possible deviations, is not necessarily virtuous and can conceal private interests and ends that are not positive on a collective level.

In conclusion, the characteristic of being a relational bank does not derive so much from the fact that loans are granted in less formal ways than other banks, but from the fact that the bank is able to create relationships in the territory that support virtuous development processes. The ability to read beyond numbers, which is the actual credit repayment possibilities, should represent a way to diversify the banking offer, especially during times of crisis, by providing a tool for the financing of companies otherwise excluded because of the credit crunch. The relationship based on mutual knowledge, in order to be effective, needs to be included in a clear strategic vision of what are opportunities and constraints of the territory. A development policy and the ability to drive the investment choices are necessary for the bank to act as a promoter of social changes.

This would allow cooperative banks to become true relational banks, capable of encouraging the creation of virtuous networks between members, relationships other than mere peer-to-peer that, on the contrary, creates a climate of mistrust and antagonism.

8.5 Cooperative Banks, Digitalization, and Fintech

In recent years, one of the major innovations in the financial field takes the name of Fintech, or Financial Technology, namely "the application of technology to the delivery of financing, payment, investment and consulting services" (Banca d'Italia 2018). Fintech is radically changing the credit market, payment services, and technologies that support banking and financial supplies. It has automated insurance, trading, and risk management. Thanks to the almost free access to the internet, the proliferation of clients and new agents has been fast and wide. The players in this new market are many and with very different characteristics: from the most informal technology start-ups to the "giants" of information technology and social media. This new concept of the credit market opens up new channels of supply, channels that allow the interconnection of dataset and subsequently a substantial reduction in costs, a higher level of inclusion and a highly customized quality of services.

Fintech calls into question the dichotomy between soft and hard information in the reduction of information asymmetry. This new way of making credit, without a bank structure behind it, bases its loans on information coming from big data. Big data includes unstructured, semi-structured, and structured data and its "size" is constantly moving. Five Vs are associated with big data: (1) Volume, that is, the quantity of data not only generated but, most importantly, stored; (2) Variety, since those data do not only include numbers but text, images, audio, and video, and they allow to complete missing parts through data match; (3) Velocity, big data are generated and immediately shared and available in real time; (4) Veracity, given the velocity and the variety of the data creation, it is difficult to guarantee their quality and reliability; and (5) Value, meaning the possibility to transform those data in business. Data are collected and sold without personal or direct knowledge between the source and the final user. However, their details are possibly deeper compared to those supply in personal relationship. Table 8.1 compares big data information and relationship knowledge towards the 5 Vs.

Table 8.1 Big data information and relationship knowledge towards the five Vs

	Big data	*Relationship knowledge*
Volume	Potentially limited only by the possibility to store	Limited by the capacity of people to know each other
Variety	Numbers, text, audio, video—codified by algorithms: objective and easy to share	Attending various aspects of life—collected through personal experience: subjective and difficult to replicate
Velocity	Generated, stored, and shared simultaneously	Slow to be collected
Veracity	Can be verified by the match with other data	Every subject can let people know what he/she wants
Value	Large market of firms interested	Difficult to trade

Notes: Authors' elaboration

Thanks to the use of computer channels and impersonal algorithms, the information collected is objective and standardized. Consumers provide their data surfing in the net, not always conscious of it. However, differently from soft information, those data are collected by machines and not by the interaction between humans. They are not based on personal experience and they can narrow unexpressed knowledge that might be otherwise inferred when the knowledge is personal.

Fintech revolutionizes the concept of relational credit. Proximity becomes virtual and no longer physical; the level of knowledge is no longer based on the direct relationship between bank and customers but on direct and indirect information obtained from the Internet. In some cases, it is possible to have a convergence in terms of business between borrower and lender, which further reduces the asymmetry information. In some countries, however, the development of Fintech is slowed by constraints linked to the high costs of investments whose profits are uncertain. Not only the Fintech market is still under development and its demand is not yet mature enough, but the future evolution of the regulatory framework is uncertainty (Banca d'Italia 2017), even because Fintech channels are more difficult to regulate, given their transnational nature. Finally, the recent scandals due to the lack of confidentiality in the treatment of personal date are negatively affecting the trust in social media companies.

Though Fintech is seen as more inclusive than the traditional banking market, it is not encompassing. Internet is yet a service used by a certain group of people in certain countries. Elderly and poor people have still difficulties in getting online and in having access to financial services. For similar reasons, cooperative banks were born. Nowadays they can help people banished by the Fintech market, finding their new *raison d' être* by going back to their original goal.

8.6 How to Limit the Regulatory Burden

Following the financial crisis of 2007, the advance of banking regulation has been substantial. Since 2014 more than 40 legislative acts have been derived from the Banking Union and the various legislative sources. These acts have not had a harmonious development within a specific plan defined on the basis of impact studies. Each new regulation has simply been added to the previous one (Hofmann 2016). In some cases, the new legislation has outlined scenarios considered unpredictable until a few years before. However, the result has been a regulation aimed at responding mainly to the needs of major banks, following the "too-big-too-fail" view. This proliferation of rules and controls, particularly complex, turned out asymmetric and penalizing for small and cooperative banks, whose work has been further burdened (Alessandrini et al. 2016) and gave rise to a clash between the need for a heterogeneous system of banks clashes and the "too-small-to-survive" vision.

The interpretation of this phase of legislative interventions seems to converge on the will to make local and cooperative financial institutions increasingly similar to the *modus operandi* of big banks, despite the greater responsibility of these latter in the instability of the financial system. Indeed, the financial crisis originated not from smallest intermediaries, but from the largest ones. Local banks mostly experienced deterioration in their performance once the crisis moved from the financial to the so-called real economy. The growth of their non-performing loans is due to the negative economic situation, to the overly optimistic assessment of credit risk, to an inadequate level of collaterals, and to criticisable behaviour of management. The new regulatory constraints, increasing compliance costs, have affected their ability to create profit, already engendered by the erosion of margins. All together these events have led to a low level of profitability, which has worsened the cost-income ratio.

Also the relationships with customers are affected by this disparity, since small banks, failing to exploit economies of scale, must increase the cost of their intermediation services, burdening in this way local businesses, unable to find alternative sources of credit. The adoption of a system of rules that penalizes the supply of credit from small banks to encourage commercial banks is then not only inadequate, but also distortive (Alessandrini et al. 2016). The lack of availability of local credit will lead to disparities between regions in terms of development. Moreover, different banks can value the creditworthiness differently and enforce disparities. On the contrary, the presence of heterogeneous actors could represent a resource to avoid idiosyncratic risks in periods of turbulence.

The introduction of the principle of proportionality, based on the assumption that "one size does not fit all", intends to apply less strict requirements to the banks of smaller size and operational complexity. It seeks to mitigate the asymmetry in the legislative burden that affects most of the smallest banks. However, as recommended at present, it does not seem to alleviate the fate of these banks. The demand for precise figures to oversee certain functions, that is, employees who can only do specific functions, like the compliance officer or the risk manager, and are required in each bank regardless its size, has in fact imposed aggregation policies to reduce the fixed costs. The dimensional growth has therefore not been determined exclusively by market logic, but by legislative choices. In this perspective, Alessandrini et al. (2016) propose a dual regulatory system to achieve the result of a symmetrical distribution among regulatory constraints, a road to which the United States has already moved.

The search for a balance between regulation and market liberalization should pursue the objective of safeguard and solidity of the credit market, trying to follow not so much a principle of proportionality, but rather of reasonableness. It is not a question of defining mathematical relations between banks, where the minimum unit of measurement is still difficult to delineate and does not define a subunit of large banking groups, as the proportionality suggests. These are different realities that pursue different goals. Reasonableness, on the other hand, should lead to consider the peculiarities of cooperative banks, both as local and not for-profit intermediaries and as a promoter of a sustainable development.

8.7 Conclusions

An advanced economy needs capitals, that is, some form of capitalism, just as it needs markets and financial operators to allocate savings among the various purposes. At the same time, a truly productive economy and finance should be responsible, that is, concerned about the consequences, that is, the externalities, both negative and positive, not only immediate, but in the long term, of their activities.

However, the current capitalist phase contradicts these assumptions. First of all, it is unbalanced on the financial side: capital allocation systems have progressively moved away from the real economy and are no longer performing effectively and efficiently their function. Finance has become progressively disinterested in its real and long-term value, when it has not started to bet against it. The growing separation between the prices of financial assets and the source of the underlying value has increased market risks: the higher the separation, the more difficult it is for markets to act in a morally responsible way. In short, financial capitalism is at the service of itself and not of value production[2]; financial systems are increasingly oriented towards redistributive goals, when not explicitly predatory (Goglio 1998; Birchall 2017; Goglio and Catturani 2017). Higher responsibility and transparency are required. By a general point of view, finance must compete to create value, not just take a non-produced value; at a lower level, banks must look for profitability in really productive realities, instead of applying margins on relatively trivial and often passive transactions. Secondly and more generally, together with the degeneration of finance, the world of the economy has shown a growing rapacity towards the other components of the human environment (the natural, social, family, political, cultural world), directing and exploiting them for their own purposes.

We can however make out in recent times signs of inversion to this trend: there is indeed a growing interest in more friendly production sectors towards other systems, such as health and prevention, green economy, education, and culture, with a growing importance of relationship-oriented services. These changes, combined with demographic changes and the state's fiscal crisis, can lead to a revaluation of the localized production and of the domestic and community dimensions as places of economic activity.[3] In general, it is emerging an economy based more on relationships than on physical products, on the prevention and the maintenance, requiring investments in health and healthcare, online assistance, green industry, environmental protection, and property. This focus on the production and marketing of specific processes related to the life cycle or to the use of a specific service constitutes a more apparent than substantial

[2] It can be said that the current capitalist phase has reversed the relationship between finance and production.

[3] Obviously these are not exclusive dimensions.

change, since the material economy has always been supported, even if not explicitly admitting it, on a relational economy (see Mulgan 2013).

The connection between economy based on relationships and cooperative economy is tight, since the origins of this last. However, during the twentieth century, governments and large private companies have often supplanted in this sector organizations with social participation, often accused, not always wrongly, of paternalism, non-professionalism or bureaucratization. Moreover, the growth of dimension may undermine their values, dedication, and sense of belonging of the members. These are the problems and accusations that cooperative banks are still facing and which are partly reflected in the ongoing reforms, not always voluntary, of the cooperative credit in some European countries.

A credible answer to these accusations and the renewal of the cooperative credit must therefore go through the promotion of an economy where the value derives mainly from relationships. This entails a new conception and a redesign of finance, where negative and positive externalities are included in the estimate of produced value, favouring social value and surplus with respect to a private one.[4] Practically, this means to finance, besides technological innovation, also social innovation—that is, new solutions that are more responsible and sustainable. The cooperative credit must therefore aim to strengthen the relationship between supply and demand for capital, overcoming the separation between investors and recipients that has been growing over the last decades. Investors should have more knowledge of specific investment fields: the more funds are aggregated by investment banks and global funds, the more it will be difficult for investors to become aware of and to be willing to risk on innovative and socially relevant projects. The ambition should be to channel capital to creativity and to utility calculated in a non-traditional way: finance must return to being "at the service" and not master. Hence, the need to spread ownership and control of financial capital and not to concentrate them.[5]

A new vision of value that takes into account the relational aspects should also give greater consideration to the value of time as a substitute for money as a unit of measure of the value itself, by setting up banks of

[4] In other words, it means to be aware of the existence of external costs and benefits, given by the difference between social costs and benefits and private ones.

[5] It is significant that very few of the recent financial innovations are aimed at the less well off.

time. Furthermore, it should consider not only efficiency in production but also in consumption—the so-called consumptivity, that is, the difference between social benefit and cost of consumption. In other words, it should be encouraged the consumption with greater productivity: for example, normally high-end consumption tends to be the least efficient, since the marginal benefit of consumption decreases with the increase in the consumption band, the absolute increase being less than proportional (see Mulgan 2013).

This work of reengineering cooperative finance requires some choices and implementations within it that clearly signal (1) what are its objectives, consequent to the evaluation of what is productive and what is predatory; (2) what are its true stakeholders; (3) what is its most appropriate form of governance and what is the selection process of its managers.

References

Alessandrini, P., Fratianni, M., Papi, L., & Zazzaro, A. (2016). *The Asymmetric Burden of Regulation: Will Local Banks Survive?* Mofir Working Paper, 125.

Alexopoulos, Y., & Goglio, S. (2011). Financial Cooperatives: Problems and Challenges in the Post-Crisis Era. *Journal of Rural Cooperation, 39*(1), 35–48.

Alexopoulos, Y., Catturani, I., & Goglio, S. (2013). Searching for a Model of Governance in Cooperative Banking. In J. Brazda, M. Dellinger, and D. Rößl (a cura di) (Ed.), *"Genossenschaften im Fokus einer neuen Wirtschaftspolitik Bericht der XVII", Internationalen Genossenschaftswissenschaftlichen Tagung (IGT) 2012 in Wien* (pp. 707–731). Im Auftrag der Arbeitsgemeinschaft Genossenschaftswissenschaftlicher Institute (AGI). Wien, Austria: Forschung und Wissenschaft.

Banca d'Italia. (2017). *Fintech In Italia. Indagine conoscitiva sull'adozione delle innovazioni tecnologiche applicate ai servizi finanziari.* Roma: Banca d'Italia.

Banca d'Italia. (2018). *Canale FinTech.* Banca d'Italia, URL consultato il 26 febbraio 2018.

Birchall, J. (2017). *Co-operation as Co-ordination Mechanism and Co-operative Governance.* Presented at EURICSE International Workshop on "Co-operation as Coordination Mechanism: Consequences on the Interpretation of the Cooperative Enterprise", Trento, 4–5 December 2017.

Goglio, S. (1998). Sistemi Locali, Nazione Economica e Nazione Politica. *Sviluppo locale, 8*, 47–74.

Goglio, S., & Catturani, I. (2016). Cooperazione di Credito. *Cooperazione Di Credito, 218–219*, 161–189.

Goglio, S., & Catturani, I. (2017). *Local Public Goods and Social Entrepreneurship*. Presented at Euricse International Workshop on Co-operation as Coordination Mechanism: Consequences on the Interpretation of the Cooperative Enterprise", Trento, 4–5 December 2017.

Hofmann, G. (2016). *Challenges and Opportunities for Co-operative Banks in a World of Change*. XV National Congress of Credito Cooperativo, 15th May 2016, Milan.

Mulgan, G. (2013). *The Locust and the Bee. Predators and Creators in Capitalism's Future*. Princeton: Princeton University Press.

CHAPTER 9

The Cooperative Banks Today in the EU Perspective

Giorgio Caselli

9.1 Introduction

A week before Northern Rock sought emergency funding from the Bank of England, prompting the first bank run in more than a century, American biologist Edward O. Wilson wrote an editorial for *The New York Times* in which he claimed:

> *[E]ach species […] is a masterpiece of evolution. Each has persisted […]. And each is exquisitely adapted to its environment and interlocks with a legion of other species to form the ecosystems upon which our own lives ultimately depend. We need to properly explore […] biodiversity if we are to understand, preserve and manage it.*

Similar to living organisms, banks and other types of financial institutions interact with each other and with the environment in which they are located. The outcomes of these interactions have an impact on their behaviour, profitability and ultimate survival (Baschieri et al. 2015). If we were to make a parallel between financial and natural ecosystems, we could

G. Caselli (✉)
University of Cambridge, Cambridge, UK
e-mail: g.caselli@cbr.cam.ac.uk

M. Migliorelli (ed.), *New Cooperative Banking in Europe*,
https://doi.org/10.1007/978-3-319-93578-2_9

argue that cooperative banks, alongside other forms of financial institutions such as commercial and savings banks, constitute a major component of the financial ecosystem. By virtue of their differences in ownership structures, business models and corporate objectives, cooperative banks vis-à-vis commercial and savings banks contribute to (bio)diversity in banking (Llewellyn 2017).

The aim of this chapter is to shed new light on the benefits that may result from a plurality of ownership types in the banking sector. To this purpose, it sets out to examine the contribution of cooperative banks to diversity in banking, to highlight differences in the degree of diversity across the major EU countries as well as over time and to identify some of the main challenges that the current competitive environment may pose to the cooperative banking model. It is hoped that the results discussed in this chapter will stimulate further interest on the part of researchers, practitioners and policymakers alike in the implications that diversity of ownership structures, business models and corporate objectives in banking may have for a range of financial, economic and social outcomes.

The remainder of this chapter is structured as follows. The next section explains in greater detail the meaning of diversity in the banking sector and offers a comparison of the degree of diversity characterising the banking sectors in 15 EU countries. It also presents an analysis of the macroeconomic impact of banking diversity during the periods before and after the onset of the global financial crisis. Specific attention is devoted to the implications of diversity for financial stability and access to credit. Section 9.3 reviews the main features of the current banking regulatory framework in the EU and identifies some of the challenges that a 'one-size-fits-all' approach may raise for smaller and less complex institutions like most cooperative banks in Europe. The principle of proportionality and its application to EU banking regulation is also discussed, along with some suggestions on how this principle could be strengthened further. Section 9.4 elucidates the value that diversity in the banking sector has for the European society. In doing so, it reviews the implications that some of the recent changes in the competitive environment within which cooperative banks operate may have for key concepts such as membership, mutuality and territoriality. The final section summarises the main arguments that are made in this chapter and concludes.

9.2 Cooperative Banks and Diversity in Banking

Among the central features of cooperative banks is that they strive to generate value for a larger array of stakeholders rather than almost exclusively for shareholders (Ferri et al. 2014). Whilst commercial banks have maximisation of shareholder wealth as their principal objective, cooperative banks tend to place stakeholder value creation at the core of their activities. A key characteristic of cooperative banks, which differentiates them from shareholder-oriented banks and other stakeholder-oriented institutions such as savings banks, is that they are owned by their members, who are entitled to only one vote and their stakes are generally not marketable. Since distribution of profits is limited, it is unlikely that the property right structure of cooperative banks will lead to profit-maximising behaviour (Amess 2002). Similar to cooperatives, savings banks operate according to a 'double bottom line', that is, a dual financial and social mission to serve the local economy in which they are embedded (Ayadi et al. 2009). At the same time, savings banks differ from cooperative institutions in that they are not owned by members, but either by a private foundation or by an organisation that belongs to the government.

The debate over the contribution of cooperatives to diversity in banking has received somewhat considerable attention most recently in a number of EU countries, where cooperative banks find themselves competing with a large and heterogeneous set of financial institutions. A case in point are countries such as Germany and Austria, in which customer-owned cooperatives and not-for-profit savings banks well exceed in number their commercial counterparts.

Figure 9.1 shows the distribution of market shares by ownership type on the loan side of banks' balance sheets in each of the 15 countries that joined the EU prior to the 2004 accession (i.e. Austria, Belgium, Denmark, Finland, France, Germany, Greece, Ireland, Italy, Luxembourg, the Netherlands, Portugal, Spain, Sweden and the UK).[1] Among the EU-15 countries, the largest market shares of cooperative banks are observed in France (39.93%) and Finland (35.58%), followed by other countries such as Austria (29.49%) and the Netherlands (22.33%). Conversely, the

[1] The values reported in Fig. 9.1 refer to average market shares over the 1999–2013 period. Loans are computed as residential mortgage loans, other mortgage loans, other retail loans, business loans and other loans (minus loan loss reserves). EA-12 are the founding euro area member countries, namely Austria, Belgium, Finland, France, Germany, Greece, Ireland, Italy, Luxembourg, the Netherlands, Portugal and Spain.

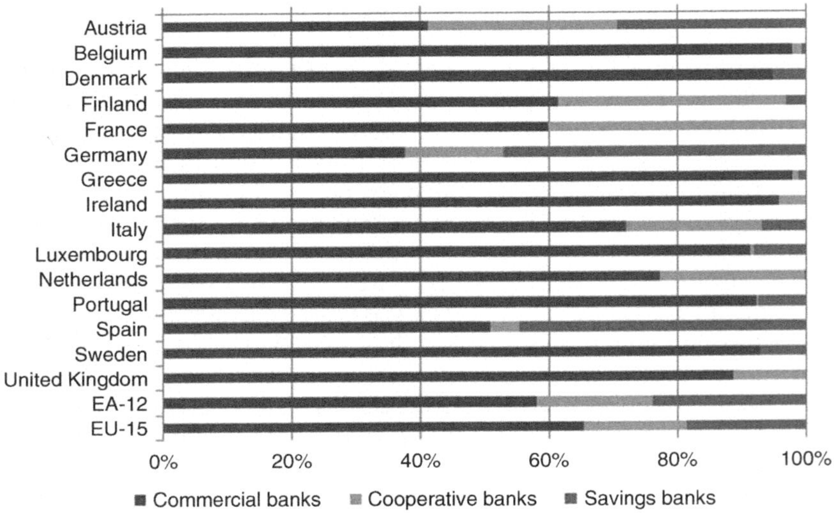

Fig. 9.1 Market share of loans by country and ownership type. Average 1999–2013. Source: Author's calculation on data Bankscope

cooperative banking sector has limited market shares in Spain (4.53%) and Belgium (1.51%), while it is virtually non-existent in Greece (0.96%) and Sweden (0.01%). Countries where commercial banks dominate the loan market are Belgium (97.96%), Greece (97.93%) and Ireland (95.76%), while savings banks have their largest presence in Germany (47.02%).[2] It is also worth noting that shares on the loan side of the market are spread more evenly across ownership types in Austria and Germany, whereas they tend to be more concentrated in one of the three ownership groups (namely commercial banks) in countries such as Luxembourg and the UK. Interestingly, the average market shares of both cooperative and savings banks are higher if countries outside the eurozone (i.e. Denmark, Sweden and the UK) are not included in the sample (18.11% versus 15.98%, respectively, if cooperative banks are concerned).

[2] The list of savings banks in Germany includes state-owned *Landesbanken*.

9.2.1 *Measuring Diversity in the Banking Sector*

A first attempt to quantify diversity in the banking sector is advanced by Michie and Oughton (2013), who introduce a measure, the 'D-Index', resulting from the combination of sub-indicators across four main dimensions:

- Corporate diversity: this sub-indicator, which is based on the Gini-Simpson index of biodiversity, quantifies the extent to which financial institutions of different ownership types (i.e. commercial banks, mutual building societies and government-owned National Savings and Investments, NS&Is) coexist within the financial system. A single indicator of corporate diversity is obtained by taking into account the number of corporate forms as well as their corresponding market shares, calculated with respect to either retail deposits or mortgages.
- Market competition: based on the Herfindahl-Hirschman index of market concentration, this measure captures the degree of competition that exists in the industry. For computational purposes, the inverse of the Herfindahl-Hirschman index for the retail deposit and mortgage markets is considered.
- Balance sheet structure and resilience: this component aims to describe differences in funding models adopted by financial institutions. To this end, it takes the funding gap, that is, the ratio of the difference between loans and deposits to total loans, as the point of departure and derives an index of funding model diversity.
- Geographic spread: as a measure of the geographical dispersion of the financial services industry, this sub-indicator estimates the distance (weighted by market share) of the institutions' headquarters from the City of London.

Michie and Oughton (2013) use their D-Index to assess how diversity in the UK retail deposit and mortgage markets has changed during the period between 2000 and 2011. They find that diversity on both the deposit and mortgage sides of financial institutions' balance sheets deteriorated substantially in the run-up to the global financial crisis. This trend was followed by an even higher decline during the crisis years, while diversity in the UK financial services sector has remained somewhat stable since 2009.

Drawing on the seminal work by Michie and Oughton (2013), this chapter sets out to estimate the degree of diversity in the banking sectors of 15 EU countries during the period from 1999 to 2013. The point of departure of this analysis is a widely held view in the field of ecology, according to which the functioning of an ecosystem is likely to depend on the diversity (or heterogeneity) of its species (Jizhong et al. 1991). Ecologists and conservation biologists have put forward a number of indicators aimed at quantifying the diversity of ecosystems. According to Whittaker (1972, p. 213), there are two aspects of biological diversity (also known as 'alpha diversity') that should be measured:

> *Diversity in the strict sense is richness in species, and is appropriately measured as the number of species in a sample of standard size. Slope measurements, in contrast, express the steepness of the importance-value sequence.*

While the 'richness' component refers to the effective number of species that are present within a certain habitat or community (Peet 1974), slope measurement (also denoted as species 'evenness') captures the extent to which individuals are distributed evenly across species (Heip 1974). A unified concept of diversity is proposed by Hill (1973), who defines 'true diversity' (D) of species (S) as the reciprocal of the weighted generalised mean (M_{q-1}) of their proportional abundances (p_i). More formally, the general equation of diversity can be written as follows:

$$D = \left(M_{q-1}\right)^{-1} = \left(\sqrt[q-1]{\sum_{i=1}^{S} p_i p_i^{q-1}}\right)^{-1} = \left(\sum_{i=1}^{S} p_i^q\right)^{1/(1-q)} \tag{9.1}$$

where q represents the order of diversity and defines the sensitivity of the true diversity index to either rare or abundant species. Broadly speaking, low values (i.e. $q < 1$) of this parameter account for a higher weight given to rare species, whereas high values (i.e. $q > 1$) put more emphasis on the extent to which the abundance is equal across species (Magurran 2004).

Some of the most popular indicators of diversity are derived from Eq. (9.1) and correspond to different values of the parameter q. Among these indicators is the Simpson index, which was first introduced by Simpson (1949) to assess the degree of concentration when individuals are classified into groups. In its original formulation, this index quantifies the probability that two individuals drawn randomly and independently from the population will belong to the same species (Simpson 1949). When the degree of diversity (rather than the degree of concentration) is of concern, the reciprocal of the Simpson index (D') is suggested for general application (Tuomisto 2010). It can be expressed as follows:

$$D' = \left(\sum_{i=1}^{S} p_i^2 \right)^{-1} \tag{9.2}$$

It can be shown that the Simpson index is a special case of the true diversity index (Eq. 9.1) with $q = 2$ (Hill 1973). It follows that, relative to other indicators such as the Shannon-Wiener index (Shannon and Weaver 1949), the measure developed by Simpson (1949) appears to be sensitive to changes in the proportional abundance among groups and is appropriate when the researcher is mostly concerned with the distribution of individuals across groups (McDonald and Dimmick 2003).

The key properties of the Simpson index make it well suited to the present empirical setting, in that for any given country and year the maximum number of species—that is, ownership types—is limited to three (i.e. cooperative, commercial and savings). By treating ownership types as analogous to species within an ecosystem, it is possible to estimate the degree of diversity in the banking sector in terms of relative market shares of cooperative banks vis-à-vis commercial and savings banks. To this end, I collect data on bank loans and deposits from Bankscope and calculate time-varying indices of ownership diversity for the 15 EU countries before the 2004 enlargement over the 1999–2013 period.[3]

Table 9.1 details the average degree and percent change in ownership diversity during the sample period in each of the selected countries. There appear to be considerable differences across EU countries in terms of the degree of diversity characterising their banking sectors. At one end of the spectrum, diversity is found to be particularly high in Austria and Germany, irrespective of whether the loan or deposit side of the market is examined. Interestingly, the Austrian banking system seems to have witnessed the greatest increase in ownership diversity between 1999 and 2013 among

[3] Data are from unconsolidated statements. Loans are defined as in Fig. 9.1, while deposits consist of customer deposits. Considering both loans and deposits is important, as evidence suggests (Michie and Oughton 2013) that market shares may differ significantly depending on whether they are calculated with respect to the asset or liability side of banks' balance sheets.

Table 9.1 Ownership diversity in EU countries

	Ownership diversity for loans		*Ownership diversity for deposits*	
	Average	*% change*	*Average*	*% change*
Austria	2.85	38.08%	2.87	32.38%
Belgium	1.06	−3.20%	1.07	−8.49%
Denmark	1.11	0.36%	1.19	6.03%
Finland	1.97	4.14%	1.99	11.43%
France	1.91	8.27%	1.97	3.03%
Germany	2.57	7.07%	2.73	9.83%
Greece	1.04	−2.54%	1.08	−12.66%
Ireland	1.08	−6.58%	1.06	−6.69%
Italy	1.73	23.26%	1.75	18.27%
Luxembourg	1.19	12.55%	1.23	11.22%
Netherlands	1.63	−13.97%	1.64	−19.04%
Portugal	1.17	2.26%	1.16	6.30%
Spain	2.10	−3.07%	2.09	5.44%
Sweden	1.15	11.24%	1.17	13.38%
UK	1.27	−3.55%	1.31	−4.57%
EA-12	2.35	−3.46%	2.43	−8.75%
EU-15	2.08	−9.50%	2.16	−14.34%

Average and percent change 1999–2013

Source: Author's calculation on data Bankscope

the sample countries, especially when diversity is calculated based on market shares for loans. At the other end of the spectrum, the ownership composition of the banking sector is more concentrated in Greece, Belgium and Ireland. These countries, along with others such as Spain and the UK, have all observed a decline in diversity on the loan side of banks' balance sheets over the 1999–2013 period. One can also notice that diversity of ownership structures in the UK is less than half the corresponding values for Austria and Germany, while it is somewhat higher in countries such as Finland, France and Italy.[4]

Figure 9.2 illustrates the trend in ownership diversity for the loan and deposit markets by considering the whole sample as well as the 12 eurozone economies separately. One can see that there has been a substantial loss of diversity in the EU, as is demonstrated by the 14.34% drop in the

[4] Since data on loans and deposits are collected for the period between 1999 and 2013, market shares of cooperative banks in Italy include those held by the country's *Banche popolari* that were forced to convert to joint stock companies through the 2015 reform.

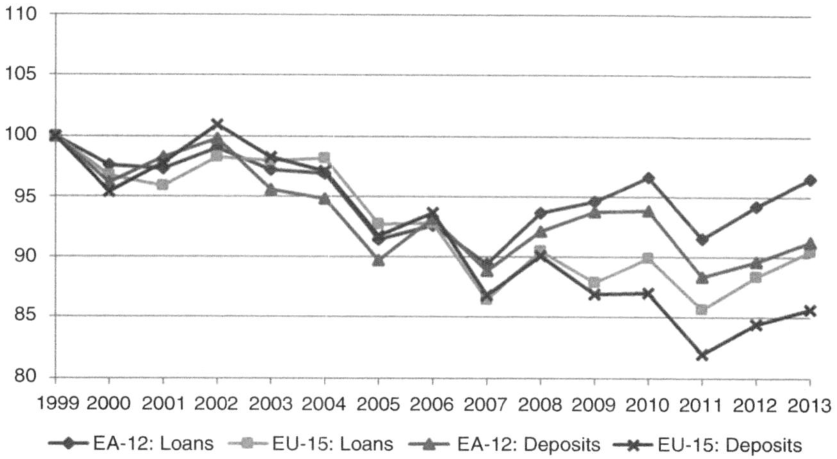

Fig. 9.2 Ownership diversity in EU countries. Index (1999 = 100). Source: Author's calculation on data Bankscope

diversity index for deposits between 1999 and 2013. On the loan side of the market, a significant fall in diversity occurred in the period leading to the crisis, with the index decreasing by 13.51% in 2007 relative to its 1999 value. This trend is mirrored by the diversity index for the group of euro area countries, although the decline in diversity appears to have been less conspicuous in these countries compared to the 15 EU economies as a whole. I now turn to some of the implications that this loss of diversity in the EU may entail for the financial and economic system.

9.2.2 *Financial and Economic Implication of Diversity in Banking*

A central theme of this chapter is that there are financial and economic benefits to be gained from having a degree of diversity in the banking sector, that is, a critical mass of cooperative banks operating alongside their commercial and savings counterparts. This section will draw attention to two main implications that diversity in banking may have, namely in terms of the stability and resilience of the financial system as well as access to credit.

Diversity in Banking and Financial Stability
Consistent with their property right structure, which makes retained earnings the main source of their equity capital, cooperative banks may have less incentives to increase leverage with the aim of maximising equity returns compared to their commercial peers (Ayadi et al. 2010). Since cooperatives tend to view the generation of profits as a necessary condition to ensure their survival and not as their primary objective (Llewellyn 2017), they are less likely to venture into riskier areas than banks that pursue shareholder wealth maximisation (Boonstra 2012).

Evidence exists in the literature for important differences in the risk profile of cooperative banks vis-à-vis other types of financial institutions. Much of this evidence is drawn from EU countries, where the large presence of stakeholder-oriented institutions has resulted into a sustained interest in the cooperative banking model. Early findings from a sample of 29 OECD countries indicate that, due to lower volatility of returns, cooperative banks are generally more stable than their commercial counterparts (Hesse and Cihák 2007). Similar conclusions are reached by Ayadi et al. (2010), who focus on a sample of six eurozone economies and show that cooperatives tend to have lower insolvency risk compared to profit-oriented banks. These results are confirmed by data for Germany (Beck et al. 2009), which suggest that cooperative banks are likely to operate farther away from default than government-owned savings banks. An explanation for the high degree of stability that characterises cooperative banks is provided by Groeneveld (2012), who contends that cooperatives may use consumer surplus as a buffer in order to maintain their profitability relatively fixed over time. Recent evidence from the UK (Casu and Gall 2016) reveals that mutual building societies appear less risky than shareholder-oriented banks on a variety of measures (e.g. volatility of earnings and of net interest margins), while their stability has increased from 2008 onwards despite the occurrence of the crisis. Moreover, support is found for cooperative banks dampening the impact of lower interest rates on systemic risk, particularly when the pre-crisis period is considered (Caselli 2018).

Table 9.2 reports, for each ownership type, the degree of bank stability before and after the onset of the crisis for the group of 15 EU countries examined in this chapter. Bank stability is measured through the Z-score, a proxy for distance from insolvency that has found enduring support in the literature (e.g. Laeven and Levine 2009). The Z-score measures the number of standard deviations that returns have to fall before equity is depleted and the bank becomes insolvent. Consistent with the approach

Table 9.2 Bank stability pre-crisis (1999–2007) and post-crisis (2008–2013) by ownership type in EU countries

	Z-score		*ROA (%)*		*Standard deviation of ROA (%)*		*Capital-to-asset ratio (%)*	
	Pre-crisis	*Post-crisis*	*Pre-crisis*	*Post-crisis*	*Pre-crisis*	*Post-crisis*	*Pre-crisis*	*Post-crisis*
Commercial banks	2.75	2.65	0.78	0.36	1.13	1.24	11.64	12.39
Cooperative banks	3.76	3.89	0.47	0.31	0.47	0.43	8.08	8.66
Savings banks	3.80	3.96	0.41	0.21	0.55	0.56	7.03	8.86

Source: Author's calculation on data Bankscope

put forward by Lepetit and Strobel (2013), which is shown to suffer from a relatively low level of intertemporal volatility at the bank level, the Z-score can be expressed as follows:

$$Z - \text{score}_{i,t} = \frac{\mu\text{ROA}_{i,T} + \text{CAR}_{i,t}}{\sigma\text{ROA}_{i,T}} \tag{9.3}$$

with $i = 1, \ldots, 15$ and $t = 1, \ldots, T$, where i is either a cooperative, commercial or savings bank, t is the year, ROA is the return on assets and CAR is the capital-to-asset ratio. Due to the Z-score being highly skewed, the use of its natural logarithm is generally recommended (Mohsni and Otchere 2014). A greater value of this indicator implies higher bank stability, that is, greater distance from insolvency.

Looking at Table 9.2, three main aspects are worth noting. First, regardless of the time period being considered, cooperative banks in the EU are found to be more stable than their commercial peers and almost as stable as savings banks. The relatively high Z-score for cooperative banks is explained primarily by the lower standard deviation of ROA compared to both commercial and savings banks, which appears to offset the lower profitability and capitalisation exhibited by cooperatives relative to the other two ownership types. Second, there is evidence that cooperative banks' probability of default has decreased in the period following the start of the crisis. This result is particularly interesting in light of the corresponding figures for shareholder-oriented banks, in that their Z-score has fallen from 2.75 in the pre-crisis period to 2.65 after the crisis. Third, it can be observed that the standard deviation of ROA has declined in the post-crisis period only for cooperative banks, whilst it has increased somewhat remarkably for commercial banks. Such evidence seems to suggest that, by lowering the standard deviation of their returns since the burst of the crisis, cooperative banks have been able to improve their stability despite the period of financial distress. Importantly, this finding provides further support to the view that cooperatives have weathered both the global financial crisis and the eurozone sovereign debt crisis relatively unscathed (Llewellyn 2012).

Taken together, the results illustrated in Table 9.2, which are in accordance with findings from the literature (e.g. Ayadi et al. 2010; Casu and Gall 2016; Hesse and Cihák 2007), imply that there are macroeconomic benefits to be gained from a plurality of ownership types in the banking industry. By way of their lower appetite for risk and ensuing higher stability, a critical mass of cooperative banks operating alongside their commercial and savings counterparts is likely to contribute to financial stability and to reduce systemic risk (Smolders et al. 2012). This point is described well by Haldane and May (2011, p. 353):

> *[E]xcessive homogeneity within a financial system—all the banks doing the same thing—can minimize risk for each individual bank, but maximize the probability of the entire system collapsing.*

Along with its direct effect on financial stability, a relatively high presence of cooperative banks may exert an indirect effect on systemic risk by influencing the risk-taking activities of other banks in the system. Some early evidence is offered by Hesse and Cihák (2007), who find support for a larger share of cooperative banks (in terms of total assets) in industrialised countries being linked to increased stability of an average bank in the system. Interestingly, this effect seems to be due to the impact that cooperatives' behaviour has on the stability of other non-profit-maximising institutions, while the soundness of weak commercial banks is adversely affected by a larger presence of cooperative banks. In a similar vein, Chiaramonte et al. (2015) draw on a sample of 26 industrialised economies and show that cooperatives have a stabilising influence on large commercial banks in the system during the crisis years, yet only above a certain market share threshold. As Chiaramonte et al. (2015) suggest, a possible explanation behind these findings is that interconnections between cooperative and commercial banks may be looser in more mutualised banking systems. Recent evidence from Western Europe is also provided by Caselli (2018), whose results indicate that—ceteris paribus—banks located in more ownership-diverse systems tend to be more stable and to take on less risk in response to expansionary monetary policy than those from less diverse systems.

It follows that diversity of ownership structures, business models and risk profiles in banking may have implications for financial stability through its effect on the nature and degree of competition in the banking system. As Groeneveld (2012, p. 272) effectively states:

> *More competition does not result from just adding more firms with the same business model but by also adding firms with different business models and meaningful market share. Diversity in ownership and business orientation leads to diversity in risk appetite, management, incentive structures, policies and practices as well as behaviours and outcomes.*

It can be argued that more diverse systems are likely to induce banks to compete for better customer service rather than higher equity returns (Berry et al. 2015). In line with Meriläinen (2016), this may relate to the fact that competition—and, with it, the degree of diversity—tends to alter banks' decisions about the relative weight assigned to profitability vis-à-vis other objectives. Inasmuch as competition between banks is focused on serving customers instead of venturing into overly risky activities, one would expect the aggregate level of risk in the financial system to be reduced. Furthermore, enhanced competition resulting from greater diversity in the banking industry may be associated with more efforts on the part of customers and/or depositors to discipline banks (Kick and Prieto 2015). If stricter market discipline prevents banks from selecting riskier projects, thus potentially decreasing their probability of default, the stability of the financial system and its resilience to external shocks might be heightened.

Diversity in Banking and Access to Credit

Alongside its implications for financial stability, a plurality of ownership types and business models in the banking sector can have positive effects in terms of access to credit. According to Michie (2011), the presence of cooperative banks, which tend to operate within a well-defined geographical area through a relatively dense branch network, provides access to borrowing, insurance and a range of other financial services. Evidence of differences in lending behaviour between cooperatives and other types of financial institutions is provided by Ferri et al. (2014), who study how the loan supply of stakeholder- and shareholder-oriented banks reacts to changes in monetary policy—that is, the so-called bank lending channel of monetary policy transmission (Bernanke and Blinder 1988). Drawing on a micro-level dataset for euro area banks over the period between 1999 and 2011, Ferri et al. (2014) find that cooperative banks adjust their loan supply to a lesser extent than shareholder-oriented banks in response to variations in monetary policy. Additional support for cooperative banks exhibiting less procyclical lending policies is advanced by Meriläinen (2016), who shows that the loan supply of cooperatives did not slow down during the global financial crisis and the eurozone sovereign debt crisis. Interestingly, the results obtained by Meriläinen (2016) also suggest that cooperative banks did not contribute to excessive credit growth in the run-up to the two crises, which appears to have been fuelled primarily by commercial and privately owned savings banks. All in all, this set of findings indicates that cooperative banks may continue to provide credit to the economy even at times of financial turmoil, whereas commercial banks are more likely to cut back on lending when the economic environment becomes more uncertain.

To shed further light on the impact that diversity in banking may have on the availability of credit, Fig. 9.3 plots the trend in bank lending in EU countries over the 1999–2013 period for each ownership type. It can be noticed

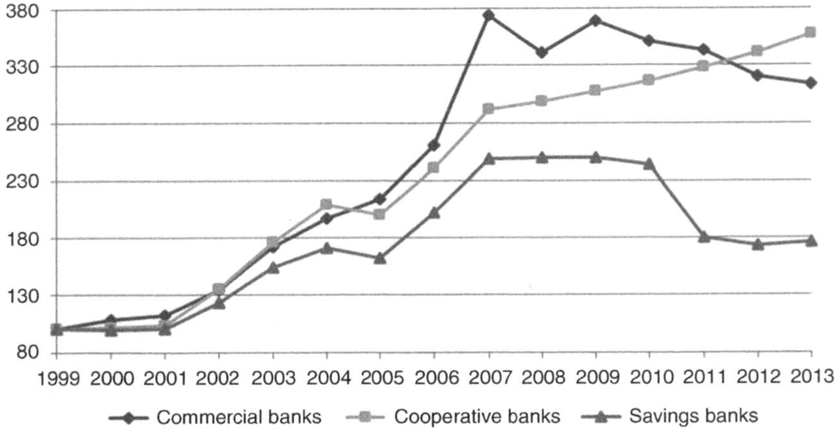

Fig. 9.3 Lending supply by ownership type in EU countries. Index (1999 = 100). Source: Author's calculation on data Bankscope

that, throughout the whole time window, commercial banks seem to have experienced a higher and somewhat more volatile growth in their loan supply compared to their cooperative and savings counterparts. However, while the amount of credit that shareholder-oriented banks have extended to the economy has increased until the mid-2000s, their lending has been characterised by a rather marked decline since the onset of the crisis. A similar picture for the post-crisis years can be observed for savings banks, whose aggregate loan supply and corresponding shares in the loan market were also negatively affected by the collapse of the Spanish *cajas* in the aftermath of the crisis. Conversely, remarkably different results can be seen for cooperative banks. Not only has their lending been more stable during the sample period relative to the other ownership types, it has also increased (at a rate between 2.18% in 2008 and 4.65% in 2013) after the start of the global financial crisis. In a nutshell, this evidence further corroborates the view that cooperative banks tend to reach segments of the market that would otherwise find it difficult to access credit. By doing so, cooperatives represent a means for channelling savings into loans at the local economy level, thereby supporting growth in those regions where they hold relatively large market shares (Birchall 2017). Consistent with theoretical predictions (Michie 2011), diversity of ownership types in banking might thus play an important role in fostering financial inclusion, customer choice and economic development.

9.3 'One-Fits-All' Regulatory Approach and Proportionality

9.3.1 Regulation and Diversity in the Banking Sector

The evidence presented in Sect. 9.2.2 suggests that macroeconomic benefits can be derived from a diversity of ownership types, business models and corporate missions in the banking industry. A critical mass of cooperative banks operating alongside their commercial and savings counterparts is likely to result in a more competitive, systemically less risky and financially more inclusive financial system (Llewellyn 2017). These findings complement existing evidence on the contribution of banking diversity to a range of other outcomes such as quality of service, fairness and customer choice (Michie 2017). For all these reasons, the ongoing discussion has important implications for banking regulation, in that it speaks to the current debate over how a more stable, resilient and inclusive financial system might be attained (Birchall 2017; Casu and Gall 2016).

Consistent with the financial and economic benefits that diversity in banking can bring about, preserving—and, even more so, promoting—a multiplicity of ownership types in the banking sector should be viewed as a major public policy objective. In the current environment, there are two main sets of interventions that appear to be particularly critical for banking regulators. If diversity is to be safeguarded, it is important that the core features of cooperative banks (e.g. member ownership, proximity to customers and support to the local economy) are not weakened by regulatory restrictions directed to and devised for their larger and internationally active competitors (often represented by commercial banks). In addition, one could contend that greater competition between different ownership types (rather than between banks belonging to the same ownership type) should be encouraged. Specifically, regulators should ensure that market shares on the loan and deposit sides of banks' balance sheets are distributed more evenly across ownership types. To this purpose, the degree of diversity in the banking industry should be quantified, monitored and disclosed at regular intervals (Michie and Oughton 2013), using diversity indices such as those reported in this chapter. At the same time, efforts may be directed at opening up opportunities for strengthening and expanding the current network of stakeholder-oriented institutions in countries where they only play a marginal role (Blisse and Hummel 2017), for example via the creation of mutually owned banks and local credit unions. Some important steps in this direction have been taken in the UK, where several community banks modelled on German *Sparkassen* and *Volksbanken*—for example, Hampshire Community Bank—are currently being set up. It is hoped that these efforts will help counteract the significant loss of diversity that has occurred in the country during the last three decades as a result of consolidations and demutualisations.

9.3.2 Challenges of a 'One-Size-Fits-All' Regulatory Approach to Diversity in Banking

In the aftermath of the recent financial crisis, the increased fragility of the banking sectors in a number of European countries, along with the problems arising from the close links between public sector finances and the banking sector, has led policymakers to review the existing regulatory framework. Among the major initiatives that have been pursued is the adoption of Basel III, which introduces tighter capital requirements compared to Basel I and II with the aim of creating a more stable and resilient financial system. An additional innovation made by Basel III is the provision of liquidity and leverage requirements (i.e. the Liquidity Coverage Ratio, Net Stable Funding Ratio and Liquidity Ratio) to ensure that financial intermediaries have sufficient liquidity during periods of financial distress and to safeguard against excessive borrowing. In the EU, the introduction of Basel III has been accompanied by the establishment of a European Banking Union. In its present form, the Banking Union involves a common set of rules for banks in all EU countries—together with a Single Supervisory Mechanism (SSM), a Single Resolution Mechanism (SRM) and a European Deposit Insurance Scheme (EDIS)—directed at strengthening banks' buffers and increasing their ability to withstand shocks.

The stricter and more complex regulatory framework that has been designed for the EU banking system, which by and large seems to follow a 'one-size-fits-all' approach, could pose significant challenges to cooperative banks. Despite the context of extremely low interest rates and limited profit margins, they will be required to retain profits in order to strengthen their capital positions further. Such requirements may be particularly costly to cooperative banks, since they cannot raise capital as quickly as their shareholder-oriented peers (Ayadi et al. 2010). An attempt to quantify the regulatory impact of rising cost of capital on bank profitability following the adoption of Basel III is put forward by Fischer (2017), who considers balance sheet data for 756 cooperative banks in Germany and finds that the new framework is likely to decrease their return on equity between 14 and 111 basis points per year (in case no countermeasures are adopted). Moreover, greater complexity in banking regulation may cause additional costs of compliance for cooperative banks. Although these costs are expected to increase for any financial institution, the operational burden may be higher for banks of smaller size—like the majority of cooperative banks in the EU—which may not be able to generate economies of scale as easily as large, commercial banks. Therefore, there are concerns that increasingly complex regulation might threaten the competitiveness of cooperative banks and reduce their ability to continue to finance the local economy (Goglio and Kalmi 2017). Support for compliance costs being not equally distributed across banks with different size exists in the literature. By measuring regulatory costs faced by German cooperative banks in complying with a number of legal requirements (e.g. risk management, security services and IT standards), Schenkel (2017) concludes that the regulatory burden varies with bank size and may make cooperative banks 'too small to survive'.

9.3.3 *Proportionality in Banking Regulation*

As the findings discussed in Sect. 9.3.2 suggest, imposing the same regulatory requirements on banks characterised by different size, ownership structure and systemic significance might produce undesired effects. These include reduced profitability and excessive costs of compliance for smaller and less systemically significant institutions like many cooperative banks, whose role in providing finance to the local economy could be hindered by disproportionate barriers in regulation. The additional complexity of banking regulation in the aftermath of the global financial crisis has triggered renewed interest in the principle of proportionality, that is, the extent to which regulatory requirements can be tailored to smaller, less complex and non-internationally active banks (Carvalho et al. 2017).

Principle of Proportionality in EU Regulation
From a broad regulatory perspective, the principle of proportionality requires that any regulatory action that is undertaken must be proportionate (i.e. commensurate) to the objectives it aims to achieve. In the EU, the principle of proportionality finds explicit recognition in Article 5 of the Treaty on European Union, which states that:

> *The use of Union competences is governed by the principles of subsidiarity and proportionality. […] Under the principle of proportionality, the content and form of Union action shall not exceed what is necessary to achieve the objectives of the Treaties.*

In line with this provision, the proportionality principle ensures that measures adopted by EU institutions do not exceed what is necessary and appropriate for achieving the legislative objectives being pursued. Although it does not tend to translate into the complete non-application of regulation if certain parameters are fulfilled, this principle enables a differentiated application of regulatory requirements to institutions with different features (e.g. in terms of complexity and size). It follows that, when a choice has to be made between alternative measures, the least onerous should be favoured. On this front, traditional tools such as cost-benefit analysis are particularly useful, in that they allow to assess whether regulation is proportionate—and hence justified—in relation to its objectives.

Application of Proportionality to EU Banking Regulation

According to a report that was recently published by the European Banking Authority's (EBA) Banking Stakeholder Group (EBA Banking Stakeholder Group 2015), there are a number of reasons that support the application of proportionality to banking regulation. These can be classified into five main areas:

- Regulatory costs: the introduction of virtually any regulation comes with a series of costs at different levels. These encompass resource costs incurred by regulatory bodies; compliance costs faced by firms being regulated, for instance in relation to the training of employees working in the compliance area or the hiring of regulatory consultants; regulatory costs that are passed on to customers in the form of higher prices for financial services; economic costs due to some of the core functions of the financial system, such as facilitating the channelling of funds from savers to borrowers, being somewhat compromised.
- Banking competition: regulation could jeopardise competition in the banking sector. As is explained in a study by the European Commission (2014, p. 260):

  > *Regulations tend to pose a disproportionate burden on smaller players in the market and new entrants, which can make it harder for them to compete with more established players.*

  Inasmuch as it imposes an excessive burden on smaller banks, regulation might force them to resort to mergers and acquisitions in order to achieve economies of scale and might thus reduce the degree of competition in the banking industry (Goglio and Kalmi 2017).
- Bank management: disproportionate regulation might cause unjustified limitations to bank managers' discretion, thereby de facto weakening the controlling role of the Board of Directors. Besides potentially leading to some degree of regulatory capture, this overlap between supervisors and supervisees could call into question the independence of the regulatory authority that is tasked with assessing the bank's financial profile.
- Bank business models: one of the possible effects of regulation is to induce changes in bank business models that are not necessary for the attainment of the given regulatory objectives. This is because banks might attempt to minimise regulatory costs by changing their

behaviour, thus giving rise to an endogeneity problem—that is, a change in regulation prompts a change in bank behaviour that itself results in a subsequent change in regulation.

- Regulatory arbitrage: if regulation has a disproportionate impact on some types of banks, it can be envisaged that some of these banks could take advantage of loopholes in the regulatory framework to avoid unfavourable rules. In turn, such behaviour could engender unanticipated effects that might be in contradiction with the initial objective that the adopted regulation was intended to address.

The principle of proportionality and its application to banking regulation are qualified further by the EBA (EBA Banking Stakeholder Group 2015), according to which five pillars of proportionality can be identified:

- Objectives: in accordance with Article 5 of the Treaty on European Union, any given regulation that applies to all banks should be proportionate with respect to the objective that it aims to achieve. To this regard, it is key to assess whether the externalities and other market failures that the regulation intends to redress offset the possible inefficiencies that the same regulation could bring about. This is an area where robust and well-devised cost-benefit analyses can offer useful guidance.
- Totality of regulation: the entire set of regulations for the banking system, as opposed to each individual regulation considered separately, should be commensurate to the objectives being pursued by the regulator. A central issue is the potential for diminishing marginal returns that may be observed if the scope and intensity of regulation exceed their optimal level. It follows that cost-benefit analyses should weigh the cumulative costs and benefits associated with all regulations making up the regulatory regime instead of only those related to any individual regulation.
- Excess complexity: banking regulation should not be unnecessarily complex in relation to the objectives that are addressed. To gauge the extent to which a certain regulatory initiative can be considered as overly complex, attention should be devoted to investigating whether the same objectives can be accomplished as effectively with less complex regulatory requirements. The issue of excess complexity is particularly critical, in that it can bear important consequences in terms of costs of compliance, banking competition and regulatory arbitrage.

- Differentiation: in the application of regulation, differences across banks should be properly taken into account while ensuring that the regulatory objectives are not compromised. These differences refer to key features such as size, ownership structure, business model, risk profile and systemic significance. The need to differentiate between types of banks when applying regulation can be found in several areas of EU banking law. For example, Recital 46 of the Capital Requirements Regulation (CRR) states that:

  The provisions of this Regulation respect the principle of proportionality, having regard in particular to the diversity in size and scale of operations and to the range of activities of institutions. [...] Member States should ensure that the requirements laid down in this Regulation apply in a manner proportionate to the nature, scale and complexity of the risks associated with an institution's business model and activities.

  Other areas where the principle of proportionality is explicitly mentioned include internal capital adequacy assessment plans (Capital Requirements Directive—CRD—IV, Article 73), recovery and resolution plans (CRD, Article 74) as well as banking supervision (SSM Regulation, Recital 55).
- Materiality: regulatory restrictions should not be applied to banks that are only marginally affected by the issue that these restrictions aim to address. More formally, the principle of materiality can be defined as follows (EBA Banking Stakeholder Group 2015, p. 29):

  [T]he requirement that particular regulation should only be directed and applied to those institutions which are relevant to the issue being addressed by the proposed regulation.

  As a case in point, regulatory requirements that are developed for and targeted to systemically significant banks should not also be applied to other banks that are not deemed to have systemic significance.

Although the principle of proportionality has found explicit recognition in a number of EU banking regulations over the last few years, there appears to be room for extending its application further. In identifying areas where scope for greater simplification in banking regulation for smaller and less complex financial institutions may exist, one should weigh the potential for reducing the operational burden imposed on regulated institutions with the need to maintain financial stability. It follows that, while minimum capital and liquidity requirements should be retained, proportionality within the EU banking regulatory framework could be strengthened further by devising greater simplifications to individual rules so as to reduce the costs that banks have to incur to comply with these rules.

A case for greater proportionality in banking regulation along these lines has been made during most recent years in countries like Germany—particularly through the Deutsche Bundesbank—and the UK—where the need for more proportionality is advocated for example by the Building Societies Association. This process, which started in 2016 with a joint initiative by the finance ministers of both countries, has also led the European Commission to launch a series of proposals in order to grant proportionality a more central role. Some of the measures that are currently being reviewed include a simplified version of the Net Stable Funding Ratio, reduced granularity of reporting requirements and exemptions from disclosure requirements. Insofar as they will help decrease the operational burden on smaller and less complex institutions, these measures could translate into a level playing field for banks of different sizes, business models, risk profiles and systemic significance. Therefore, measures such as those mentioned above might constitute a necessary—but not sufficient—condition to ensure that the diversity of ownership types characterising the banking sectors in a number of EU countries will not be impaired.

9.4 Diversity in Banking and Impact on Society

The discussion about the consequences that an insufficient application of the proportionality principle in banking regulation might have for diversity in banking achieves even more prominence if one reflects over the role that cooperative banks (along with other types of stakeholder-oriented institutions) play within the European society. Since the launch by Friedrich Wilhelm Raiffeisen of the first modern credit cooperative in Germany in 1864, cooperative banks have become a key component of the European society by bringing about benefits that go well beyond financial and economic implications such as those described in Sect. 9.2.2 of this chapter. The motivation behind the establishment of the first credit cooperative, that is, alleviating poverty among the rural population, helps itself explain the value that the cooperative movement has taken on in the European society.

Among the mechanisms that may elucidate the contribution of cooperative banks—and, with them, diversity in banking—to the wider society is the concept of 'social capital' (Bourdieu 1986). According to Bourdieu (1986, p. 51), social capital can be defined as follows:

> *Social capital is the aggregate of the actual or potential resources which are linked to possession of a durable network of more or less institutionalized relationships of mutual acquaintance and recognition—or in other words, to membership in a group—which provides each of its members with the backing of the collectivity-owned capital, a 'credential' which entitles them to credit, in the various senses of the word.*

The accumulation of social capital is at the heart of credit cooperatives, since it underpins key concepts such as membership, mutuality and territoriality. These concepts embody the essence of the cooperative banking model, which is based on equal rights of each member (membership), the pursuit of mutual benefits that might not be achieved otherwise (mutuality) and a scope of operation that tends to be focused on a geographically well-defined area (territoriality). It can be argued that, by facilitating the creation and accumulation of social capital, cooperative banks have the potential for engendering important benefits for the communities within which they operate. These benefits, which are in line with the dual financial and social mission that characterises stakeholder-oriented institutions (Ayadi et al. 2009), take the form of support to a range of social, cultural and environmental activities that could produce beneficial spillover effects for the local community.

Recent years have witnessed some profound changes in the competitive environment within which cooperative banks operate, with possible implications in terms of the meaning that concepts such as membership, mutuality and territoriality may take on. The remainder of this section will focus on three trends that are likely to be reshaping some of these concepts, namely the evolution of regulation, the occurrence of the global financial crisis and the development in technology.

A first source of change that might have a bearing on the fundamental underpinnings of the cooperative banking model is banking regulation. As has been discussed in Sect. 9.3, one of the main responses to the global financial crisis on the part of policymakers has been the provision of tighter and more complex regulatory requirements for financial institutions. Although somewhat greater recognition has been granted over the past few years to the principle of proportionality, smaller and less complex institutions such as cooperative banks are too often perceived as a form of banking organisation to be guarded against. For instance, cooperative banks are regarded with scepticism by some as they are deemed to have low market discipline, limited incentives to prioritise profitability objectives and substantial difficulties in raising external capital in the form of common equity (Véron 2017). This line of reasoning might have been somewhat reinforced by the regulatory regime that has been adopted in the EU in the aftermath of the crisis, which appears to be largely dominated by a 'one-size-fits-all' approach. Concerns can be expressed that the scarce recognition by EU regulators of the distinguishing features of cooperative banks could weaken their role further, while possibly leading more observers to call into question the desirability of structuring bank operations around the cooperative model.

A concurrent impact on the concepts of membership, mutuality and territoriality might have originated from the recent financial meltdown. There tends to be agreement among researchers and policymakers alike that a major cause of the global financial crisis is the adoption of overly aggressive and risky policies by a number of financial institutions, in many cases large, listed and shareholder-oriented banks. At the same time, there is evidence suggesting that stakeholder-oriented banks did not contribute to the build-up of the crisis (Meriläinen 2016) and were able to navigate through the recent period of financial turmoil relatively unaffected (Casu and Gall 2016). An important example is the high resilience shown by cooperative banks, which were responsible for a somewhat limited share of the total losses incurred by European banks during the crisis and hardly necessitated government support (Smolders et al. 2012).[5] For these reasons, recent events have sparked greater debate over the relative weight that should be given to social objectives vis-à-vis the generation of profits. There seems to be increasing awareness of the potentially negative effects that a culture centred on the mere maximisation of shareholder wealth could have for financial stability, economic welfare and—not least—societal well-being. Therefore, an opportunity exists for cooperative banks to capitalise on these trends and voice the benefits that a focus on values such as membership, mutuality and territoriality may have for the broader society.

[5] According to Smolders et al. (2012), cooperative banks in European countries accounted for 7% of total losses and write-downs between the third quarter of 2007 and the first quarter of 2011.

Alongside the evolution of regulation and the occurrence of the global financial crisis, cooperative banks have been presented with a number of opportunities and challenges arising from recent developments in technology. The banking business is increasingly moving away from a traditional approach whereby services are provided to customers through face-to-face interactions at local branches towards a more virtual relationship that can take place almost at any time and from anywhere. These changes appear to be particularly significant for cooperatives and other stakeholder banks that are oriented towards relationship banking (Ferri et al. 2014), given that developing long-term relationships with customers and collecting soft information to support lending decisions tend to occur via a series of exchanges at the bank's branches. While technological developments might pose some considerable challenges to the mutual banking model, there seems to be scope for cooperative banks to take advantage of recent changes in technology to deliver better value to customers as well as to the community within which they operate. For example, the advent of 'FinTech' could offer some key opportunities for customer-owned cooperatives, in that it makes available innovative techniques such as loan price optimisation or big data analytics that could be used to improve customer satisfaction. On this front, one of the key challenges that lie ahead for cooperative banks is how to maintain close relationships with their customers while fully embracing new, promising technologies.

9.5 Summary and Conclusions

A key distinguishing feature of a number of banking sectors in the EU is the coexistence of banks that are driven primarily by shareholder wealth maximisation with banks that strive to create value for a larger set of stakeholders. Similar to natural ecosystems, the presence of different ownership types competing between one another is likely to have positive effects on the functioning of the financial ecosystem. The results presented in this chapter suggest that—ceteris paribus—a financial system populated by a multiplicity of ownership types tends to be more stable and financially inclusive than one where any single type dominates. It follows that attaining a more diverse banking sector should be regarded as an important public policy objective. This notwithstanding, the more stringent and complex regulatory framework that has been adopted in the EU in the aftermath of the global financial crisis presents cooperative banks with considerable challenges, including reduced profitability and increasing costs of compliance. As a response to the concerns expressed by some researchers and policymakers alike, the past few years have seen renewed interest in how the principle of proportionality—which is also explicitly acknowledged in the Treaty on European Union—can be more effectively applied to EU banking regulation.

Although some steps have been made during the last few years towards the design of a regulatory framework that can successfully take into account differences between financial institutions, much still remains to be done if we are to ensure that the business model of cooperative banks and other similar institutions is not compromised by disproportionate regulatory barriers. As has been argued in this chapter, the risk associated with a 'one-size-fits-all' approach to banking regulation is reduced competitiveness of smaller and less complex institutions like the majority of cooperative banks, with a potentially adverse impact in terms of their ability to continue to serve the local economy. At the same time, the events that led to the recent financial turmoil have shown that there are financial, economic and social benefits to be gained from placing stakeholder value creation rather than shareholder wealth maximisation at the core of bank operations. The most recent history should teach us that a nearly blind focus on maximising profits with only marginal consideration of social objectives is neither a sustainable nor a desirable approach. It is now time for cooperative banks, along with their stakeholder-oriented peers, to capitalise on these developments and explain further the contribution that a banking sector populated by a (bio)diversity of ownership types—in which cooperative banks play a major role—may have for financial stability, economic performance and societal well-being. To use the words of Edward O. Wilson:

> *We should preserve every scrap of biodiversity as priceless while we learn to use it and come to understand what it means to humanity.*

References

Amess, K. (2002). Financial Institutions, the Theory of the Firm and Organisational Form. *Service Industries Journal, 22*(2), 129–148.

Ayadi, R., Llewellyn, D. T., Schmidt, R. H., Arbak, E., & De Groen, W. P. (2010). *Investigating Diversity in the Banking Sector in Europe: Key Developments, Performance and Role of Cooperative Banks.* Brussels: Centre for European Policy Studies.

Ayadi, R., Schmidt, R. H., & Carbó Valverde, S. (2009). *Investigating Diversity in the Banking Sector in Europe: The Performance and Role of Savings Banks.* Brussels: Centre for European Policy Studies.

Baschieri, G., Carosi, A., & Mengoli, S. (2015). Local IPOs, Local Delistings, and the Firm Location Premium. *Journal of Banking and Finance, 53*, 67–83.

Beck, T., Hesse, H., Kick, T., & von Westernhagen, N. (2009). *Bank Ownership and Stability: Evidence from Germany.* Unpublished Manuscript.

Bernanke, B. S., & Blinder, A. S. (1988). Credit, Money, and Aggregate Demand. *American Economic Review, 78*(2), 435–439.

Berry, C., Ryan-Collins, J., & Greenham, T. (2015). *Financial System Resilience Index: Building a Strong Financial System.* London: New Economics Foundation.

Birchall, J. (2017). The Performance of Member-owned Businesses Since the Financial Crisis of 2008. In J. Michie, J. R. Blasi, & C. Borzaga (Eds.), *The Oxford Handbook of Mutual, Co-operative, and Co-owned Business.* Oxford: Oxford University Press.

Blisse, H., & Hummel, D. (2017). Raiffeisenbanks and Volksbanks for Europe: The Case for Co-operative Banking in Germany. In J. Michie, J. R. Blasi, & C. Borzaga (Eds.), *The Oxford Handbook of Mutual, Co-operative, and Co-owned Business.* Oxford: Oxford University Press.

Boonstra, W. (2012). Cooperative Banking in Times of Crisis. In J. Mooij & W. W. Boonstra (Eds.), *Raiffeisen's Footprint: The Cooperative Way of Banking.* Amsterdam: VU University Press.

Bourdieu, P. (1986). The Forms of Capital. In J. G. Richardson (Ed.), *Handbook of Theory and Research for the Sociology of Education.* New York: Greenwood Press.

Carvalho, A. P. C., Hohl, S., Raskopf, R., & Ruhnau, S. (2017). *Proportionality in Banking Regulation: A Cross-country Comparison* (p. 1). FSI Insights.

Caselli, G. (2018). *Ownership Structure and the Risk-Taking Channel of Monetary Policy Transmission.* Unpublished Manuscript.

Casu, B., & Gall, A. (2016). *Building Societies in the Financial Services Industry.* London: Palgrave Macmillan.

Chiaramonte, L., Poli, F., & Oriani, M. E. (2015). Are Cooperative Banks a Lever for Promoting Bank Stability? Evidence from the Recent Financial Crisis in OECD countries. *European Financial Management, 21*(3), 491–523.

EBA Banking Stakeholder Group. (2015). *Proportionality in Bank Regulation.* London: European Banking Authority.

European Commission. (2014). *Economic Review of the Financial Regulation Agenda.*", Commission Staff Working Documents (p. 158).

Ferri, G., Kalmi, P., & Kerola, E. (2014). Does Bank Ownership Affect Lending Behavior? Evidence from the Euro Area. *Journal of Banking and Finance, 48*, 194–209.

Fischer, M. (2017). The Impact of Financial Regulation on Business Models of Cooperative Banks in Germany. *Journal of Financial Transformation, 46*, 116–127.

Goglio, S., & Kalmi, P. (2017). Credit Unions and Co-operative Banks Across the World. In J. Michie, J. R. Blasi, & C. Borzaga (Eds.), *The Oxford Handbook of Mutual, Co-operative, and Co-owned Business*. Oxford: Oxford University Press.

Groeneveld, H. (2012). European Cooperative Banks and the Future Financial System. In J. Mooij & W. W. Boonstra (Eds.), *Raiffeisen's Footprint: The Cooperative Way of Banking*. Amsterdam: VU University Press.

Haldane, A. G., & May, R. M. (2011). Systemic Risk in Banking Ecosystems. *Nature, 469*(7330), 351–355.

Heip, C. H. R. (1974). A New Index Measuring Evenness. *Journal of the Marine Biological Association of the United Kingdom, 54*(3), 555–557.

Hesse, H., & Cihák, M. (2007). Cooperative Banks and Financial Stability. *IMF Working Papers*, (2).

Hill, M. O. (1973). Diversity and Evenness: A Unifying Notation and Its Consequences. *Ecology, 54*(2), 427–432.

Jizhong, Z., Shijun, M., & Changming, C. (1991). An Index of Ecosystem Diversity. *Ecological Modelling, 59*(3–4), 151–163.

Kick, T., & Prieto, E. (2015). Bank Risk and Competition: Evidence from Regional Banking Markets. *Review of Finance, 19*(3), 1185–1222.

Laeven, L., & Levine, R. (2009). Bank Governance, Regulation and Risk Taking. *Journal of Financial Economics, 93*(2), 259–275.

Lepetit, L., & Strobel, F. (2013). Bank Insolvency Risk and Time-Varying Z-Score Measures. *Journal of International Financial Markets, Institutions and Money, 25*, 73–87.

Llewellyn, D. T. (2012). UK Building Societies: The Strengths of Mutuality. In J. Mooij & W. W. Boonstra (Eds.), *Raiffeisen's Footprint: The Cooperative Way of Banking*. Amsterdam: VU University Press.

Llewellyn, D. T. (2017). Conversion from Stakeholder Value to Shareholder Value Banks: The Case of UK Building Societies. In J. Michie, J. R. Blasi, & C. Borzaga (Eds.), *The Oxford Handbook of Mutual, Co-operative, and Co-owned Business*. Oxford: Oxford University Press.

Magurran, A. E. (2004). *Measuring Biological Diversity*. Oxford: Blackwell Publishing.

McDonald, D. G., & Dimmick, J. (2003). The Conceptualization and Measurement of Diversity. *Communication Research, 30*(1), 60–79.

Meriläinen, J.-M. (2016). Lending Growth During the Financial Crisis and the Sovereign Debt Crisis: The Role of Bank Ownership Type. *Journal of International Financial Markets, Institutions and Money, 41*, 168–182.

Michie, J. (2011). Promoting Corporate Diversity in the Financial Services Sector. *Policy Studies, 32*(4), 309–323.

Michie, J. (2017). The Importance of Ownership. In J. Michie, J. R. Blasi, & C. Borzaga (Eds.), *The Oxford Handbook of Mutual, Co-operative, and Co-owned Business*. Oxford: Oxford University Press.
Michie, J., & Oughton, C. (2013). *Measuring Diversity in Financial Services Markets: A Diversity Index*. Centre for Financial and Management Studies Discussion Paper Series, 113.
Mohsni, S., & Otchere, I. (2014). Risk Taking Behavior of Privatized Banks. *Journal of Corporate Finance, 29*, 122–142.
Peet, R. K. (1974). The Measurement of Species Diversity. *Annual Review of Ecology and Systematics, 5*, 285–307.
Schenkel, A. (2017). *Proportionality of Banking Regulation: Evidence from Germany*. Unpublished Manuscript.
Shannon, C. E., & Weaver, W. (1949). *The Mathematical Theory of Communication*. Urbana, IL: University of Illinois Press.
Simpson, E. H. (1949). Measurement of Diversity. *Nature, 163*(4148), 688.
Smolders, N., Koetsier, I., & de Vries, B. (2012). Performance of European Cooperative Banks in the Recent Financial and Economic Crisis. In J. Mooij & W. W. Boonstra (Eds.), *Raiffeisen's Footprint: The Cooperative Way of Banking*. Amsterdam: VU University Press.
Tuomisto, H. (2010). A Consistent Terminology for Quantifying Species Diversity? Yes, It Does Exist. *Oecologia, 164*(4), 853–860.
Véron, N. (2017). *The Governance and Ownership of Significant Euro-area Banks*. Bruegel Policy Contributions, 15.
Whittaker, R. H. (1972). Evolution and Measurement of Species Diversity. *Taxon, 21*(2–3), 213–251.

CHAPTER 10

Cooperative Banking in Europe Today: Conclusions

Marco Migliorelli

10.1 Stressing the Importance of Cooperative Banks in Europe

Cooperative banking in Europe is today in a phase of transformation. Such a transformation was mainly triggered by the economic and financial crisis started in Europe in 2008 and is not yet completed. Nevertheless, after more than ten years after the beginning of the Great Crisis, a number of lessons learned can be drawn and some considerations can be stated as concerns the possible way forward for cooperative banks.

First and foremost, the systemic relevance of cooperative banking in many European countries needs to be reaffirmed. The importance of cooperative banks is not only due to the large base of clients served or to the size of their balance sheets. It has indeed to be found in the unique capacity to reach the real economy, in particular by providing credit to households and small and medium enterprises (SMEs). In many cases, through relationship lending, cooperative banks represent an effective means to reduce the market failures that characterise the credit sector and affect in particular small

M. Migliorelli (✉)
IAE Université Paris 1 Panthéon-Sorbonne (Sorbonne Business School), Paris, France

M. Migliorelli (ed.), *New Cooperative Banking in Europe*,
https://doi.org/10.1007/978-3-319-93578-2_10

economic agents (e.g. Boot 2000; Berger et al. 2001). These market failures are typically linked to the information asymmetries that usually feature the relation between small economic agents and financial intermediaries (and that can induce the latter to limit credit) and to the high costs to access directly the financial markets for small companies (which normally restrict the possibilities of financing for SMEs to bank lending). In addition, the systemic importance of cooperative banks should be further assessed as following an emerging strand of literature aiming to demonstrate that diversity in banking can bring significant advantages in terms of financial stability, systemic risk management and easiness for the economy to respond to economic downturns (e.g. Ayadi et al. 2010, 2016). The observed countercyclical role played by cooperative banks in many countries and widely discussed in literature (e.g. Bolton et al. 2013; Ferri et al. 2014) can be also analysed in this light.

10.2 An External Environment That Carries Unprecedented Challenges

Many factors have been threatening cooperative banks since the beginning of the financial and the economic crisis. Some of them are country-specific. To this extent, a direct link between general economic conditions in a country and the capacity of cooperative banks to keep delivering a distinctive value proposition has progressively emerged (e.g. Migliorelli and Brunelli 2016). As a matter of fact, cooperative banks have suffered the most in the areas of the continent in which the crisis hit more severely business and households (e.g. in many south-European countries), while they remained relatively shielded in countries in which a robust economic recovery followed the economic downturn (e.g. in Germany). Non-performing loans have represented in this respect the key channel of transmission of the recession from the real economy to the cooperative banks' balance sheets. Differences in national legislation, organisational models and market positioning have further contributed to the observed country-level heterogeneity in the resilience of the cooperative banking business model over Europe. Hence, a strong argument should be made in favour of the idea that any discussion on the future of cooperative banking in Europe needs to take into account specificities and constraints existing in each national context and no universal solutions exist. Such an argument is also supported by the factual evidence that all the reforms launched in the cooperative banking sector since the beginning of the Great Crisis have had a country-specific perimeter and approach.

However, a few trends have been impacting indistinctively all cooperative banks in Europe. The first is increasingly tightening regulation. The heightening of the banking regulatory standards at European level have affected many critical elements of the cooperative banking business model, in particular as concerns governance requirements, capital and liquidity adequacy and evaluation of the risks. In this respect, many observers claimed that European legislation, being mainly drafted on the model of the joint-stock companies, is contributing to progressively weaken the cooperative distinctiveness in banking and is indirectly pushing towards a convergence of the different business models (e.g. De Ory et al. 2012; Richez-Battesti and Leseul 2016). Nonetheless, it is likely that regulation will remain one of the major items in the cooperative banks' agenda in the next years. In fact, some of the legislative initiatives launched since the start of the Great Crisis are under a process of refinement or definition of relevant secondary provisions (e.g. in the case of the Capital Requirements Directive,[1] the Capital Requirements Regulation[2] and the Bank Recovery and Resolution Directive[3]), while some more major actions are already foreseen (e.g. the further revision of the Basel framework[4]).

A second trend affecting all cooperative banks is the gradual change that has been observed in the last decade in the fundamentals of certain segments of the banking market. In particular, this is the case for the more traditional banking services (e.g. payment services, cash withdrawals, internet banking) and for the ordinary lending activity (e.g. loans, residential mortgages). In both cases, a significant reduction in the economic

[1] Directive 2013/36/EU of the European Parliament and of the Council of 26 June 2013 on access to the activity of credit institutions and the prudential supervision of credit institutions and investment firms, amending Directive 2002/87/EC and repealing Directives 2006/48/EC and 2006/49/EC.

[2] Regulation (EU) No 575/2013 of the European Parliament and of the Council of 26 June 2013 on prudential requirements for credit institutions and investment firms and amending Regulation (EU) No 648/2012.

[3] Directive 2014/59/EU of the European Parliament and of the Council of 15 May 2014 establishing a framework for the recovery and resolution of credit institutions and investment firms and amending Council Directive 82/891/EEC, and Directives 2001/24/EC, 2002/47/EC, 2004/25/EC, 2005/56/EC, 2007/36/EC, 2011/35/EU, 2012/30/EU and 2013/36/EU, and Regulations (EU) No 1093/2010 and (EU) No 648/2012, of the European Parliament and of the Council.

[4] A new agreement on the partial revision of the Basel Accord was reached the 7th of December 2017, consisting in a proposal on risk evaluation methods that will probably lead to a non-negligible increase in risk weighted assets for nearly all banks.

returns has gradually materialised over the years. As concerns the more traditional banking services, this tendency has been driven by progressive standardisation of the offer (supported by enhanced processes automation) as well as an increasing perception of these services by clients as a form of *modern commodity*. On the other hand, the decline in the return on the banks' ordinary lending activity has been mainly triggered by the reduction in the interest spreads following the ultra-accommodating monetary policy adopted by the European Central Bank (ECB) in particular since 2009 in the attempt to contain the effects of the crisis. This has resulted in a generalised contraction in the banks' interest income. As traditional banking services and ordinary lending represent the backbone of the cooperative banking offering, this shift in the remuneration patterns has implied for cooperative banks a change in the competitive scenario of a significant greater extent than for other kinds of banks (and in particular if compared to commercial banks).

A third trend common to all cooperative banks regards increasing digitalisation and the incoming competition from *fintech* companies. Surprisingly, the potential impact of such a trend is much less debated in the cooperative banking industry (and among the researchers active in this field) than regulation or economic performances. Indeed, the strategic consequences for cooperative banks might be even more relevant. Following this trend, two main components of the cooperative banking traditional competitive advantage risk to be put under unprecedented pressure. The first is *proximity*. The possibility to access an increasing number of banking services directly via the internet has, in the last 20 years, drastically reduced the number of visits to the banks' physical branch (the typical client passed from "a couple of visits a month" to only "a couple of visits a year" to the bank). Such a change, in addition to other evolutions in customers' behaviour,[5] makes delivering *distinctive proximity* an increasingly challenging task for cooperative banks, in particular in the retail segment. The second component of the cooperative banking traditional competitive advantage that may face new challenges is the established *bank-client relationship*. In fact, *fintech* companies will progressively tend to position themselves in the (incipient) space existing between client and financial institution, by creating internet-based interfaces or platforms and relegating the financial institutions' infrastructure to functions of information provider and back office manager. *Fintech* companies will

[5] See Sect. 10.4.1.

indeed try to emerge as the primary contact point for clients in the management of their financials and establish a sustainable competitive advantage with respect to incumbent players. This competitive advantage will be eventually backed by enhanced user-experience and data-driven offering. As a matter of fact, this pattern can be similar to the one already observed in other industries.[6] The entering into force of the revised Payment Services Directive[7] (PSD II) in 2018, which opened the market of payments to Third Party Providers (TPPs), will be a concrete example of whether and how *fintech* companies can effectively drive disruption in the market of banking services.

10.3 The Imperative of Restoring Profitability

One of the most important lessons learned by cooperative banks from the Great Crisis is that *profitability* must be considered as an essential precondition for sustaining their unique business model. Limited risk appetite and profit retention practices do not exempt cooperative banks to be able to generate an adequate level of profits over time. To this extent, the main lever used so far by cooperative banks in the attempt to restore in their economic equilibrium has been a reduction in operational cost. All the reforms undertaken in the cooperative sector to date have included in particular measures impacting the number of branches and other items considered in the administrative expenses. The issue of non-performing loans has also been (partially) addressed, even though it mainly required public intervention, in particular in the form of national level regulatory initiatives allowing for a more favourable treatment of impairments and specific programmes launched in order to facilitate the sell-off of these loans. However, less has been done on the revenues side. In this respect, no prevalent solutions have arisen so far. The significant shift towards fee-based, high-value-added services that can be observed in the case of many

[6] This technology-driven tendency can be observed in other industries. Noteworthy are the cases of Airbnb, leader in the short-term real estate renting sector without owning any real estate; Netflix, leader in the home entertainment sector producing only a portion of the contents proposed to its clients; or Uber, emerging leader in the urban transportation sector without owning any car.

[7] Directive 2015/2366 of the European Parliament and of the Council of 25 November 2015 on payment services in the internal market, amending Directives 2002/65/EC, 2009/110/EC and 2013/36/EU and Regulation (EU) No 1093/2010, and repealing Directive 2007/64/EC.

commercial banks in the attempt to sustain *profitability* by strengthening the intermediation income has not been observed in the cooperative banking sector.

10.4 The Call for Challenging the Cooperative Business Model

Are the cooperative principles of *membership*, *democratic governance*, *proximity*, *commitment to social values*, *prudent management* still appealing in the post-crisis banking market in Europe? When analysing the possible dimension of cooperative banking in a long-term perspective, answering this simple question seems increasingly relevant. Nevertheless, any answer different from "*yes, of course (!)*" would seem unduly provocative and result to be factually mistaken. However, the sustainability of cooperative business model in banking as it has grown and consolidated in more than one century cannot be given for granted in the post-crisis world. As a matter of fact, the constantly evolving competitive scenario requires cooperative banks to challenge substantial parts of their business models. In doing so, they must anchor the change to their inherent values. Otherwise, the only concrete alternative they would have in order to survive is a progressive convergence towards the model of *shareholder value bank* (and many examples in this sense can be already observed[8]).

10.4.1 Rethink Proximity

A first element of the traditional cooperative banking business model that would benefit from a reassessment is *proximity*. The evolution in technology patterns and in lifestyles experienced in particular in the last decades can hardly be considered as neutral with respect to the traditional concept of *proximity* as used in cooperative banking and backed by focus on local community and physical interaction with stakeholders. Some examples of these changes in technology patterns and in lifestyles are the possibility to access an increasing number of services through the internet, the tendency to vehiculate communication and social interaction via internet-based

[8] See in this respect the reform of *Banche Popolari* launched in Italy in 2015 (where all the *Banche Popolari* with total assets higher than EUR 8 billion have been transformed in joint-stock companies) or the high level of hybridisation already reached by some large cooperative banking groups or networks.

platforms (e.g. social networks) or the propensity of people and businesses to move and change location at a much higher pace than it happened in the past (and several times in a lifetime).

As a matter of fact, the determinants of the concept of *proximity* continuously evolve alongside changes in the society. In this respect, two considerations seem particularly relevant. On the one hand, a decisive contribution to the evolution of the concept of *proximity* will be probably given by the consolidation in the use of new communication channels and their impact for banks as concerns the way to effectively engage customers. To this extent, for a bank reaching its customers will be increasingly linked to an active presence on the internet-based platforms used by customers to access banking services or simply to get in contact, collect information and share experiences. Already today, the number of bank-client interactions through internet-based platforms is in many cases higher than the number of interactions via physical branches. Paradoxically, for an increasing number of people, a sentiment of *proximity* with respect to their bank will materialise first and foremost through adapted digital communication and not through physical interaction. On the other hand, the exact identification of a *local community* is becoming increasingly challenging. What in the past could have been easily recognised as such (and summarised as "a group of people living in the same territory and sharing the same values") today seems much harder to circumscribe. The link with the territory, even though it remains a crucial element of determination of a local community, is progressively transforming. To this extent, the constant presence of an individual in a territory may be seen less important than social involvement or family roots (e.g. the case of an active member of a community that spends a great part of his/her time in another city for business reasons).[9]

For cooperative banks, rethinking and adapting the concept of *proximity* to the evolution in technology patterns and in lifestyles becomes progressively necessary in order to preserve and keep leveraging one of their crucial sources of distinctiveness. In practical terms, a review of the concept of *proximity* may lead to a change in the way the bank communicates

[9] Even identifying what are the shared values of a local community is becoming more complicated, in particular due to the increasingly cultural heterogeneity that can be today observed in the citizenship composition, even at local level. To this extent, it is worth mentioning that the first cooperative banks adopting the Raiffeisen model were mainly created by rural communities sharing Cristian values and practices.

(in terms of channels and contents) and even to a refinement of some statutory provisions concerning member composition or definition of territorial ties.[10]

10.4.2 Embrace Sustainability

In recent years, the issue of the sustainability of human activities has been increasingly debated by policy makers, practitioners and academicians, in particular following the Paris Agreement reached in the United Nations Framework Convention on Climate Change (UNFCCC) in December 2015[11] and the final adoption of the Sustainable Development Goals (SDGs) in the context of the United Nations Development Programme (UNDP) in January 2016.[12] In Europe, sustainability has become a policy priority. To this extent, and among other initiatives, the European Commission (EC) published in March 2018 its first *Action Plan for a Greener and Cleaner Economy*. This plan has in particular the merit to specifically address the crucial role of finance in reaching climate and environmental goals.

Cooperative banks are naturally inclined to promote sustainability. The cooperative principles of *commitment to social values*, *stakeholder involvement*, *prudent management* convey a strong indication towards the support of some key sustainable objectives, such as the preservation of the environment, the promotion of the equality, the responsible consumption. Furthermore, cooperative banks already play a crucial role when it comes

[10] As an example, for the Italian *Banche di Credito Cooperativo* members must have their domicile and/or continuative business within the territory where the bank operates and 95 per cent of the lending must be in the municipalities where the bank has a branch and the neighbouring ones.

[11] The Paris Agreement's aim is to strengthen the global response to the threat of climate change by keeping a global temperature rise this century well below 2 degrees Celsius above pre-industrial levels and to pursue efforts to limit the temperature increase even further to 1.5 degrees Celsius. Additionally, the agreement aims to strengthen the ability of countries to deal with the impacts of climate change. To reach these ambitious goals, appropriate financial flows, a new technology framework and an enhanced capacity building framework will be put in place, thus supporting action by developing countries and the most vulnerable countries, in line with their own national objectives. The Agreement also provides for enhanced transparency of action and support through a more robust transparency framework (Source: UNDP website, http://unfccc.int/paris_agreement/items/9485.php).

[12] While the SDGs are not legally binding, governments are expected to take ownership and establish national frameworks for their achievement.

to the financing of sustainable projects. In this respect, their operational relevance is given in particular by their unique capacity to reach SMEs and households, which are often pivotal actors for the success of sustainable policy actions.[13]

Embracing sustainability (by endorsing, communicating and financing sustainable initiatives) could have two advantages for European cooperative banks. On the one hand, it would represent an enrichment of their cooperative identity in the banking market. This would further strengthen market positioning and distinctiveness with respect to ***shareholder value banks***. On the other hand, it would permit to leverage the increasingly favourable policy scenario in Europe. In this respect, the number of policy initiative to finance a sustainable economy will probably keep increasing in future, representing a concrete business opportunity for banks in terms of funds intermediation. In addition, a promising movement in research, supported by policy makers, is emerging trying to link sustainability risks and financial risks (e.g. by considering that sustainable investments may reduce the frequency and the incidence of catastrophic natural events, in this way also reducing their economic consequences). In the longer term, and as a measure to further encourage sustainable finance, regulatory provisions for a different prudential treatment of the exposures related to sustainable projects might even be introduced to the benefit of financial intermediaries (e.g. in case of more favourable requirements in terms of capital absorption for loans issued to finance sustainable projects).

10.4.3 Learn to Communicate the Cooperative Difference in Banking

In point of fact, the distinctive characteristics of cooperative banking (and their impact on banking operations) are often underestimated by a great part of the population in Europe, in particular when comparing cooperative banks to commercial or savings banks. This is in part due to the high level of hybridisation reached by many cooperative banking groups or networks, especially in some European countries, but also (and in some cases principally) to the way the cooperative banking difference is usually communicated.

[13] A possible distinctive role of cooperative banks in helping SMEs to reach the financial markets in the framework of the introduction of new market-oriented financing instruments in the EU agriculture has been recently analysed by Migliorelli and Dessertine (2017).

Traditionally, industrial communication and advertising strategies were developed to induce clients to buy a product or a service. Nevertheless, in the last two decades the importance of the valorisation of the *brand* has constantly increased. In particular, the *brand image*, usually declined in its components of *brand identity*, *brand experience* and *brand communication*, has been progressively recognised as one critical success factors for a company in the market (e.g. Zhang 2015). In this respect, an argument can be made according to the idea that the banking industry, and in particular the retail banking industry, still largely adopts an approach to communication substantially based on the promotion of products or services, and less on the valorisation of the *brand image*.

When prompted by cooperative banks, such an approach risks to be particularly ineffective. In fact, little differentiation exists when comparing many of the products and services offered by a cooperative bank to the ones offered by other kinds of financial institutions (e.g. loans, mortgages, short-term deposits, current accounts). On the contrary, a substantial room for differentiation can exist when addressing *brand identity*, *brand experience* and *brand communication*. An approach based on the valorisation of the *brand image* (within an adapted strategic framework and operational cycles) would have two main advantages for cooperative banks. First, by leveraging the cooperative distinctiveness, it would enhance perceived differentiation and hence reinforce positioning. Second, it would contribute to transform the unique cooperative banking values in intangible earning-maker assets. As a matter of fact, a market premium for banks backed by unique principles such as *membership*, *democratic governance*, *proximity*, *commitment to social values*, *prudent management* can today indeed be justified, in particular when assisted by a coherent value proposition and communication approach.[14]

10.4.4 Do Not Leave Fintech Companies Leading the Change

The consolidation of the presence of *fintech* companies in the banking market in the next few years will probably bring a certain degree of disruption. Even though it can be argued that banks will maintain a strong

[14] A similar phenomenon can be already observed in other industries. For example, Anselmsson et al. (2014) showed that in the fast-moving consumer goods (FMCG) industry, a market premium exists for companies that are able to be perceived as having a positive social image, being unique, having a link with the home country or having a positive corporate social responsibility (CSR) approach.

competitive advantage in the business areas for which customers will keep prising physical interaction and support (e.g. mortgages, specialised financial counselling), in other segments of the market the shift in competitive scenario could be substantial (e.g. payment services, unspecialised financial counselling). Cooperative banks should not ignore the potential impact of the digitalisation in terms of service innovation and customer satisfaction. As a matter of fact, it becomes increasingly evident that innovative financial services at fair prices are prerequisites for every bank.[15] Yet, the market of digitalisation in banking is still in an early phase and it is difficult to predict how it will grow and consolidate, as well as to identify the best strategic response for banks. Nevertheless, the main risk for cooperative banks is to adopt a *wait-and-see* approach and not to be able to bridge the gap with new entrants once the market shifts in an advanced growth phase. Such a risk will be even higher for smaller cooperative groups and networks with relatively limited investment capacity.

The key question for cooperative banks today should hence be *how* to take part to the *digital move*, more than *if*. In this respect, *fintech* companies could emerge both as competitor and business partners. More in detail, two main possibilities seem viable for cooperative banks. The first is to develop internally digitalisation-based solutions with the aim to propose innovative services to existing clients. In doing that, cooperative banks would benefit from their positioning of incumbents and would probably be able to shield (at least partially) their base of clients from potential new entrants. Following this option would require to take-in highly technical competencies and accept a higher level of risk on the investment. The second possibility is to acquire or enter into a partnership with specialised *fintech* companies that already have or are better positioned to develop the required technology. Nevertheless, this second option may result not to be effective in particular in the case the winning market solutions will be provided by high-tech giants with large investment possibilities and innovation capacities (e.g. Apple, Facebook, Google, Microsoft).

[15] On the other hand, digitalisation as a lever of cost reduction and streamlining of operational processes is something that the banking industry has already largely embraced to support reorganisation initiatives.

References

Anselmsson, J., Bondesson, N. V., & Johansson, U. (2014). Brand Image and Customers' Willingness to Pay a Price Premium for Food Brands. *Journal of Product and Brand Management, 23*(2), 90–102.

Ayadi, R., De Groen, P. W., Sassi, I., Mathlouthi, W., Rey, H., & Aubry, O. (2016). *Banking Business Models Monitor 2015 Europe.*

Ayadi, R., Llewellyn, D., Schmidt, R. H., Arbak, E., & De Groen, P. W. (2010). *Investigating Diversity in the Banking Sector in Europe: Key Developments, Performance and Role of Cooperative Banks.* CEPS Paperbacks.

Berger, A., Klapper, A., & Udell, G. (2001). The Ability of Banks to Lend to Informationally Opaque Small Businesses. *Journal of Banking and Finance, 25,* 2127–2167.

Bolton, P., Freixas, X., Gambacorta, L., & Mistrulli, P. E. (2013). *Relationship and Transaction Lending in a Crisis.* BIS Working Papers, No. 417.

Boot, A. W. A. (2000). Relationship Banking: What Do We Know? *Journal of Financial Intermediation, 9,* 7–25.

De Ory, J.-N., Serres, A., & Jaegger, M. (2012). Comment Résister à l'Effet de Normalisation des Banques Coopératives? *La Revue des Sciences de Gestion, 258,* 69–82.

Ferri, G., Kalmi, P., & Kerola, E. (2014). Does Bank Ownership Affect Lending Behavior? Evidence from the Euro Area. *Journal of Banking and Finance, 48,* 194–209.

Migliorelli, M., & Brunelli, S. (2016). The Transmission of the Monetary Policy in the Euro Area: The Role of the Banks' Business Model. *Annals of Public and Cooperative Economics, 88*(3), 303–322.

Migliorelli, M., & Dessertine, P. (2017). Time for New Financing Instruments? A Market-Oriented Framework to Finance Environmentally Friendly Practices in EU Agriculture. *Journal of Sustainable Finance and Investment, 8*(1), 1–25.

Richez-Battesti, N., & Leseul, G. (2016). Cooperative Banks in France: Emergence, Mutations and Issues. In S. Karofolas (Ed.), *Credit Cooperative Institutions in European Countries.* New York: Springer.

Zhang, Y. (2015). The Impact of Brand Image on Consumer Behavior: A Literature Review. *Open Journal of Business and Management, 3,* 58–62.

Index[1]

[1] Note: Page numbers followed by 'n' refer to notes.

M. Migliorelli (ed.), *New Cooperative Banking in Europe*,
https://doi.org/10.1007/978-3-319-93578-2

The manufacturer's authorised representative in the EU is Springer Nature Customer Service Centre GmbH, Europaplatz 3, 69115 Heidelberg, Germany. If you have any concerns regarding our products, please contact ProductSafety@springernature.com

Printed and bound by CPI Group (UK) Ltd, Croydon, CR0 4YY
30/09/2026
02225439-0006